The Collapse of
the Middle Way

The Collapse of the Middle Way

Senate Republicans and the
Bipartisan Foreign Policy, 1948–1952

DAVID R. KEPLEY

CONTRIBUTIONS IN AMERICAN HISTORY, NUMBER 126

GREENWOOD PRESS
New York · Westport, Connecticut · London

Library of Congress Cataloging-in-Publication Data

Kepley, David R.
   The collapse of the middle way.

   (Contributions in American history, ISSN 0084-9219 ;
no. 126)
   Bibliography: p.
   Includes index.
   1. United States—Foreign relations—1945–1953.
2. Republican Party (U.S. : 1854–   )—History—
20th century.   3. United States.   Congress.   Senate—
History—20th century.   I. Title.   II. Series.
E813.K47   1988   327.73   87-23665
ISBN 0-313-25784-1 (lib. bdg. : alk. paper)

British Library Cataloguing in Publication Data is available.

Library of Congress Catalog Card Number: 87-23665
ISBN: 0-313-25784-1
ISSN: 0084-9219

First published in 1988

Greenwood Press, Inc.
88 Post Road West, Westport, Connecticut 06881

Printed in the United States of America

∞™

The paper used in this book complies with the
Permanent Paper Standard issued by the National
Information Standards Organization (Z39.48-1984).

10 9 8 7 6 5 4 3 2 1

I dedicate this book to the memory of my father, Rodney Strickler Kepley (1915–1987). He would have been proud to see this.

Contents

Preface

This study began in the mid-1970s as an examination of the role of Congress in foreign policy. In those days, right after the resignation of President Richard Nixon, it was popularly assumed that presidents had manipulated Congress and the American people into wars. It was in this spirit, for instance, that the War Powers Act of 1973 was passed. I thought it might be useful, therefore, to examine the relationship between President Harry S Truman and the Congress (particularly the Senate) during the previous Asian war in Korea. Like the Vietnam conflict, the Korean War featured an attempted communist takeover of a pro-Western regime. It also became an exercise in limited war and soon became a political albatross around the neck of the president. Finally, in each conflict, questions of the constitutional prerogatives of the president and Congress were raised. This is not to say that there were not important differences between these two conflicts, only that the similarities are worth studying.

During my research I came across numerous references to the bipartisan foreign policy. I was fascinated with how this device for achieving consensus on foreign policy issues was initiated in the mid-1940s, came under massive attack during the late 1940s and early 1950s, and later re-formed around some new assumptions in the early 1950s. The history of this process sheds valuable insights into a variety of issues that are central to our understanding of the Cold War. How did the Cold War consensus develop, and how was it sustained? What was the political, ideological, and personality mix that accounts for the attack by the McCarthyites on the bipartisan foreign policy? To what extent did the bipartisan foreign policy stifle the development of alternatives to the Truman administration's containment strategy?

How and to what extent did the Republican party change from being a haven for the isolationism of Gerald P. Nye during the 1930s, to the nationalism of Robert A. Taft during the mid-1940s, to the party of universal, militant, anticommunism represented by William Knowland and Barry Goldwater in the 1950s and 1960s? What is the constitutional relationship between the president and Congress on foreign affairs in an age when America's enemies can strike so swiftly? Finally was there a way in which the United States could have been spared the excesses of the McCarthy period? This book by no means provides final answers to these questions, but I hope that it will stimulate further scholarship.

One of the pleasures of working on a large project is acknowledging those who have provided much help and a great many kindnesses. I want to express my thanks to the Harry S Truman Institute for providing me with a grant-in-aid that enabled me to travel to the Truman Library in 1981. Librarians in the following institutions were professional, courteous, and generous with their resources: McKeldin Library, University of Maryland; Paley Library, Temple University; Beaver College Library; the Library of Congress; the National Archives Library; and George Mason University Library. I also had the pleasure of meeting numerous archivists across the country whose work in processing materials, promptly providing them to me, and sharing their many insights was invaluable. I wish to express my thanks in particular to the following: Dennis Bilger, Truman Library; Allen Kenyon, Eisenhower Library; Robert Wood, Hoover Library; and George Perros, Debra Leahy, and Ron Swerczek, National Archives. I also had rewarding and pleasant experiences at the Bentley Historical Collections, Ohio State Historical Society; Western Historical Collections, Indiana Historical Society; Nebraska State Historical Society; Massachusetts Historical Society; Wisconsin State Historical Society; New England College Library; Manuscripts Division, Library of Congress; Columbia University Library; Seeley G. Mudd Manuscript Collection, Princeton University; and McKeldin Library, University of Maryland.

I wish to thank the editor of *Prologue: The Journal of the National Archives* for the inclusion of chapter 7 in this volume.

I am also indebted to J. Samuel Walker, Donald Ritchie, Nathan Einhorn, E. B. Smith, Keith Olson, and Wayne Cole, who read all or parts of the manuscript. Professor Cole commented on this project at an earlier stage with great patience and intelligence; his influence is undeniable. I was fortunate enough to have Dennis Burton type the entire manuscript—his diligence, patience, and knowledge were a source of support. I will miss him.

I am lucky enough to have a good many friends and loved ones whose importance to this project was incalculable. Robert Plowman and his family extended many kindnesses to me. My parents have been a constant source of encouragement and support in this project, as in anything I have ever attempted. Typing the entire rough draft, helping me proofread the text, and overall in more ways than I can express, my wife, Brenda, was indispensable. (I hope my sons Andrew and Patrick will forgive me for not spending more time with them; I almost finished this before they were born!) Of course, I am solely responsible for any errors of content or style in this work.

March 1985
Annandale, Virginia

The Collapse of
the Middle Way

Introduction

From the time of Pearl Harbor to the 1960s, the Republican party underwent important changes in its approach to foreign policy. Despite a strong internationalist wing, the "Grand Old Party" (GOP) has been the traditional home of the most prominent nationalists of the twentieth century. During the 1940s the nationalists, spiritual heirs of the isolationists of the 1930s, followed the lead of Republican Senator Robert A. Taft of Ohio. They opposed much of President Harry S Truman's containment policy because it called for political commitments, such as the North Atlantic Treaty; expensive foreign aid programs, such as the Marshall Plan; and a dramatic growth in presidential power. By the 1950s and 1960s, however, the nationalists argued that the fatal flaws in Truman's containment policy were that it had been too narrowly defined (covering only Europe and not East Asia) and was too passive. This new militancy, articulated by California Senator William Knowland, General Douglas MacArthur, and John Foster Dulles, later manifested itself in the rhetorical aggressiveness of the 1950s and ultimately in the nomination of Senator Barry Goldwater of Arizona in 1964. The "fall of China," the Korean War, and the rise of McCarthyism were crucial events in effecting the party's transformation from noninterventionism to globalism.[1]

In order to describe and analyze these changes, this study focuses on how Republicans in the Senate reacted to and were influenced by major foreign policy issues from 1948 to 1952. In the American constitutional system, it is, of course, difficult to identify "spokesmen" for the party that is not in control of the White House. During these years, however, there were a number of influential Republicans in the Senate, including, in particular, Senators Arthur H. Vandenberg of Michigan, Robert A. Taft, William Knowland, Henry Cabot Lodge, Jr., of Massachusetts, and Kenneth S. Wherry of Nebraska, who played key roles on foreign policy questions. Also, Senate leaders are discussed because of their institution's role in foreign affairs, which is traditionally greater than, for instance, the House of Representatives.

In examining the senatorial documentation of this period, this author was struck by the constant reference to the term "bipartisan foreign policy." The bipartisan foreign policy that developed in the late 1940s had a dual meaning: It referred to an executive-legislative process, as well as to the diplomatic goals of the Truman administration. Bipartisanship in foreign affairs required prior consultation between responsible members of the two parties to attain a consensus. According to the theory, both parties would then refrain from introducing foreign policy issues into politics, especially at election time. Vandenberg explained that if the bipartisan formula were followed it would "unite our official voice at the water's edge so that America could speak with maximum authority against those who would divide and conquer us and the free world." Its adherents hoped to avoid what they regarded as the tragic and unnecessarily partisan controversy that accompanied the rejection of the Treaty of Versailles in 1919. It became a powerful tradition on the Senate Foreign Relations Committee that persisted into the 1970s.[2]

Republican defenders of the bipartisan foreign policy were stout internationalists. While many of them were liberals on domestic issues, some, such as Vandenberg and Smith, were as fiscally conservative as Taft. Their leader was Vandenberg and their numbers included Senators Henry Cabot Lodge, Jr., and Leverett Saltonstall of Massachusetts, H. Alexander Smith of New Jersey, William Knowland of California, Wayne Morse of Oregon, George Aiken and Ralph Flanders of Vermont, Charles Tobey of New Hampshire, Irving Ives and John Foster Dulles of New York, and Margaret Chase Smith of Maine. They vigorously supported Truman's programs to revive Europe economically through the Marshall Plan in 1948, and to protect it militarily through the North Atlantic Treaty and Military Assistance Program in 1949.

Defending the Democrats' foreign policies, however, placed them in a politically vulnerable position. On the one hand, any backsliding might bring charges from the administration that the GOP had reverted to the isolationism of the 1930s, a black mark bipartisan Republicans were trying desperately to erase. On the other hand, when they supported the Democrats, their more isolationist colleagues criticized them for not developing a genuine Republican alternative to Truman's foreign policy. Political survival, therefore, dictated that the bipartisan Republicans urge consideration of foreign policy decisions strictly on their merits, regardless of which party sponsored them. Issues that aroused partisan sentiment, such as McCarthyism, were anathema to their political position.

By the late 1940s, most of the dissenters to the bipartisan foreign policy were fiscal conservatives. The opponents were led by Taft, Wherry, and former president Herbert C. Hoover. Their followers included Republican Senators John W. Bricker of Ohio, Homer Capehart and William Jenner of Indiana, Arthur Watkins of Utah, Milton Young and William Langer of North Dakota, Bourke Hickenlooper of Iowa, Karl Mundt of South Dakota, and George Malone of Nevada. Since the advent of the New Deal, they feared that America had strayed from "liberty" (by which they meant the liberty of individuals to operate freely in the market place) toward what they called "statism" (which they defined as government interference in the economy). The New Deal-Fair Deal, in "unholy alliance" with organized labor, they believed, had brought the United States perilously close to British socialism.

Their foreign policy concerns were similarly tightfisted. As heirs to the nationalist-isolationist tradition in American foreign policy, which had been so powerful in the years between the wars, they were leery about political commitments such as the North Atlantic Treaty. As conservatives, they opposed outright or at least sought to circumscribe such foreign assistance programs as the Marshall Plan. Finally, as men who had battled Franklin D. Roosevelt, they were deeply suspicious of any accretions of presidential power, such as in the "troops to Europe" controversy in 1951. By 1949 and 1950, Taft and Hoover developed an alternative to Truman's containment policy; scorning commitments to countries on the Eurasian land mass, they instead relied on America's air-sea-atomic power in conjunction with Britain, Japan, and the islands of the western Pacific to protect the United States from the communists.[3]

Despite their common heritage, Taft Republicans were divided over the extent to which America should follow Truman's lead. More moderate members, the nationalists (which included Taft, Hickenlooper, Capehart, Young, and Mundt) did support some aspects of the president's program. Taft, for instance, voted for the Marshall Plan in 1948 and later favored sending a small American ground contingent to Europe in 1951. In those cases, however, the Ohioan voted for amendments that would circumscribe the commitment as closely as possible. More extreme members of the group, the isolationists (which included Wherry, Watkins, James Kem and Forrest Donnell of Missouri, Malone, and Jenner) found little of Truman's foreign policy to their liking. They introduced amendments or reservations to each program designed sharply to reduce its scope. The differences between these two groups of Taftites was one of degree.

In voicing these concerns, however, the Taftites faced some imposing obstacles. To oppose the North Atlantic Treaty or the Marshall Plan, one risked being branded an "isolationist" and a disrupter of bipartisanship, a term that had assumed patriotic proportions at the hands of the Democrats and bipartisan Republicans. The Taftites, countering that the voters and the party deserved an alternative to Truman's liberalism and internationalism, in turn scorned bipartisan Republicans for favoring a "me too" foreign policy. During 1948 and 1949, bipartisan Republicans effectively muzzled the dissenters. But during 1950 and 1951, by focusing on the administration's failures in East Asia, such as the fall of China, the Korean War, and allegations of spies in the American foriegn policy establishment, Taftites wrecked the bipartisan coalition of 1948 and 1949. A new bipartisanship emerged around somewhat different principles during 1951 and 1952.

Throughout the 1940s and 1950s, Taft Republicans fought a rearguard action. By the late 1940s, the internationalists' arguments were especially persuasive to Americans who in the space of a generation had fought two world wars to subdue a dangerous enemy in Europe. The Soviet Union, whose institutions were so diametrically opposed to those of the United States, seemed like yet another power that threatened to dominate western and central Europe. Each aggressive move by the Soviets or any communists, such as the Czechoslovakian coup and the Berlin blockade in 1948, the fall of China in 1949, and the North Korean attack in 1950, reinforced the internationalists' explanation of Soviet behavior and their prescriptions for handling it. Politically, the Taftites made their greatest impact only when they could appeal to some of the bipartisan Republicans, such as the China bloc; when they could arouse partisan sentiment, as they did with McCarthyism; or when they could raise the spector of an imperious president, as in the case of the great debate of 1951.

1

The Origins of Bipartisanship, 1942–1948

The bipartisan foreign policy had its origins in the domestic political situation in the United States during the Second World War. From Pearl Harbor until the election of 1942, President Franklin D. Roosevelt could ignore Republican views on foreign affairs because the GOP was so badly divided and discredited. During 1943 and 1944, Senator Arthur H. Vandenberg played a key role in unifying and strengthening his party on foreign policy questions in a meeting at Mackinac, Michigan, and at the Republican National Convention in 1944. Such efforts brought a handsome return, encouraging Roosevelt and his Secretary of State Cordell Hull to consult the Senate on the United Nations Treaty and on appropriations for the United Nations Relief and Rehabilitation Administration (UNRRA). During 1947 and 1948, bipartisanship flowered. A popular consensus developed behind the administration's foreign policy programs and leaders of the two parties in the Senate worked closely with Secretary of State George Marshall and his Undersecretary, Robert Lovett. Vandenberg and the bipartisan Repblicans also came to dominate their party on foreign policy concerns.[1]

Crucial to the development of bipartisanship was the rise of Vandenberg to a prominent position in his party. The elections of 1940 found the Republican party rent by the effects of the Great Debate of 1940–1941, which had pitted Wendell Wilkie's internationalists against Midwestern isolationists. By 1943, Vandenberg believed that his party needed to discover a "middle ground" between "the internationalist extremists . . . and the nationalist extremists who can still [only] think exclusively in pre-Pearl Harbor terms." It was appropriate that Vandenberg would take the leading role in developing that "middle ground," since his whole career had been that of a man who had moved within the mainstream of his party. As a young man, he had been a Theodore Roosevelt progressive and had favored American entry into World War I in 1917, as had most members of his party. In the period between the wars, Vandenberg stood shoulder-to-shoulder with most Republicans, being strongly probusiness and every bit as much an isolationist as Republican Senators Gerald P. Nye of North Dakota and George W. Norris of Nebraska. By 1943, Vandenberg's prewar isolationism gave way to a limited internationalism; the shift came about for reasons of political expediency and because he genuinely believed that technology had rendered isolationism obsolete. In appearance, Vandenberg looked Churchillian; he clad his portly frame in beautifully tailored suits set off with a snappy bow tie and a cigar. While knowledgeable about foreign affairs, the senator could be pompous, egotistical, and overly susceptible to flattery. By the late 1940s, Vandenberg had become a real power in the Senate, his stature being equalled only by Robert A. Taft.[2]

The beginnings of bipartisanship during the Roosevelt years were but a backdrop to the golden age the concept enjoyed during 1947 and 1948. Bipartisan cooperation worked in those years because a unique set of circumstances and individuals allowed it to work. The new president, Harry S Truman, had spent a decade on Capitol Hill and was more favorably disposed toward Congress than Roosevelt. Also, in January 1947 the Republicans controlled Congress for the first time since 1931 and believed they could beat the Missouri haberdasher handily in the election of 1948. That predisposed them to cooperate with the Democrats probably so they could demand the same when a Republican took over the White House in January 1949. The dominant elements of both parties agreed on the major objectives of American foreign policy and were delighted to use bipartisanship, a concept that was fast becoming synonymous with patriotism, to silence opposition.

Occurrences in Europe, such as the Greek crisis in 1947, and the Czech coup and Berlin blockade in 1948 confirmed the prevailing view of communist behavior and hence the administration's solution to it. Also in 1947 and 1948, exactly the right men were in exactly the right positions in the government to effect bipartisanship. For the Republicans, Senator Vandenberg was the leading senatorial spokesman on foreign affairs, and he was also chairman of the Foreign Relations Committee. Truman's Secretary of State, George C. Marshall, and his Undersecretary, Robert Lovett, were both ideologically and personally compatible with the Michigan senator. These two years, therefore, witnessed the passage of a remarkable spate of legislation that shaped the direction of American foreign policy for a generation.

The Greek-Turkish crisis of 1947 provided the Eightieth Congress with its first challenge. During the winter of 1946–1947, the British informed Truman that because of the grim economic situation in the home islands, they could not aid either the Greeks in their struggle against a left-wing uprising, or the Turks in their resistance to Soviet pressure on their borders. British statesmen confronted Truman with the dual problem of stabilizing the eastern Mediterranean and, more importantly, of relieving the economic woes of Britain and Western Europe. Truman quickly came to the conclusion that the United States had to fill Britain's shoes in the Middle East by bolstering the Greek and Turkish governments with military aid. Realizing that such a program violated both the American tradition of political isolation and the fiscal conservatism of the Eightieth Congress, the president moved circumspectly to consult with congressional leaders.[3]

On February 22, 1947, the administration met with a delegation from Capitol Hill.[4] Marshall commenced the session with a dry, logical analysis of America's interests in the Middle East that fell flatly on congressional ears. Undersecretary of State Dean G. Acheson then delivered an impassioned argument describing the program's passage as critical to the entire free world. Should Greece and Turkey fall to the communists, he argued, it "might open three continents to Soviet penetration." The congressmen, impressed by the dangers Acheson outlined, agreed to support the program. Two days later, the president announced that "it must be the policy of the United States to support free peoples who are resisting attempted subjugation by armed minorities or by outside pressures."[5]

Once he submitted the legislation to Congress, Truman proved he could be most accommodating to Vandenberg's suggestions. Although Acheson later disdainfully asserted that the changes Vandenberg made in the Greek-Turkish aid bill were advanced only to make it a "Vandenberg product," that contention revealed more about Acheson's attitude toward the senator than about Vandenberg's contributions. For instance, the Michigan senator was concerned that the Greek-Turkish aid program circumvented the United Nations, so he proposed that the aid be cut off if the United Nations moved in to handle the problem. Vandenberg had a personal stake in the United Nations, since he had played an important role in founding the organization and the United Nations Treaty had been among the first bipartisan measures. The Michigan senator tried to square most of the major programs he sponsored with the principles of the charter. By so doing, he could argue on the floor of the Senate that new programs such as the Greek-Turkish aid bill and the Marshall Plan stemmed from the United Nations commitment, which had passed the Senate by a healthy margin. During the late 1940s, the United Nations also enjoyed widespread support among the American people.[6]

The bipartisan foreign policy experienced no finer moment for its adherents during the Eightieth Congress than in the passage of the Marshall Plan, in which all the major ingredients in the bipartisan recipe were scrupulously blended. During the planning of the program, administration figures conferred with and heeded the advice of key Republican leaders, especially Vandenberg. When the bill went to Congress, Truman demonstrated admirable flexibility in letting the adroit senator get it through its legislative hurdles with just the right compromises to minimize dissent. The result was that the bill carried the Senate Foreign Relations Committee by a unanimous vote and was passed on the floor by an impressive margin. Even world events had a way of helping. While the bill was under sharp scrutiny in the House, Czechoslovakia fell to the communists, causing the bill's opposition to collapse. In short, passage of the most ambitious peacetime foreign aid program in American history owed much to the bipartisan approach.

The weaknesses displayed by the British in the Greek-Turkish situation was but a symptom of a general economic malaise that affected the entire Continent. The European economy had, since the sunny days of the 1920s, been hit by two jackhammerlike blows: the Depression of the 1930s, followed by the most destructive war in history. Little wonder that, as the first snows fell upon the Continent in the winter of 1946–1947, Europeans peered up at the skies with considerably less enthusiasm than the owners of a Vermont ski lodge. Even as the administration charted its Greek-Turkish legislation, plans were afoot for a program to rescue Europe. In the spring of 1947, Acheson and Marshall revealed the State Department's thinking in speeches at Harvard University and Cleveland, Mississippi. Acheson and Marshall proposed that America take a lead in resuscitating Europe with a vast aid program designed to stimulate European industries and revive trans-Atlantic trade. In that manner, the administration hoped to put Europe's economy back on its feet.[7]

The next month, in a meeting with Democrats Tom Connally of Texas and Alben Barkley of Kentucky, and Republicans Vandenberg and Wallace White of Maine, Truman informed them that he was going to appoint a nonpartisan advisory council to assess "the limits within which the United States may safely and wisely plan." The president invited the senators to comment on his tentative list of appointments to the council. Vandenberg was delighted and asked only that former Senator Robert M. La Follette, Jr., of Wisconsin be added to Truman's list, to which the president graciously concurred. The council was then set up under the leadership of W. Averell Harriman, Secretary of Commerce. Vandenberg was, however, vexed at the scope of the program and the prospect of having to steer a bill of that magnitude through the Congress so late in the session. In a private meeting at the Blair House, Marshall quieted the senator's fears, assuring him that the State Department would only introduce an interim aid measure during that session of Congress and that he had every intention of conferring with a wide range of public and private figures. The department got along so well with Vandenberg in the fall and early winter months of 1947–1948 that it even wrote some speeches for him on the Marshall Plan.[8]

Opposition to the Marshall Plan centered in the Taft wing of the Republican party. Although he rarely expressed an opinion on the plan, Taft favored the program in general, but believed the administration's version was too costly. The Ohioan, preoccupied by the Republican presidential primaries of 1948, played a relatively inactive role in the debates. Contributing to Taft's reticence was an

informal understanding he had developed with Arthur Vandenberg
during the Eightieth Congress to divide party leadership between
them, with Taft taking the leading role in domestic matters while
Vandenberg led the party on foreign policy issues. Consequently,
congressional opponents of the plan rallied around Kenneth S.
Wherry of Nebraska with ex-president Herbert C. Hoover playing
a behind-the-scenes role. During the second week of January 1948,
Wherry called a meeting of the dissenters at Kansas Senator Clyde
Reed's Washington, D.C., apartment.[9] They agreed that the bill
was far too costly, that a four-year plan was excessive, and that the
State Department exercised far too much control over it.[10]

Vandenberg understood Taft, Wherry, and Hoover's objections
and moved adroitly to counter them. Concerning the amount of
the appropriation, the Michigan senator worked with the State Department to pare the Europeans' initial request of $24 billion down
to $17 billion. In addition, Vandenberg convinced Truman that it
would be easier to pass the funds on a yearly basis than to present
Congress with one enormous appropriations bill for the whole four-
year program; he also pointed out that one Congress could not
legally bind another to an approriation. The only major direct confrontation between Taft and Vandenberg on the Marshall Plan took
place when Taft made an unsuccessful attempt to cut funding for
the program. The party split twenty-four to twenty-three in Vandenberg's favor. After having made that brief sally, Taft retired
from the field.[11]

The Michigan senator proved equally adept at meeting criticisms directed at the State Department's role in overseeing the
Economic Cooperation Administration (ECA), the agency in charge
of administering the plan. Vandenberg clearly recognized the dilemma, noting that while "the business side of this essentially business enterprise [should] be under the effective control of adequate
business brains, . . . we cannot have two Secretaries of State." To
bridge the gap, Vandenberg asked the Brookings Institute to propose a solution. The Institute suggested that the head of the ECA
be accorded cabinet-level status and that he consult with the secretary of state; the plan won the support of Vandenberg and Truman. Owing largely to those judicious compromises, the bill passed
the Senate Foreign Relations Committee unanimously, and passed
the full Senate by a sixty-nine to seventeen margin.[12]

The Marshall Plan then went to the House of Representatives where Christian Herter, backed by Herbert Hoover, girded himself for a fight to trim the appropriation. However, the best-laid plans of congressmen and ex-presidents were reduced to a shambles by events in central Europe. On February 25, 1948, the communists seized power in Czechoslovakia and within a month Jan Masaryk, the living symbol of Czech independence, died an unnatural death under circumstances that pointed to murder. Marshall asserted that recent events made it imperative that the Congress pass the plan immediately. Truman further dramatized the situation in a nationally broadcast speech before a joint session of Congress. In it, he darkly declared that the Czech incident was part of Moscow's larger expansionist activities. The president implored the Congress to "speedily complete its action on ERP (European Recovery Program) and universal military training. In such an atmosphere, Herter and Hoover did not stand a chance.[13]

As in the election of 1944, an important test of bipartisanship was in the behavior of the parties during the national elections of 1948, but the results of that test were mixed. Bipartisanship could claim yet another triumph in the potentially volatile Berlin blockade crisis. Truman had consulted with Dewey's people early on, so each side refrained from exploiting the issue for political advantage to the benefit of American diplomacy. Both nominees, however, bent the rules of bipartisanship. The overconfident Dewey refrained from attacking Truman's foreign policy, even in those areas where there had been little bipartisan consultation, such as China and Palestine. Truman, too, bent the rules by taking major credit for recently passed programs, including aid to Greece and Turkey and the Marshall Plan, while castigating the Republican-controlled Eightieth Congress. Although the president waged his battle against the Eightieth Congress mostly over domestic issues, he made little effort to correct the impression that Congress did little more than tag along in foreign affairs.

In 1948, the bipartisan Republicans backed Dewey's bid for their party's presidential nomination. Dewey, Dulles, and Vandenberg, the leading lights on Republican foreign policy, determined early in the campaign that they would pursue a strategy of support for bipartisanship and its achievements. They did so because they wanted to prove that the Republican party had purged itself of its isolationist past and was therefore worthy of holding power. The glaring state of disarray in which the Democratic party found itself also helped shape Republican campaign strategy. In 1948, the Democratic party had split three ways, with some liberals following Henry Wallace's Progressive party and many conservative Southerners joining South Carolina Senator Strom Thurmond's States' Rights Democratic party. What was left of the Democratic party listlessly nominated the feisty Missourian. Dewey's strategists reasoned, therefore, that he should set his speeches on a high plane to avoid alienating the huge numbers of voters most pollsters had told him he had already won.[14]

As in 1944, Vandenberg played a key role in drafting the foreign policy plank for the Republican platform. The Michigan senator made it clear that he would fight any who tried "to upset any sort of enlightened foreign policy and return to the 'good old days' when it took two weeks to cross the ocean." Although Vandenberg worked closely with John Foster Dulles and Lodge, who headed the Resolutions Committee, the final version of the plank showed the unmistakable marks of Vandenberg's ideas. The platform supported aid to free peoples under a "businesslike and efficient administration of all foreign aid," one of the formulae Vandenberg had championed to obtain passage of the Marshall Plan. It also advocated American participation in "collective security [organizations] against aggression, . . . particularly commend[ing] the value of regional arrangements as prescribed by the Charter," of the United Nations, while extending the open hand of the Grand Old Party to "invite the Minority [Democratic] party to join in under the next Republican administration in stopping partisan politics at the water's edge."[15]

Those Republicans who had been critical of bipartisanship on the grounds that it was of little use in a presidential election against an incumbent had their worst fears confirmed by the Democratic platform that year. The foreign policy segments of the Democratic platform took major credit for the United Nations, the Marshall Plan, and aid to Greece and Turkey. Truman's acceptance speech followed in much the same vein, slapping the Republicans with one hand, while extending the other in the sacred name of bipartisan cooperation. The president condescendingly noted that his party had "turned away permanently from isolationism, and we have converted the greatest and best of the Republicans to our viewpoint on that subject." After having eaten so much of his cake, Truman quickly demonstrated that he could have it too. The president confessed that the major foreign policy programs of his presidency were bipartisan and that his practice had always been that: "Partisanship should stop at the water's edge." In both the platform and the presidential acceptance speech, the Democrats had clearly bent the rules of the bipartisan covenant.[16]

As one might expect, the Republican high command grimaced over those Democratic indiscretions. The same day that Truman delivered his acceptance speech, Dulles fired off an angry letter to Vandenberg, saying that he and Dewey "were both rather disturbed by the tone of the draft Democratic plank and its effort to take total credit for everything good, both in the war and in the conduct of foreign policy." Lovett confidentially told Dulles of "his chagrin at the Democratic platform on foreign policy, saying that he and M[arshall] were bitterly disappointed; that they had worked with the President to get a decent platform which would not claim all credit for the results of bi-partisan cooperation; that they thought they had Truman's support, but that in the end the political advisers had written it their way." Dulles retorted to Lovett that "if the President went on through the campaign in that way, it would be disastrous for the country."[17]

In a July speech from Albany, New York, Dewey gave evidence that he had his own ideas about how the campaign should be run. He indicated that those foreign policy programs to which bipartisan consultation had contributed, such as the United Nations Treaty and the Marshall Plan, would not be subject to a partisan attack. To underscore that point, Dewey encouraged his chief foreign affairs advisor, John Foster Dulles, to accept a position on the American Delegation to the United Nations. In those areas, however, where there had been little consultation, such as China, Palestine, and the aid to Greece and Turkey program, the New York governor promised a sharp attack. Vandenberg, alarmed at Dewey's tone, reminded Dulles that

the next Republican Secretary of State is going to need Democratic votes in the Senate just as badly as the present Administration has needed Republican votes. I have no illusions that the Republican isolationists have surrendered. . . . It is peculiarly our job—yours and mine—to see that bipartisan liaison in the next Congress does not become impossible. Otherwise, November will represent a Pyrrhic victory.

In short, Vandenberg's campaign strategy rested on the belief that, as scores of journalists and pollsters could confirm, Dewey just could not lose.[18]

Most authors agree that Dewey's loss was due to his failure to attack Truman's policies, foreign or domestic. Dewey could also have tried to pursue the China issue which bore his party such bittersweet fruits over the next four years. However, aside from providing some aid earlier in the year, the GOP had yet to show much interest in China by the fall of 1948. Dewey also might have pointed out that it was Truman's failure to gain the access rights to Berlin at Potsdam in 1945 that had caused the blockade, but most Americans would not have been impressed by such technicalities in the midst of a crisis. Truman cleverly shut off that avenue of attack by handling the situation in the best bipartisan tradition— by holding prior consultations with responsible members of the opposition party. Also, to have criticized Truman on Berlin would have given the Missourian a golden opportunity once again to hang the albatross of isolationism around the Republicans' necks, as Roosevelt had done so effectively.[19]

Dewey's passivity is, however, less justified on domestic issues. In retrospect, it was clearly a serious error in political judgment for Dewey to have avoided fighting back when Truman blasted what he called the "good for nothing Eightieth Congress." Although Truman focused most of his criticism on domestic matters, Vandenburg proudly retorted that the Eightieth Congress had compiled "the most amazing record of constructive congressional cooperation ever written in any Congress," especially considering the number of unanimous Senate Foreign Relations Committee votes on a list of far-reaching foreign policy programs. Instead of retaliating, Dewey got the Republican National Committee to withdraw its endorsement of a pamphlet it had written blasting Democratic foreign policy blunders. In short, Dewey, Dulles, and Vandenberg all wanted to "have it both ways." They wanted to be tough enough to win the election, but nice enough to be in a position to demand maximum cooperation from the Democrats after

January 1949. All the eventualitites for the upcoming Dewey administration were neatly arranged except for the most important one—winning the election.[20]

By election day in 1948, the bipartisan foreign policy had become an important force. Vital to that concept's origins had been the growth of a Republican leadership that could speak with authority for the party on foreign policy. Vandenberg provided the leadership and the unity Republicans required to demonstrate to Roosevelt that they had to be consulted if he wanted passage of certain pieces of legislation, such as UNRRA and the United Nations Treaty. From that fragile seedling, bipartisan cooperation matured into a sturdy sapling during the term of the Eightieth Congress. Those years were fruitful in part because Truman and his advisors were more amenable to cooperation than Roosevelt had been, and because the Republicans controlled both houses of Congress. Most leading Republicans, too, were disposed toward bipartisanship because they hoped to beat Truman in 1948 and wanted to be able to demand a similar cooperative arrangement from the Democrats in 1949. In addition, the dominant elements of both parties were close in their ideas about leading issues in American foreign policy. The result was the overwhelming adoption of such crucial cold war measures as aid to Greece and Turkey, and the Marshall Plan.

In 1948, bipartisanship helped account for one of the "cleaner" campaigns on foreign policy issues in recent years. The parties acted admirably in the touchy Berlin situation and, in general, conducted themselves with restraint, even if they did occasionally bend the rules of the game. Dewey, Dulles, and Vandenberg had exhorted their fellow Republicans to eschew partisan attack on Truman's foreign policy on the grounds that in doing so they were both performing a patriotic service and following the wisest course politically. The result on election day in 1948, however, was disastrous for the bipartisan approach. If bipartisanship could not win an election against so vulnerable a foe as Truman, many Republicans reasoned, perhaps a more partisan approach was necessary.

2

The North Atlantic Treaty and the Military Assistance Program, January–September 1949

In the wake of New York Governor Thomas E. Dewey's defeat in 1948, the bipartisan Republicans fell on hard times. In the space of three months, they lost a bid to oust Republican Senator Robert A. Taft of Ohio and his followers from their Senate leadership positions. They were then humiliated when the Democrats reorganized the Foreign Relations Committee, and were unhappy over the appointment of Dean Acheson as the new secretary of state. From January through July, the bipartisan Republicans led by Republican Senator Arthur H. Vandenberg of Michigan, again reigned supreme during the Senate's deliberations on the North Altantic Treaty. Working closely with the administration, Vandenberg helped devise the strategy for an overwhelming legislative victory. In the passage of the Military Assistance Program (MAP) of 1949, however, the bipartisan coalition faltered because of a lack of consultation with key Republicans. By late 1949, cracks appeared in the once solid bipartisan edifice.

The election returns registered on November 5, 1948, did more than just embarrass the owners of the *Chicago Tribune* (which had the temerity to go to press early on election day with the headline "Dewey Defeats Truman"); they reopened old wounds within the Republican party. While superficially amiable during the campaign, the two wings of the party turned viciously on each other in assessing the causes of defeat. Deweyites believed the loss was due in large measure to the identification of the party in the popular mind with the "reactionaries" of the Eightieth Congress, who fought both the New Deal and the bipartisan foreign policy. A new leadership in Congress was needed, they argued, to refurbish the party's image. Taft and his followers, however, believed that when the Republicans ran a "me too" bipartisan campaign they would never win. Taft contended that the party should vigorously attack the administration's foreign policy errors. Such internal disharmony boded ill for the bipartisan foreign policy.

Less than a fortnight after the election, a gathering of bipartisan Republicans laid plans to challenge the Taftites' hold on the Senate Republican leadership posts. Senator H. Alexander Smith of New Jersey noted that the consensus of the meeting was that it would be "wise to have a change [in the Republican Senate leadership] and not have it appear to the country that Taft, [Colorado Senator Eugene] Millikin, and [Nebraska Senator Kenneth] Wherry are the spokesmen for the party." Instead they proposed the following slate: Millikin, a moderate Taftite, as president of the Republican Conference; and three bipartisan Republicans: Vandenberg as chairman of the Policy Committee, Massachusetts Senator Leverett Saltonstall as Floor Leader, and California Senator William Knowland as Whip. The challengers hoped that Taft, the current chairman of the Policy Committee, would voluntarily step down, since his term as chairman had expired and he faced a tough reelection fight in Ohio in 1950.[1]

Ultimately, thirteen senators supported the challenge to Taft's leadership. Senator Henry Cabot Lodge, Jr., of Massachusetts became the unofficial leader. Lodge was the grandson of the distinguished Boston patriarch, Senator Henry Cabot Lodge, who in 1919 had fought President Woodrow Wilson's Treaty of Versailles. The elder Lodge bequeathed to his grandson an education befitting a member of the Boston elite—preparatory schools and Harvard University. Before Pearl Harbor, Lodge, Jr., was a noninterventionist who had spoken on behalf of the America First Committee, but by the late 1940s he had become a moderate liberal who supported Truman's foreign policy. Vandenberg believed that the tall, lean, handsome Lodge was certain to become a future leader of the bipartisan Republicans and perhaps even president.

Lodge explained the group's rationale in an article for the *Saturday Evening Post*. The Massachusetts senator warned his fellow

Republicans that although the party had lost in 1948, it "was not a result that calls for coroners. But it does call for soul searching." He castigated those Republicans "who have fought every piece of New Deal reform legislation with uncompromising and myopic fury," giving the party the undeserved reputation as a "rich man's club." Although Lodge characterized the fight as one between "liberals" and "conservatives," the presence of such conservatives as H. Alexander Smith, William Knowland, and Milton Young of North Dakota in the group made it clear that it was really a fight between "internationalists" and "nationalists."[2]

The man caught in the middle of the controversy was Vandenberg. In reflecting on the events of 1948, the Michigan senator admitted that he had "thought the Dewey campaign strategy was sound. . . . But our premise was wrong and, as a result, so was our strategy. However, let him who is without sin throw the first stone. We are all to blame." In mid-November 1948, Vandenberg asserted that the "GOP must present a more aggressive, progressive program in the domestic field, just as it has in foreign affairs . . . [and] it has to do this despite the ideological pain it will mean to the party's elder members," a clear reference to the Taft-Wherry leadership. The Michigan senator believed that if the challengers worked quietly, they would have their best chance of persuading Taft to retire gracefully from contention. In any case, Vandenberg wanted the reorganization resolved "by unanimous agreement." He had worked too long for unity in the party to take a hand in its disruption.[3]

By November 1948, Taft and his followers had experienced frustration in four successive bids for the Republican presidential nomination at the hands of the internationalists. They were in no mood, therefore, to suffer Lodge's accusations that they had been the cause of their party's defeat and should pay for it with their positions of power. In assessing the party's performance in 1948, Taft berated Dewey for having failed to make "an aggressive campaign . . . in answer to the president's attacks on Congress and in fact [he should have given] more than an answer affirmatively claiming credit for that record." During the fall, however, Taft had been conspicuously silent about Dewey's campaign tactics and was as prone to overconfidence as Dewey. Despite Taft's irritation with Dewey's attempts to disassociate himself from the record of the Eightieth Congress, if Dewey had won the election of 1948, there was a good chance for amiable relations between Taft and Dewey.[4]

In mid-December 1948, Taft returned to Washington from a European vacation amidst talk that changes in the Senate Republican leadership were long overdue. In a personal letter Lodge reassured Taft that "my warm and friendly feeling and my admiration for your character and industry are strong," but Lodge pointed out that the American people believed "the Republicans, like the Bourbons of old, had 'forgotten nothing and learned nothing' . . . [and that] 'regardless of the desires of the people, so recently demonstrated, we are going to give you the same old management.' " Lodge was certain that such an attitude could only "insure the defeat of Republicans generally whenever the voters have a chance to do so." While the Massachusetts senator had no specific proposals, he transparently suggested to Taft that "if you agree with any or all of my viewpoint, you will know how to implement it."[5]

In late December, Taft's followers demonstrated their contempt for such notions. They announced that they planned to amend party rules to permit Taft to succeed himself as chairman of the Policy Committee in the upcoming January meeting of all Republican senators. In a gesture of conciliation, they proposed that the committee membership be expanded from seven to nine to allow for the possibility of two additional senators from Lodge's camp.[6]

Lodge's followers, however, were in no mood to douse their war fires. On December 30, Lodge and Senator Irving Ives of New York held a two-hour meeting with eleven of their colleagues, where they agreed that they would oppose any changes on the rules. H. Alexander Smith was excited enough about their prospects to estimate that Republicans would probably divide "about 50-50" between Lodge and Taft. Smith also believed that it was imperative for the future of the party that a leadership change be made, but emphasized that his objections to Taft stemmed from his "isolationism," not his "conservatism." The battle placed Vandenberg in a difficult position. Although he sympathized with Lodge, Vandenberg refused to oppose Taft openly; he did not want to jeopardize his good working relationship with Taft. The Michigan senator, however, had much graver doubts about Wherry, whom he privately called "one of the last remaining symbols of Republican isolationism." Vandenberg noted privately that of the ten Republican senators who voted against the Marshall Plan, nine had been defeated and only Wherry had won reelection. Surely it was unwise, he reasoned, to place Wherry in a prominent position.[7]

When the smoke cleared on January 3, Taft's forces had scored a decisive victory, capturing three of the four leadership posts. Taft was reelected as chairman of the Republican Policy Committee, while Wherry was chosen as Republican Floor Leader, both by twenty-eight to fourteen margins. Millikin became chairman of the Republican Conference by default. As a sop to the challengers, Hugh Butler of Nebraska, a Taftite, nominated Leverett Saltonstall as Republican Whip, which passed without debate. To underscore the meaning of their victory, Millikin reported that Taft said: "We could have an entirely progressive and forward-looking . . . social and economic program, but that the main difference with the Democrats was that the Republicans would not infringe upon the liberties of the people in achieving this."[8]

Still recovering from their scrape with Taft, the bipartisan Republicans suffered new injuries at the hands of the Democrats. At the beginning of the Eighty-First Congress, Republicans became indignant when the Democrats reorganized the Senate Foreign Relations Committee with eight Democrats and only five Republicans. When the Republicans had been in control during the Eightieth Congress, they had set up the same committee on a seven to six basis. On the floor of the Senate, Vandenberg snapped that "the Democratic Conference has seen fit in this connection to take the first partisan action in opposition to the theory and spirit of bipartisan cooperation in foreign affairs which has prevailed in the past 2 years." The implication of the move, the Michigan senator growled, was that Republican Senators are not quite trustworthy and that there must be faithful partisan Democrats, to the maximum, put upon the committee for the sake of the national welfare."[9]

Democratic Senator Alben Barkley of Kentucky, soon to be sworn in as vice president, explained that since the Republican majority in the Eightieth Congress had been six, only three committees had had to endure the eight to five split, but the Democrats now enjoyed a majority of twelve which, they determined, could best be resolved into eight committees based on an eight to five ratio. Although Barkley's arguments may have been mathematically correct, they missed the point made by Republican Senator Wayne Morse of Oregon that 'the action of the Democratic Senators has weakened the position of the Senator from Michigan [Vandenberg] so far as concerns his leadership in support of what Democratic Senators will in the future contend to be a bipartisan policy." Morse emphasized the critically important role Vandenberg played in the bipartisan relationship because of the respect he could command from the diverse elements of his party. It behooved the Democrats, he asserted, to aid him in his juggling act, for in so doing they smoothed the way for their own foreign policy. [10]

More crucial for the future of bipartisanship was the attitude of Senator Tom Connally of Texas, the new chairman of the Senate Foreign Relations Committee. Connally looked like a caricature of a senator: he wore a white suit with a black string tie, had long, flowing, white hair, and perpetually chewed on a cigar. In debate his quick and acerbic tongue often left the galleries in stitches and his opponents looking foolish. Connally usually opposed New Deal-Fair Deal measures, but was a staunch internationalist. After the war, he rose to national prominence in his work for a United Nations Organization.

During the Eightieth Congress, however, Connally became jealous of seeing Vandenberg bask in the limelight of publicity as the "isolationist" who had become a "bipartisan statesman." With Democrats again in control of the Senate, he was determined to elevate his own stature. In one instance, at a White House function in February 1949, Connally upbraided a protocol officer who had permitted Vandenberg to proceed him in a presidential reception line. The Texan snarled that he thought things had changed now that the Democrats had captured control of the Senate. When the officer explained that the order of the legislators was determined strictly by their seniority and that Vandenberg had served about a year longer than Connally, the Texan shook with rage and threatened to have the man fired. It was Connally who had fought the hardest in the Democratic Conference for the eight to five ratio. [11]

The retirement of General George Marshall and Robert Lovett, the outgoing secretary and undersecretary of state, also hurt bipartisanship. Personally and ideologically committed to working with the Republican-controlled Eightieth Congress, Marshall and Lovett skillfully cultivated Vandenberg's good will, especially during the critical negotiations surrounding the Berlin blockade and the passage of the Marshall Plan. The State Department sought out and followed the Michigan senator's advice on a variety of issues to strengthen its foreign policy and blunt congressional opposition. In looking back on those days, Vandenberg agreed with Marshall when the general said that "it would have been a great relaxer to sit down and have a drink with you and Lovett and decide just how we are going to manage the world and then have done it."[12]

The views of the new secretary of state, Dean Acheson, on the role of Congress in foreign policy were quite different from those of his predecessor. Acheson's life was a textbook example of a successful son of the Eastern elite, having been educated at Groton, Yale, and Harvard Law School. He served as Supreme Court Justice Louis Brandeis's law clerk, before joining the prestigious Washington law firm of Covington and Burling. Acheson soon complemented a successful law practice with a career as an effective government administrator, working in the Treasury Department in the 1930s and the State Department in the 1940s. Acheson's background, however, bred in him a lack of respect for those who had attained government service through the elective process. At one point in the 1940s, for instance, he described his work with Congress as "a low life, but a merry one."[13]

More important for the history of bipartisanship in 1949, Acheson did not appreciate Vandenberg's talents, something the Michigan senator sensed and resented. The secretary's description of Vandenberg's behavior on one issue is typical: "Vandenberg's opening attitude of histrionic opposition was his usual one—as I have pointed out before—to any proposal. It usually preceded embracing the proposal and making it his own with a Vandenberg amendment, which gave it saving grace." In another instance, he had kinder words for the Michigan senator: "There was no more effective advocate" than Vandenberg on an issue, but he was "not a creative person. He did not himself originate policies." Acheson had scant appreciation of the critical role the Michigan senator played in the Republican party, as a man who commanded the respect of Taft and Dewey. Vandenberg commented to a friend that "Mr. Acheson would not have been my choice for Secretary of State."[14]

Despite some rocky beginnings for bipartisan Republicans in 1949, the passage of the North Atlantic Treaty saw them at the peak of their power. In the early stages of the negotiations, Acheson consulted closely with Vandenberg and Connally, incorporating some of their ideas into the language of the treaty. Once wedded to it, the two senators beat back attempts to change the treaty in committee and on the floor. Their opponents, denigrated as "isolationists," were reduced to a small, ineffectual group. The treaty passed after two weeks of debate, with only thirteen opposed.

By 1948, those Americans who had placed great faith in the United Nations as an instrument for checking aggression were disillusioned when the threat of a Soviet veto had prevented the organization from acting in the Greek crisis of 1947 and the Czech coup in 1948. Marshall, Lovett, and Vandenberg contemplated ways of circumventing the veto. Their efforts culminated in Senate Resolution 239, the Vandenberg Resolution, that recommended that the United States associate itself with regional collective security organizations as outlined in Article 51 of the charter. In effect, the resolution signaled the willingness of the Senate to align the United States with the Brussels Pact, an alliance of France, Britain, Belgium, the Netherlands, and Luxembourg. In May 1948, the resolution passed by a lopsided sixty-four to four margin after only one day of debate. The State Department immediately opened negotiations with the Europeans to develop what would become the North Atlantic Treaty. Less than a month later, the Berlin blockade added greater urgency to their deliberations. By late 1948, the State Department and the Europeans had devised a tentative treaty.[15]

During February and March 1949, the State Department opened talks with Vandenberg and Connally on the treaty. Their initial reactions were favorable towards all aspects of the treaty except Article 5, which stated that an attack against one member of the treaty "shall be considered an attack against all." The senators feared that the article automatically committed the United States to war and circumvented Congress's war-making prerogatives. State Department officials were successful in working with the senators to rephrase Article 5 to make it less offensive, while retaining the sense of the original draft.[16]

The senators were completely won over and became powerful allies of the administration in committee hearings. When his colleagues raised questions about these issues in committee, Vandenberg at one point confessed that at first he and Connally, too, believed the "the language regarding military action stuck out like a sore thumb, and we insisted that it be put in its proper connotation. Even that request raised a storm of suspicion that we were trying to water this thing down." Therefore, Vandenberg urged his colleagues "not to change a word, unless it is very important."[17]

Significantly, the only areas of discord with the Senate came over an upcoming arms bill about which senators had not been consulted. Lodge, Connally, and Vandenberg were irritated that the newspapers had learned about the details of the arms bill before they had and that it was being discussed in the middle of the treaty debates. The next week, the senators were further aggravated when, after the formal treaty-signing ceremonies, the Europeans announced their military shopping lists. Connally lectured Ernest Gross of the State Department: "one of my complaints is this: . . . You folks come up here and say, 'we want to advise with you' after something is already done. . . . I just do not appreciate that attitude." Vandenberg was more succinct: "The thing that astounds me about it fundamentally is that this Committee was scrupulously consulted regarding every detail of the Atlantic Pact, and yet I do not recall a single word submitted to us . . . regarding this military implementation."[18]

On April 21, Acheson and Secretary of Defense Louis Johnson appeared before the committee to straighten things out. Acheson argued that since Europe was the "keystone" of America's security, developing a sense of confidence among the Europeans was crucial in achieving economic recovery. Important in building confidence was countering the Soviet military presence on the Continent with the pact and an infusion of arms. Getting to the root of the senators' problem, Acheson assured them although the aid was justified under Article 3 of the treaty, the Senate was not automatically obliged to vote for the arms bill if it ratified the treaty. However, the secretary stated: "My own judgment and I presume the judgment of many Members of Congress, will be that the United States can and should do something to assist the other countries in the pact to maintain and develop their collective security."[19]

During the last two weeks of May, the committee staff developed a report on the North Atlantic Treaty that, in Vandenberg's words, would "mobilize our position so strongly that we could say to a reservation or to any resolution, 'It isn't necessary.' " When the report was presented to the committee, most of the attention again focused on Article 5. During the public hearings, Senators Arthur Watkins of Utah and Forrest Donnell of Missouri, two of the most extreme isolationists in the Senate, had raised some tough constitutional questions about the war powers of the president and congress that still vexed the committee. Would the United States be committed to declaring war if Paris were attacked in the same way that it would be if New York were bombed? In the skillful hands of Vandenberg and Gross, the report judiciously defused the issue, noting that "the President and the Congress, within their sphere of assigned constitutional responsibilities" would take the appropriate action to protect the country. The report concluded that "nothing in the treaty . . . increases or decreases the constitutional powers of either the President or the Congress or changes the relationship between them."[20]

The committee report also sought to allay any fears aroused by Article 3 which related to military aid. To meet the objection that ratification of the pact obligated the Senate to pass the arms bill, the report stated that although there was a "definite obligation . . . to contribute, individually and collectively, to the defense of the North Atlantic area. . . . There is no specific obligation as to the timing, nature, and extent of assistance." Another section of the report also asserted that since economic recovery was of paramount importance, arms aid would not take precedence over the Marshall Plan and that the arms could not be used by the Europeans to build up "military establishments for use in their overseas territories."[21]

On June 6, the committee unanimously passed the treaty and the report, permitting an ebullient Senator Connally to exclaim that the treaty "will promote the cause of peace and will contribute toward stability and concord in the North Atlantic area." Despite a few rough spots, especially in the way the arms bill was handled, the State Department and the committee worked together well and with impressive results. In February and March when Connally and Vandenberg had pointed out difficulties in Articles 3 and 5, efforts were made to meet their objections without injuring the substance of the treaty. By June 6, Vandenberg had what he wanted, a unanimous committee vote and a powerful report.[22]

In the face of such a combination, the opponents to the treaty appeared as forlorn as waifs. At first, few of them came out publicly against the treaty, although the addition of Taft in mid-July gave them more respectability. The core of the group included Republican Senators Taft and John W. Bricker of Ohio, Kenneth Wherry of Nebraska, Arthur Watkins of Utah, George Malone of Nevada, Forrest Donnell and James P. Kem of Missouri, William Jenner of Indiana, Ralph Flanders of Vermont, William Langer and Milton Young of North Dakota, and Edwin Johnson of Colorado; Progressive Senator Glenn Taylor of Idaho; and Democratic Senator Harry Byrd of Virginia. While most of these senators agreed that Western Europe was important to America's security, they believed it could be adequately protected by extending the Monroe Doctrine to Europe, rather than having a formal alliance. They were also suspicious that the "mutual self-help" section of Article 3 presaged an expensive military arms program for Europe.[23]

Nonetheless, on July 11, Watkins introduced a reservation (later cosponsored by Wherry and Taft) that was aimed at circumscribing Article 3. It stated that nothing in the treaty would create "a legal or moral obligation on the part of the United States to furnish or supply arms, armaments, military, naval, or air equipment or supplies to any party or parties to said Treaty." Vandenberg argued that the reservation was unnecessary since Article 3 was not so open-ended as Watkins, Wherry, and Taft implied. The Michigan senator pointed out that since the article stressed "self-help and mutual aid," it guaranteed that no one got a "free ride." Vandenberg warned his colleagues not "to invite misgivings that, though we ratify the pact, we shall have no sense of mutual concern in the defense problems of those brave countries which sit in the immediate shadow of jeopardy, which wherever it may break, is aimed finally at us. The consequences [of that] could be appalling." The reservation was defeated soundly, but it mustered twenty-one votes, more than any of the others.[24]

Watkins then introduced a reservation aimed at Article 5, which stated that the United States would assume "no obligations to restore and maintain the security of the North Atlantic area . . .

unless the Congress . . . shall by act or joint resolution so provide." Successive speeches by Connally, Democrat Elbert Thomas of Utah, and Lodge hammered away at the reservation. Thomas brushed aside the constitutional issue, arguing that "no treaty has ever been entered into which does not imply mutuality of some kind." Lodge described the extension of the Monroe Doctrine to Europe as "extraordinary," since it would mean that "we should undertake the defense of Europe singlehandedly without the cooperation of the Europeans." Connally too scoffed at the reservation, claiming it would "tie the hands of the Congress and the President." The reservation and another like it were crushed eighty-four to eleven and eighty-seven to eight.[25]

On July 21, 1949, the Senate ratified the North Atlantic Treaty by an impressive eighty-two to thirteen margin. It was a classic example of how powerful bipartisanship could be when the proper elements fell into place. A year before, the Senate had anticipated the treaty in their passage of the Vandenberg Resolution by an impressive margin. Public opinion polls demonstrated that a considerable sentiment had developed among the American people for a political relationship with Western Europe. At the same time, the Soviet Union's aggressive behavior in the Berlin blockade made the pact appear more urgently needed. With the specter of another world war hanging over Europe, the notions of the nationalists seemed dangerously outdated to most Americans. The administration had consulted with Vandenberg and Connally before submitting the treaty to the Senate and heeded their advice on language and tactics. The two senators, armed with language they could defend and a strong committee report, were able to strike down every reservation by lopsided margins. Watkins complained to one State Department official that with the press carrying the administration line almost exclusively, "anyone who questioned the Pact or what lay behind it was being put in the position of being pro-Russian."[26]

Less than a week after the ratification of the treaty, the administration introduced its arms bill. While the passage of the North Atlantic Treaty provided a good example of executive-legislative cooperation, the arms bill episode showed just the opposite. The State Department had already irritated Vandenberg and Connally by leaking information about the arms program during the treaty debates. By June, the administration, which was fearful that it could not get a military assistance bill before the end of the congressional session, was desperate to move quickly. Because the administration had not consulted the Foreign Relations Committee before releasing the bill, it was embarrassed to learn that Vandenberg had major objections to it. Momentarily bereft of Vandenberg's support, the Military Assistance Program (MAP) was left to the "tender mercies" of the Taftites and Southern Democrats, a coalition that was skilled in paring down programs with big appropriations and increases in presidential authority. Acheson at first clung to his initial proposal, but quickly realized that if he wanted a program he would have to mollify Vandenberg and his colleagues.

Vandenberg initiated the attack on the MAP, calling it "too wide in scope and too general in [its] grant of power," while it ignored "the machinery that the pact provides for its own implementation." The Michigan senator commented that the bill had to be "re-written and curtailed to get action at this session" of Congress. He suggested that only an interim program be considered for now. John Foster Dulles, who had recently been appointed to the Senate to replace outgoing Senator Robert Wagner of New York, released a similar statement, while Taft added that the bill "demands that Congress substantially abdicate all functions relating to foreign policy, and authorize the State and Defense Departments to make alliances throughout the world." Lodge underscored the same points, noting that the department had "ignored the facts of life . . . [since it] overlooked the recent expression of legislative sentiment on the Hill." Privately, Vandenberg explained:

I served blunt notice today that I simply would not support the president's bill. It's almost unbelievable in its grant of unlimited power to the Chief Executive. . . . The old bipartisan business is certainly "out the window" on this one. Yet I don't want to be shoved over into a position of seeming hostility to the objective (in which I deeply believe). So it's a pretty tight "poker game" between Acheson and me.[27]

On July 29 and August 2, during the executive session meeting of the combined Foreign Relations and Armed Services Committees, Vandenberg outlined his objections. Although he supported arms aid, the Michigan senator argued that the administration's program would strengthen "those [in Congress] who want to beat the whole show. That is the hell of this situation. . . . [Section 3] will just inflame this country to a point where you will have an isolationist country all over again. You sure will out my way!" Noting that Dulles, Lodge, and H. Alexander Smith were behind him, the Michigan senator asserted that the department's only hope to pass anything during that session was to draft a new bill. Specifically, he argued that the bill should eliminate Section 3; its language should be more in line with the United Nations Charter and Articles 3 and 9 of the North Atlantic Treaty; in addition, the program should not proceed until a strategic plan was developed by the North Atlantic Advisory Council. Vandenberg described the encounter to his wife: "I gave 'em an ultimatum—write a new and reasonable bill or you will get no bill and it will be your fault! Both Committees backed me up—and at the end of a rather dramatic session, they went downtown to write a new bill. It was a very tense session."[28]

The progress of the arms bill gave evidence of the new realities that had developed in the bipartisan relationship since Truman's reelection. Connally, who had been jealous of the attention Vandenberg had received during the Eightieth Congress, made it difficult for the State Department to consult with Vandenberg. The Michigan senator recognized the problem: "I feel rather sorry for Acheson. I think he would like to carry on in the old pattern. But it just isn't possible under the new set-up [with Connally as chairman]." At one point, however, Acheson did stop at Vandenberg's apartment to discuss the world's problems. Vandenberg described it as "slightly reminiscent of the old Lovett days. . . . I didn't let him unload them [the problems] on me in any such fashion as Marshall and Lovett did. But I tried to be both genial and helpful." Nonetheless, Acheson had little appreciation for Vandenberg's position; he denigrated the Michigan senator's opposition to the arms bill, as his "going through the familiar gambit of opposing and obtaining an amendment before he could support it." To Acheson, the arms program was vital in meeting the Soviet menace, so he expected its immediate passage with few congressional restrictions.[29]

Vandenberg's perspective was much different. The Michigan senator had a keen sense of where his party stood on foreign policy questions and was determined to move cautiously in an internationalist direction to pass each program by an overwhelming majority. In debates, Vandenberg used each new internationalist measure as a building block for the next step, arguing that the new programs were logical extensions of past decisions. This explains his insistence that Senate Resolution 239 conform to the framework of the United Nations Charter, that the North Atlantic Treaty borrow the language of both the charter and Senate Resolution 239, and that the arms bill become the logical extension of Articles 3 and 9 of the treaty. Such techniques became the grist for the powerful floor presentations for which the senator was famous. When Acheson disdainfully described Vandenberg's notions about tailoring the arms bill to the wording of the North Atlantic Treaty as "wholly without merit," he revealed a good deal about his inability to perceive the constraints under which Vandenberg operated.[30]

The lack of consultations and the clash with Acheson had, as Vandenberg put it, some "collateral advantages" for the senator. Since the election of 1948, the Taftites had attacked bipartisan Republicans for mimicking the administration's foreign policies while making few contributions of their own. Taft's major objections to containment (that its cost threatened the American economy, its increases in presidential power menaced Americans' freedoms, and its internationalism compromised the country's freedom of action) were particularly acute in the case of the arms bill. Vandenberg, having himself spent many years in the nationalist camp, clearly perceived these flaws in the administration's bill. It was also a relief for him to join Taft for a change in attacking a Democratic program. In a letter to columnist Walter Lippmann, the Michigan senator explained that the quarrel over the arms bill has "demonstrated that the Republicans' contribution to so-called 'bi-partisan foreign policy' is not on a 'me too' basis. This 'me too' charge has been the most successful criticism which the isolationist wing of the Republican Party has been able to throw at me. I have never felt free to answer. Now events have answered for themselves."[31]

During August, the State Department had to give in on MAP. On August 5, the department introduced a new bill that met many of Vandenberg's objections. Acheson explained that he reduced the "breadth of powers which the former act gave the President," and gave a clearer indication of which countries would receive aid. While

the Michigan senator greeted the new proposal enthusiastically
(saying, "I think you have done a swell job"), he maintained that
the program was still too expensive and that it did not follow the
procedure laid out in Articles 3 and 9 of the treaty, which stipulated that an Advisory Council would determine arms requirements first and would then present a coherent request to the United
States government. The House gave the State Department another
shock by cutting the arms appropriations in half. Vandenberg crowed
to his wife:

The House sure "put the crimps" into the arms bill! . . . And I don't
blame 'em much—the thing has been so miserably handled. Now Acheson
and company are yelling to high heaven for help. [John] Foster [Dulles]
and I can "write our own ticket." But I don't propose to let them belatedly
dump their problem in my lap. We'll help 'em trim their bill . . . into
possible shape. But it's not going to be *my* bill.

Faced with the House and Vandenberg in revolt, Acheson again
surrendered; he telephoned Connally saying that "he did not feel
the changes [proposed by Vandenberg] did much harm."[32]

On August 25, Vandenberg formally introduced his amendments
to the bill in committee, again maintaining that the aid earmarked
for Europe should be funneled through the pact. Tydings weakly
objected, declaring that "in this interim period time is too pre-
cious, and the agreements between the military people are already
made, and I do not think we ought to lose that time." Only Connally joined Tydings in voting against the amendment. The Michigan senator also got his way on two other amendments, providing
that Congress could cut off aid to a country by concurrent resolution and that the total appropriation would be $1 billion.[33]

Although the arms bill ultimately passed Congress, it faced greater
obstacles than the treaty. The bill that emerged closely resembled
Vandenberg's ideas and passed the committee with only conservatives Walter George and Richard Russell of Georgia and Harry
Byrd of Virginia opposed. In the floor debates, Connally and Vandenberg argued that the arms program was a critical adjunct of the
Marshall Plan and North Atlantic Treaty, insuring the security of
Western Europe. Vandenberg added that it was the logical extension of the North Atlantic Treaty, which had passed by an over-

whelming margin. Vandenberg dwelled at great length on the glaring inadequacies of the initial bill and emphasized how the new bill corrected those problems.[34]

A coalition of Taft Republicans and southern Democrats opposed the bill. Their leader, Walter George, was a conservative who had a traditional southerner's taste for a strict interpretation of the constitution. An eloquent orator known for speaking his mind, his colleagues referred to him as the "conscience of the Senate." In the late 1930s, George (like many other Southerners) was initially reticent to support Franklin Roosevelt's foreign policy, but ultimately he became a staunch internationalist. During the debate on MAP, George introduced several amendments to cut the appropriation; he argued that the larger amount would necessitate prohibitively high taxes that would undermine American prosperity. While most of the opponents to the program highlighted the economy argument, the Taftites among them also questioned the wisdom of the internationalists' strategy. Wherry and Watkins, for instance, believed that since any attempt to compete with the Soviets' enormous ground strength in Europe was ludicrous, the money should instead go toward stronger American air and atomic forces. Taft added that the program seemed provocative. More irritating to the Ohioan and his colleagues, however, was the internationalists' implication that "anyone who opposed an international measure is an isolationist."[35]

The fight over the arms bill testified to the new strength and assertiveness that Taft Republicans had acquired since the 1948 elections. In the debates over aid to Greece and Turkey, the Marshall Plan, and the North Atlantic Treaty, Vandenberg and the administration had cultivated public opinion and carefully tailored the language of each program to minimize dissent. The results were lopsided legislative victories. On the MAP, however, Taftites found a common ground with some Southern Democrats, and put up a much better fight. While the MAP passed by a comfortable fifty-five to twenty-four, the tallies on the amendments to cut the appropriation were closer (forty-six to thirty-two and forty-seven to thirty-one). Had Vandenberg not altered those sections of the initial bill concerning the president's authority and the program's relationship to the treaty, the arms bill would probably have been defeated.[36]

By September, it was apparent in the debates on the arms bill that the Taftites would not be stifled. The split in the party, evident in December 1948 in the fight over Senate Republican leadership posts, was only papered over during the debates on the North Atlantic Treaty. The bipartisan coalition had triumphed because a popular consensus existed and careful State Department consultations had wedded Connally and Vandenberg to the treaty. However, the tribulations of the arms bill showed that bipartisanship was fragile and that the Taft Republicans were growing stronger. Events in East Asia coming on the eve of an election year brought the split into full relief by January 1950.

3

The Senate and the Fall of China, 1949

Cardinal principles of Republican politics of the 1950s and 1960s included staunch support for Generalissimo Chiang Kai-shek, hostile opposition to the Chinese Communist regime, and a belief that Chiang had been "sold down the river" by either incompetent or traitorous Democratic politicians of the 1940s. Events of the period 1949–1951, which featured the collapse of the Nationalist military position on the mainland, the advent of the Korean War, and the rise of McCarthyism, played key roles in shaping Republican notions about China. Before 1950, however, the overwhelming number of Senate Republicans (all but the China bloc) opposed large-scale American assistance to China, but they were uncomfortable about cutting free of Chiang. By late 1948, bipartisan Republicans likewise doubted that sending more aid to China would do any good, but they were also leery about cutting Chiang off.

Vandenberg faced an ambitious legislative calendar in 1949 that included such major measures as the annual appropriation for the Marshall Plan, the ratification of the North Atlantic Treaty, and the Military Assistance Program. In an effort to minimize criticism, therefore, the Michigan senator reluctantly supported small concessions to the China bloc. While Taftites occasionally lent rhetorical support to the China bloc during 1949, they also remained unenthusiastic about foreign aid regardless of its destination. It was not until early 1950 that the Taftites aggressively seized upon the arguments of the China bloc with the vicious partisanship of McCarthyism.[1]

The China-bloc members, relatively recent converts to Chiang's cause, also supported Truman's containment program for Europe. A glance at the index to the *Congressional Record* for the period 1945–1947, for instance, reveals that of the four senatorial leaders of the bloc in 1949 (Republicans William F. Knowland of California, Styles Bridges of New Hampshire, and H. Alexander Smith of New Jersey; and Democrat Pat McCarran of Nevada) only Bridges showed much interest in China prior to 1948. In the 1950s, Knowland was called the "senator from Formosa," but in 1946–1947 he concentrated most of his efforts on atomic energy. The Californian often boasted of his record of support for the bipartisan foreign policy; on domestic issues he was a moderate conservative. Smith of New Jersey, whom Woodrow Wilson had hired as a history professor at Princeton, became intensely interested in China in the spring of 1949 when he was hospitalized for phlebitis. Only a year before (in February and March of 1948) in discussions on the China Aid Act of 1948, Smith had been as unenthusiastic about aiding China as Vandenberg and Lodge. McCarran also won his reputation in the Senate for issues quite unrelated to China. The Nevada senator was famous for championing such Western issues as water rights and the remonetization of silver, prompting one columnist to quip that he was "silver-haired, silver-tongued, and silver-minded." Bridges of New Hampshire was the only one of the four to have a longer standing affinity for East Asian problems, having spoken out in defense of Patrick Hurley in 1945. Although he had earned a reputation as a fiscal conservative and staunch anti-Communist, he also voted for the containment program during 1947–1949.[2]

The China-bloc senators believed that America's interests in East Asia would best be protected by having a strong and independent China not under the control of any hostile power. Since they were convinced that the Communist Chinese were only the "pawns" of Moscow, the bloc's members argued that the United States had to stop the communists' advances at all costs. Some of the supporters of the Nationalists outside the Senate, such as General Claire L. Chennault, favored dispatching 20,000 American advisors into China to administer a huge aid program while permitting Americans to join a volunteer air force to fight the Chinese Communists. Although the China-bloc senators admitted that Nationalist leader

Chiang had his faults and had made grievous errors of judgment, they nonetheless argued that as a World War II comrade-in-arms and a fervent anticommunist, he deserved American support. In 1949, the bloc introduced two major aid programs, one by Mc-Carran in March and one by Knowland in August.[3]

Opposing the China bloc were the East Asia experts of the State Department. Like the bloc, they also believed that America needed a strong and independent China, and many of them were appalled at the thought of a communist takeover, but they became convinced that Chiang's regime had become too weak and corrupt to stop the communists. During World War II, some of the "old China hands" such as John Carter Vincent and John Paton Davies were impressed by the toughness and dynamism of the Communist Chinese forces, especially when compared to the lazy incompetence that pervaded the Nationalist regime. While Secretaries of State George C. Marshall and Dean G. Acheson were never as enamored of the Communist Chinese as were the "old China hands," they nonetheless became convinced that Chiang's was a losing cause.[4]

It was during the period from late 1948 to spring 1949, as the communist forces swept through Manchuria and appeared ready to swallow up China proper, that the positions that the administration and the senatorial factions would later assume became evident. Styles Bridges, as chairman of the watchdog committee on the Economic Cooperation Administration, appointed two men already well known for their Nationalist sympathies to conduct separate fact-finding missions in China. The two, former ambassador to the Soviet Union William Bullitt and former Democratic Senator D. Worth Clark of Idaho, reported that while the situation in China was desperate, American aid administered by American advisors might yet turn the tide against the communists. Bullitt made this appeal: "I plead for a bipartisan policy in China and rapid action. It is very late. It is not yet too late." Bridges then requested that Truman call Congress back into special session to consider a China aid bill.[5]

Truman and Vandenberg, however, remained unenthusiastic about Bridge's ideas. The president refused to call the Eightieth Congress back into session, while Vandenberg noted that public discussions of Chiang's situation would only undermine the Nationalists' morale. In an off-the-record press conference the Michigan senator argued that "our mistakes have been made over a period of time, and we can't recoup them between now and New Year's. . . . And would more money alone solve the problem? It certainly hasn't up to now!" In his correspondence Vandenberg observed, much as the State Department would do later in the *China White Paper*, that since 1945 the United States had provided some $2 billion in aid to a government so demoralized by corruption that many of its American-equipped divisions had surrendered without firing a shot.[6]

The new year brought Truman a new secretary of state, Dean Acheson, who held strong views on China. Acheson, always more interested in events in Europe than in China, had even less patience than Marshall with the irresponsible corruption and Byzantine politics that characterized Chiang's regime. As the Generalissimo's forces fell apart during 1949, therefore, Acheson believed that the best way to further American interests in China was to cut free of Chiang, while keeping the avenues of communication to the Chinese Communists open. This meant that during 1949 the secretary opposed two aid programs advanced by the China bloc and sought to keep his options open on the question of recognition until the Nationalist government was properly buried. Acheson hoped that if Communist China showed its intention to be a responsible member of the world community, then American recognition might be forthcoming, probably after the 1950 congressional elections. The Korean War rendered such a course impossible, however. While Acheson enjoyed great success in implementing his China policy during 1949, he failed to develop a working relationship with those Republicans who shared his point of view, leaving his policies open to the ravages of McCarthyism in 1950.[7]

By early February 1949 the military situation had become even more serious, and the National Security Council recommended to the president that shipments of military aid to the Nationalists be in large part suspended. Before making the decision, however, Truman conferred with the congressional leadership. On February 5, Truman explained to a congressional delegation that if he did not suspend aid, it would only fall into communist hands. While several congressmen agreed, Vandenberg presented stern objections. The Michigan senator, like Truman, was convinced that the Nationalists were doomed and that more aid probably would not alter the situation, but he wanted to avoid "the charge that *we* are the ones who gave poor China the final push into disaster. . . . This blood must not be on *our* hands." Vandenberg believed that the Senate and the American people were unaware of Chiang's true situation and would not understand abandoning the former World War II ally. The president acceded to the Michigan senator's wishes and agreed not to suspend aid, but he also ordered that no shipments be expedited.[8]

In early February, Acheson adeptly identified the political difficulties that the China situation presented the administration. In a conversation with Truman about a letter the president had received from a number of House Republicans criticizing China policy, the secretary outlined the administration's alternatives:

To make a non-committal reply which would result in the publication of the correspondence and the charge that the Administration had no policy on China; the second course was to make a vigorous reply setting forth the facts. This inevitably would harm the Chinese Government. A third possible course was for me to get in touch with the signers of the letter and try to have an off-the-record and very frank discussion with them.

From February through April, Acheson pursued the third alternative three times (once with House Republicans, once with the Senate Foreign Relations Committee, and once with Bridges and Wherry) while quietly preparing for the second option (the publication of the White Paper).[9]

Therefore, on February 25, Acheson held a confidential meeting with House Republicans to respond to the major points of the letter. The secretary argued that since America's ability to control events in a country as vast as China was limited, further efforts would probably not change the outcome of the war. In trying to explain to the congressmen that the American position was necessarily in limbo until the confusion of the civil war subsided, Acheson employed an analogy that, as he later put it, furnished the China bloc "with a weapon beyond their dreams." The secretary compared the China situation to a great oak tree falling in the forest, where it was difficult to see clearly "until the dust settles." Advocates of more aid for Chiang later pointed to that "dust settles" phrase as proof that the administration had adopted a do-nothing policy.[10]

The China bloc had not given up. In late February, Pat Mc-
Carran introduced a bill he called the "China Aid Act of 1949."
The bill envisioned giving China $1.5 billion worth of aid, as well
as a considerable loan. In a clear concession to the argument that
such aid would only be lost to Nationalist graft, McCarran proposed that the military aid be provided only "under American military supervision," that Americans collaborate with Chinese experts to overhaul their tax structure, and that the aid be contingent
on Chiang's guarantee of the "revenues of the major ports of central and south China . . . as collateral for the repayment of debts"
incurred under the program. As McCarran explained in letters to
some of his colleagues: "It seems to me that we have done much
talking about the Communist threat in the Orient, but we have
been dilatory in acting. I trust my bill will start something and
may lead to concertive [sic] and constructive action."[11]

The bill was referred to the Foreign Relations Committee where
Democratic chairman Tom Connally of Texas promptly pigeon-
holed it. McCarran, however, secured the signatures of fifty senators (twenty-five Republicans and, including himself, twenty-five
Democrats) on a letter requesting the committee to hold hearings
"on the general China situation and on the bill." Conspicuously
absent from the letter were the signatures of the Republican party's top leadership, notable Taft, Vandenberg, Kenneth S. Wherry
of Nebraska, Eugene Millikin of Colorado, and Leverett Saltonstall
of Massachusetts. Comments by some of the signers of McCarran's
letter clearly indicate that they were more interested in obtaining
information on China than in providing huge amounts of aid.
McCarran himself admitted as much to Chinese Ambassador Wellington Koo, explaining that what most of the signers of the letter
"meant was that they were sympathetic with the Chinese cause
which was of importance to the United States and that they would
like to see something done to help China."[12]

In mid-March, the Foreign Relations Committee therefore commenced closed meetings that gave the State Department another
opportunity to describe very frankly its assessment of the situation.
Dean Acheson summarized his objections to the bill in a tersely
worded letter to Chairman Connally. He argued that the Mc-
Carran proposal was "of such a magnitude and character [as to be]
unwarranted by present circumstances." Administration witnesses

explained that since it was fruitless to extend further aid to Chiang, it was in America's interest to stay aloof from the civil war. That way, they argued, any antiforeign sentiment that developed would be focused on the Soviets. Acheson concluded that the only way to save the Nationalists would be to introduce "an unpredictably large American armed force in actual combat," something, of course, that he flatly opposed. Committee members posed few challenges to Acheson's assessment.[13]

Vandenberg's main concern about the McCarran bill was its possible impact on the Marshall Plan appropriation bill for 1949 which was scheduled shortly for consideration on the floor. "There will just be an uproar and confusion galore," the Michigan senator complained in secret committee sessions. "There will be China amendments." A week later, as the administration finished its briefing on China, Vandenberg reminded his colleagues that "the ECA bill comes up at noon. We will be asked 'What about China?' " Vandenberg recommended simply extending the April 2, 1949, deadline of the China Aid Act of 1948 to permit the president to use the unexpended portion of the $125 million fund. Vandenberg defended his proposal by saying: "The only case for it is not to put ourselves in a position where they can prove that we ran out on the Nationalist Government at the last minute before it had disintegrated." That afternoon on the Senate floor, Connally mentioned that the committee favored an extension of the China Aid Act of 1948; the McCarran bill was scarcely heard from again.[14]

In mid-April, Connally routinely released the letter Acheson had written on the McCarran bill. Bridges, trying to keep the issue alive, charged that "it is final and absolute proof that there ought to be a full dress investigation by the Congress of the State Department position towards China and its reasons therefore," regardless of "the merits" of the McCarran bill. In late April, the issue surfaced again in a meeting of the Senate Republican Policy Committee that saw Vandenberg and Bridges square off. Most of the meeting was devoted to European matters with Vandenberg asking his colleagues not to abandon the "nonpartisan foreign policy." In an obvious reference to Bridges, the Michigan senator berated the inconsistency of those who opposed the Military Assistance Program while at the same time advocating huge outlays of military hardware for China. Bridges delivered a sharp rebuttal to

Vandenberg. "We don't have a nonpartisan foreign policy in this country," he snapped, "What we have is a one-party foreign policy—the Truman Administration foreign policy. It is this one-party foreign policy that is responsible for the mess our country and the rest of the world is in today." The New Hampshire senator also retorted that it was Vandenberg who was being inconsistent in opposing communism in Europe while ignoring its spread in Asia. Although such Taftites as Wherry, Millikin, Harry P. Cain of Washington, and William E. Jenner of Indiana, lent some verbal support to Bridges, they remained deaf to his call to arms. Scarcely a year later, in a much different political atmosphere, however, Taft's allies were more eager to embrace Bridges's ideas when they were proposed by Wisconsin Senator Joseph McCarthy.[15]

In late April, Acheson and Truman tried to quiet their critics by confidentially showing them proof of Chiang's incompetence. In a Blair House meeting with Bridges and Wherry, the president and the secretary revealed a variety of cables from China and other secret information that supported the department's position. While reports of the senators' reactions varied, they were probably not won over. Many newspapers conveyed the impression that Bridges and Wherry had been taken aback, quoting Wherry as saying that he "had a fine and interesting conference. I learned some things I didn't know before." However, veteran syndicated columnist Frank McNaughton probably came closer to the truth; he reported that Bridges and Wherry were "puzzled" at the special treatment they had received and "remained unconvinced as to the wisdom of the State Department's course in failing to take action to stop the spread of Chinese Communism."[16]

While the Taftites were cool to the ideas of aid and an investigation, they did lend occasional rhetorical support to the China bloc. One of the best examples of that collaboration during 1949 was in their mutual opposition in May to the appointment of W. Walton Butterworth to be assistant secretary of state for Far Eastern affairs. Although Butterworth's credentials were impressive, his sympathy with Acheson's policy of curtailing aid to Chiang made his nomination anathema to the China bloc and an affront to others who had questions about America's China policy. The China bloc, assisted by Wherry and occasionally by Taft, postponed consideration of the nomination for nearly three months. In late September,

Butterworth was finally confirmed in a nearly straight-party-line vote, forty-nine to twenty-seven. The China bloc and most Taft Republicans opposed Butterworth, but not a single Democrat joined them. Bipartisan Republicans, however, were split with two voting against the nomination (Irving Ives of New York and Leverett Saltonstall of Massachusetts), three in favor of it (Margaret Chase Smith of Maine; and George Aiken and Charles Tobey of Vermont), and four not voting at all (Vandenberg, Lodge, Wayne Morse of Oregon, and John Foster Dulles of New York). The vote symbolized the political dilemma of the bipartisan Republicans, for while many of them had misgivings about China policy, they did not believe that directly challenging the administration would improve the situation.[17]

Having tried on three separate occasions to develop a confidential understanding with its critics, the State Department went public with its case. Although the White Paper was completed in mid-July, the department delayed its release while it awaited Ambassador John Leighton Stuart's return from China, the concurrence of the Defense Department, and the support of Congress. Butterworth, for instance, favored striking a deal with Vandenberg whereby the department would delay the publication of the White Paper until after the Nationalists fell if the senator would quell Republican attacks on China policy. On July 19, Acheson met with Connally to inform him that the White Paper would be released soon and that he wanted to meet with the committee on the "development of Far Eastern policies in the future." Connally liked the idea of consultation, believing it would be good to "get the Republicans in" on China.[18]

On July 22, Acheson conferred with Vandenberg at the senator's apartment, but no record was kept of the substance of the meeting. It probably did not go well for the secretary since at that point the administration was on the verge of introducing its Military Assistance Program, about which Vandenberg had serious misgivings. If the "deal" that Butterworth recommended was broached, it probably got nowhere since Acheson later did release the White Paper prior to the collapse of the Nationalists. With something as critical to European policy as the MAP in the offing, the ever-cautious Vandenberg did not relish giving the opponents of the bipartisan foreign policy such a tempting target.[19]

On August 5, the State Department released the *China White Paper*. It included 1,054 pages of classified government documents and a letter of transmittal by Acheson that pinned the causes of Chiang's collapse squarely on the Generalissimo. Much of the argument contained in the letter would have been acceptable to bipartisan Republicans, except that the secretary defended every major decision the administration had made on East Asia since World War II. That stance gave his letter more of the appearance of an apology than an analysis. At the same time, Acheson announced the formation of an Advisory Council on East Asian policy that mocked the spirit of bipartisanship. The council consisted of Raymond Fosdick and Everett Case, both university presidents and Republicans, with Philip C. Jessup as their chairman. Since Case and Fosdick held little real standing in the GOP, however, the gesture rang hollow.[20]

Although the secretary feared that the White Paper would be greeted by a "storm of attack," the attack was brief and confined to the China bloc. Throughout August Knowland castigated the White Paper as self-serving, but few of his senatorial colleagues joined him. On August 22, the China bloc made an impassioned rebuttal in its "Memorandum on the White Paper," blasting it as "a 1,054 page whitewash of a wishful do-nothing policy which has succeeded only in placing Asia in danger of Soviet conquest." Vandenberg straddled the positions of the bloc and the department. He noted that the White Paper recorded "tragic, however . . . well-meaning mistakes" by the United States, but that the Nationalist government had also erred "in its failure to clean its own house." Opinion polls taken in August showed, however, that the bloc had scored points. Nearly twice as many Americans believed that their government had handled the China situation poorly as thought it had done well. By the same margin, however, Americans were also convinced that Chiang was a poor leader and that there was nothing the United States could to "stop China from going Communist."[21]

In early August, with the Nationalists apparently in their death throes, the China bloc made the last attempt of 1949 to secure funds for China. William F. Knowland led the fight to add a China section to the pending MAP bill. One of the youngest members of the Senate, Knowland had risen to prominence as a journalist in his father's newspaper, the *Oakland Tribune*, and in state politics. In 1945, he was appointed to the United States Senate by California governor Earl Warren following the death of the venerable Hiram Johnson. Knowland was a moderately conservative, bipartisan Republican who later developed an obsession with Nationalist China.[22]

With the MAP, the China bloc was tactically in a stronger position than it had been when the McCarran bill had been introduced, since three of its members, Knowland, Bridges, and Smith, sat on the combined Armed Services and Foreign Relations Committees which considered the bill. As before, Vandenberg wanted the bill reported out of the committee with as near to a unanimous vote as possible, so he was willing to appease the China bloc. By late August, Knowland and the State Department were at loggerheads over the amount of China aid, how it was to be accounted for, whether advisors were needed, and where in East Asia it could be used. The California senator favored a $175 million fund for China, to be administered by American advisors, and $18 million more to oppose communism in the rest of East Asia. The State Department, backed by Senator Connally, would accept a small unvouchered fund (preferably under $50 million) to be placed at the president's discretion for combating communism anywhere in East Asia.[23]

On September 9, Connally rammed his measure through the whole committee by slender votes of twelve to nine and eleven to nine, although the California senator seemed willing to compromise and was sympathetic to the larger MAP bill. Vandenberg, appalled by the chairman's high-handed tactics, sided with Knowland. In a final attempt to win the China bloc over to the MAP, the Michigan senator pleaded with the Democrats: "Don't you think it would be wise to wait 24 hours for a vote on the whole bill and see whether there is any remaining chance to liquidate any of these difficulties?" Over the weekend, Vandenberg, Smith, and Knowland arrived at a compromise that provided for an unvouchered fund of $75 million to be spent at the president's discretion "in the general area of China." The MAP bill then passed the combined committees by a healthy nineteen to three vote that saw Knowland, Vandenberg, and Smith siding with the majority.[24]

In August, when Knowland had begun the fight, there was no mention of China in the MAP bill; consequently, the allocation of any aid had to be regarded as a victory for him. The Californian persuaded the State Department, Connally, and Vandenberg, none of whom favored his program, to establish a fund for China. The administration gave away little, however, since it did not have to spend any of the money or even account for its expenditure. Indeed, evidence suggests that Acheson was interested in having such a fund to use against communist forces elsewhere in Asia. The amendment's passage owed a large measure to Vandenberg's desire to minimize dissent to the MAP and to the Republicans' growing belief that the administration's China policy was badly flawed. The Michigan senator was willing to set up a fund that would probably never be used to avoid the charge that he had partaken in the "last push" of China and to win the votes of three influential Republicans: Knowland, Smith, and Bridges.[25]

While, on the question of recognition, the China bloc may have had more success in influencing the administration than on providing funds for Chiang, other factors were far more decisive in explaining the administration's course. In late 1949, the department moved cautiously on recognition because it believed that "precipitous" action, as its officials called it, was not in the best interests of the United States. While the administration would have encountered political opposition had it suggested recognition of the Peiping government during the autumn of 1949, it had plenty of other reasons for proceeding slowly, too: Chiang's government was still in existence, the communists had neither complete control over the entire mainland nor were they observing the amenities of diplomatic protocol, and the administration did not want to seem to be rushing into things.[26]

In mid-October, during a confidential meeting with the Foreign Relations Committee, Acheson summarized the department's attitude to a sympathetic audience. He reported the deteriorating military situation in China and the great difficulty of making American military aid effective. "By the time you have made up your mind that somebody is a pretty 'stout fellow' and is going to stay with you," the secretary complained, "he is over on the other side." Acheson was careful to emphasize that, although he refused to rule out the possibility of recognition, the behavior of the Chinese communists represented a gross violation of international law. The secretary again promised that he would not take any action on recognition without first consulting the committee.[27]

The only senator who challenged Acheson's assessment was Republican Bourke Hickenlooper of Iowa, a moderate Taftite, but even his questions were far from harsh. The Iowa senator asked if the United States planned to retain "a foothold [in China] . . . from which we can launch any counter information or counter offensive of any kind, propagandawise or otherwise? It seems to me that we are letting nature take its course in China." When Connally replied, "What else can you do but withdraw?" Hickenlooper acquiesced: "I am not quarreling about it one way or the other. I am trying to get my understanding straightened out." Acheson added that it would be "unwise" to consider any ambitious military schemes such as those advanced by Chennault. Hickenlooper concluded: "It is possible that while the doctors are in consultation the patient may die?" Acheson replied "It may be but I think it is not the consultation." In several months, as the political forces that spawned McCarthyism took shape, Hickenlooper's tone would change from that of a tentative questioner to that of an accusing prosecutor during the Tydings subcommittee hearings on the loyalty of State Department employees. That change was mirrored in other Taftites, too.[28]

As in the beginning of 1949, when it came to providing funds for Chiang the appeal of the China bloc was confined to its members. Had Knowland or Smith been present in the meeting, the secretary would certainly have received a more intense grilling. Of the Republicans present, however, (Alexander Wiley of Wisconsin, Lodge, and Hickenlooper) only Hickenlooper posed objections to the administration's China policy. No one condemned Acheson for having deliberately or otherwise "given" China to the communists. With the nationalist regime rapidly collapsing in 1949, only a small group urged that more aid be extended to it. Despite introducing two major aid programs and playing on popular sympathies toward China, the China bloc got only an extension of the 1948 aid program and the establishment of a fund that the president was not compelled to spend nor to report on if he did so. Had it not been for the critical European aid measures then moving through Congress, it is doubtful if the China bloc would have secured even that much for the Nationalists. The Taft Republicans, who within a year became such vociferous champions of the Nationalists, were in 1949 nearly as unenthusiastic about extending aid to them as the administration.

Many of the problems that complicated Truman's foreign policy from 1950 to 1952 stemmed from the inability of his administration to convince the American people, and particularly the Republicans, that it had followed the wisest course in China. Public opinion polls taken in August 1949 demonstrated that most Americans believed that the Chinese situation had been caused at least in part by the administration's mistakes. The September vote on Butterworth's nomination and the Republicans' support of Knowland's amendments to the MAP were also ominous harbingers of the deadly combination that would dog Truman's East Asian policies for the balance of his second term—the China bloc joined by an aggressively partisan group of Taftites.

It is debatable whether the administration could have prevented this coalition from forming during 1948 and 1949 before the China issue became politicized. Its best bet would have been to have followed the example of its highly successful European policy, winning the support of prominent Republicans sympathetic to its cause. From 1947 to 1949, the administration had meticulously stroked the oftentimes pompous Senator Vandenberg with brilliant results for its European programs. The senator also agreed with the administration's China policy, asking only that the break with Chiang be less precipitous than Acheson would have liked. The administration, of course, had made overtures in this direction, confidentially conferring with its critics on several occasions. But it waited until the eve of the release of the White Paper, however, before it made a real effort to "get the Republicans in" on China. By then it was too little, too late. The appointment of Butterworth and the tone of the letter of transmittal to the White Paper erased any positive influence the consultation might have engendered.

The problems in achieving a bipartisan approach for China should also not be overlooked. When it came to "massaging" Vandenberg, Acheson was not as patient as his predecessor, George Marshall, had been. In addition, the major issues of China policy such as recognition, the suspension of aid, and the suppression of new aid measures, required much less consultation with Congress, especially compared to what was needed to implement the European program. Further, with the Democrats now in the majority in the Senate, there appeared less need to consult with the Republicans. On the Foreign Relations Committee this problem became particularly acute, considering Connally's jealousy of Vandenberg. Given such circumstances, a liaison with the bipartisan Republicans on the committee would have been difficult.

While the Taftites had begun to grasp the political possibilities inherent in the China issue during 1949, most of their attacks on Truman centered on his domestic policies. Traditionally more attuned to domestic concerns, the Taftites inveighed against "statism" while they sharpened their swords for the elections of 1950; events in East Asia were not, however, to leave them alone.

4

The Republicans and Formosa, October 1949–January 1950

While 1949 saw some spectacular successes for the bipartisan coalition, such as the passage of the North Atlantic Treaty and the Military Assistance Program, the year also revealed significant weaknesses. The coalition was heavily dependant on having exactly the right people (Vandenberg and Marshall) in exactly the right places, on keeping the Taftites off stride by always being tougher on the communists than they were, and on being able to say that bipartisanship was not only patriotic but also smart politics. The events of 1948 and 1949 dealt setbacks to each of these conditions. While the election results of 1948 had proven to the Taftites that bipartisanship did not pay political dividends, events in East Asia conspired to deal what would ultimately be a mortal blow to the bipartisan foreign policy as it existed in 1947 and 1948.

Between the autumn of 1949 with the establishment of the People's Republic of China until the Formosan crisis exploded in January 1950, the China bloc fell on hard times. The two problems that most distressed the China bloc in late 1949 were whether the administration would recognize the Chinese Communist regime and whether it would permit the Nationalists' last stronghold on Formosa to fall. As early as June 1949, in a letter to the administration, twenty-one senators staunchly opposed recognition. On this occasion and several others in 1949, Secretary of State Dean Acheson coolly informed the senators that the government had no intention of recognizing the communists and that it would certainly consult the Congress if that policy changed. The issue became more acute in the autumn, when the People's Republic of China formally invited diplomatic recognition and several Western countries, especially Britain, moved in that direction. In addition to concerns about recognition, the China bloc feared that Truman would allow the communists to take over Generalissimo Chiang Kai-shek's last bastion on Formosa.[1]

Of critical importance to the bloc during late 1949 was the leadership of Republican Senators H. Alexander Smith of New Jersey and William Knowland of California. Smith and Knowland were in key positions because they were China bloc sympathizers who also supported bipartisanship and Truman's containment policies in Europe: When they spoke, the administration could not dismiss them as isolationists and disrupters of bipartisan unity. Smith's main contribution in the autumn of 1949 was that he, more than anyone else, kept the issues of recognition and Formosa before the public. He was also important because, despite his criticisms of the administration, he resolved to accomplish his goals within the bipartisan framework. In later months, although the excesses of McCarthyism appalled him, Smith agreed that the State Department had played a role in the fall of China.[2]

Smith first made his presence felt on the China issue during the White Paper controversy. Before serving in the Senate, Smith had been a history professor at Princeton University and had worked with Herbert Hoover on food relief problems in 1919. In appearance, Smith was a lean, bald man with a stern countenance. Ideologically, Smith's approach to foreign policy had been profoundly influenced by the man who had brought him to the faculty of Princeton in 1905, Woodrow Wilson. Like Wilson, Smith was a deeply religious man who believed that America had a special mission to spread the ideas of Christianity and democracy to the world, and that such principles could be furthered by an international organization. By the late 1940s, Smith had found that some of his ideas put him in close touch with his Foreign Relations Committee colleague, Vandenberg. Both men were conservatives on domestic policy and favored internationalism through the medium of bipartisanship. When Vandenberg became sick in late 1949, Smith attempted to fill the void, prompting some journalists to call him "the poor man's Vandenberg."[3]

By August 1949, Smith's thinking on East Asia stood between

that of Vandenberg and Bridges. He became far more critical of administration policies than Vandenberg, denigrating the White Paper as an apology of America's "bankrupt" East Asian policies. In his correspondence, however, Smith also revealed his distrust of Brewster and Bridges. He feared they were

motivated . . . by the desire to make the China crisis a partisan issue in the campaigns of 1950 and 1952. It is my own judgment that if we are to get positive results, we cannot mix the situation up with partisan politics. I am therefore working for a bypartisan [sic] approach if we are going to get any practical results at all.[4]

In the fall, both Smith and Knowland took separate trips to the Orient. Smith embarked on a six-week tour with stops in Japan, the Philippines, and Formosa. The trip featured several lengthy conversations with Chiang and General Douglas MacArthur. Smith and MacArthur saw eye to eye on most of the problems confronting America in the Pacific, which reinforced Smith's already strong China-bloc proclivities. When he returned home, Smith made a public report to the Senate Foreign Relations Committee on conditions in East Asia. Smith charged that, despite the administration's excellent record of bipartisan consultation on European measures, bipartisanship had "been completely lacking insofar as the Far East is concerned." Although Smith embraced many of the ideas of the China bloc, he was neither blind to Chiang's weaknesses nor extreme in his criticisms of the administration. The two points that Smith stressed most in his report (and for which he subsequently fought hardest) were nonrecognition of the Communist Chinese and the defense of Formosa.[5]

Smith and the China problem notwithstanding, most Republicans had far different matters on their minds during the fall of 1949. October 1949 brought an end to the first session of the Eighty-first Congress. The fears that had tormented the Taftites since Truman's 1948 victory had been realized; the administration had secured more of its legislative program than during any previous session of the Truman presidency. A minimum wage, expanded war powers, and federal aid to hospitals all became law along with such dramatic foreign policy measures as the yearly extension of the Marshall Plan, the initiation of a massive Military Assistance Program, and the ratification of the North Atlantic Treaty. The president crowed that he expected the second session to bring the repeal of Taft-Hartley, a civil rights act, compulsory national health insurance, and increases in social security coverage. The "calamity of the 80th Congress" had, he declared, been reversed. Truman concluded: "I am certain that in 1950 the people will express themselves even more clearly, in favor of progress against reaction."[6]

Within a month, Republican spirits had sunk even lower with the news of Democrat Herbert Lehman's defeat of John Foster Dulles in a special election in New York which was held to fill Robert Wagner's Senate seat. The reactions of Republican leaders to the news gave evidence of the deepening splits within the party and the sense of desperation over the flow of events toward "Trumanism." Just before the election, the *Chicago Tribune* (a principle organ of Midwestern, conservative, nationalist Republicans) called it a contest between a "foe of statism" (Dulles) and the protégé of Truman's "welfare state" (Lehman). Afterwards, however, Colonel Robert McCormick's newspaper concluded that the party "is floundering in the morass of 'me tooism' " and that bipartisanship was part of the "me too" malaise. Dulles, of course, had been close to Dewey and a key participant in the bipartisan foreign policy. Moderate bipartisan Republicans, while also gloomy, pointed hopefully to Alfred Driscoll's victory in the New Jersey gubernatorial race. To Republican Senator Henry Cabot Lodge, Jr., of Massachusetts, for instance, it showed "that Republicans can win when they have a modern approach and affirmative program, and they can't win if they don't."[7]

In October 1949, at a time when the bipartisan Republicans were losing influence in the party, they received a serious blow; Vandenberg was hospitalized for a cancerous tumor on his lung. The surgeon's scalpel, however, only prolonged his life for a year and a half, during which time the senator's energies dwindled. The champion of bipartisanship became physically unable to man the battlements against his foes and was reluctant to be a combatant from the sanctuary of his sickbed. This happened at a time when, as Vandenberg noted, "The GOP show[ed] signs of splintering into various degrees of isolationism which could be ominous for a free America in a free world."[8]

An exchange of correspondence with journalist David Lawrence revealed how sensitive Vandenberg had become to growing criticisms of bipartisanship. In a November 1949 column, Lawrence had written that "Senator Dulles and Senator Vandenberg have not been permitted to participate in the making of much policy by the Administration." In a telegram to Lawrence, Vandenberg contradicted that assertion by listing the various programs and treaties in which bipartisanship had played a key role. In subsequent correspondence, Lawrence retorted that "there seems to be growing up a belief that bipartisan policy is gagging honest debate on foreign policy issues both before and after decisions are made." He ended the letter by asking Vandenberg to comment in an interview "because more and more people are beginning to ask questions as to what the bipartisan policy says so far as campaigning is concerned."[9]

Fully alive to the meaning of that last sentence in light of the upcoming congressional elections, the Michigan senator penned a terse defense of bipartisanship. Vandenberg denied that bipartisanship "gagged honest debate," admitting only that it "may *shorten* 'free debate' through the effective advance clarification of the issues involved. . . . but I think there is a vast difference between *shortening* debate and gagging debate." He went on to assert that "a *unanimous* bipartisan Committee report . . . creates an impetus which discourages *partisan* attack (if such be warranted) through a clarification of the *real* issues involved." He ended his letter with a ringing exhortation: "I want ultimate *unity* in foreign policies because without it the voice of America lacks the authority essential to peaceful success."[10]

His assurances to the contrary, Vandenberg and the administration had used tactics that made opposition to containment policies, once given bipartisan sanction, quite difficult. The most effective tactic used by both Truman and Vandenberg was to publicly label the opponents of containment policies as "isolationists." For instance, in a press conference held that November, Truman was asked if he "saw any reason for modification of the bipartisan attitude on foreign policy." The president countered: "Why certainly not. Of course there isn't any reason except in Bertie McCormick's [owner of the *Chicago Tribune*], or [William Randolph] Hearst's [the owner of a California chain of newspapers] mind. They are isolationists, if you remember."[11]

Foreseeing what was to come in January when Congress convened, Vandenberg issued a call to arms to his chief bipartisan lieutenants, Dulles and Lodge. In a letter to each, the Michigan senator asked them to "*specifically identify* Republican contributions to 'bipartisan foreign policy,' " to counteract the

increasingly persistent attempts to support the fiction that bi-partisan foreign policy is entirely "me too" on the part of its Republican participants. There is evidently a rugged fight ahead in our own Party to break down the *unity* which we have created for the voice of America at the water's edge. I do not have the remotest idea of surrendering to any such self-serving isolationism.[12]

Within a month, the opening shots of the "rugged fight" that Vandenberg anticipated, echoed throughout the party. The previous August, the Republican National Committee had selected Guy Gabrielson, a New Jersey businessman and state politician who had supported Taft in 1948, as its new National Chairman. Gabrielson's victory came after eight stormy months of debate over replacing Dewey's National Chairman, Congressman Hugh Scott of Pennsylvania. Not long after Dewey's defeat, a number of Republicans narrowly failed to oust Scott in a mid-January meeting in Omaha, calling him the "symbol of Dewey misrule." By August, however, the pressure on Scott became too much; he agreed to step down if a consensus could be reached on a replacement. After weeks of frantic activity, Gabrielson finally put together a winning coalition. The new chairman firmly declared that the Republican party's main issue was "freedom against statism" and that the party should aggressively attack the Democrats. "We are going to have an affirmative program," the new chairman asserted. "We may turn out to be a failure, but we are going to make a hell of a lot of noise doing it."[13]

In late November, Gabrielson gave evidence of his approach, proposing that the party draft a statement of principles for its candidates to use as a platform in the elections of 1950. Arthur Summerfield, head of the Republican Strategy Committee, spoke in full support of Gabrielson at a party gathering: "There is little dispute in Washington that if the Democrats make any gains whatsoever in the House and the Senate in 1950, there is likely to be a pell-mell rush to get on the socialist bandwagon." Although most of the speeches at the meeting dwelt on the evils of the "socialist" Fair Deal, the tone was omnious to the defenders of bipartisanship.[14]

On December 20, in the face of such opposition and with the next congressional session less than two weeks away, Vandenberg disregarded his doctor's orders and flew to Washington to defend bipartisanship. Beset with pain and having lost much weight and energy to his illness, and senator delivered a rousing defense of bipartisan foreign policy at a press conference. He again maintained that bipartisanship did not involve the "remotest surrender of free debate." In the same press conference, Vandenberg attempted to resolve an issue that threatened bipartisan unity—the recognition of Communist China. Playing his familiar role, the Michigan senator outlined a compromise. In phrases designed to win the assent of the State Department, he asserted that "recognition of the foreign government does not involve our approval of that form of government." To mollify the China bloc, Vandenberg was careful to note that "in neither respect does [Communist China] now qualify for recognition." Significantly, the Michigan senator did not attempt to untangle the more explosive Formosa controversy.[15]

Vandenberg matched his public attempts at establishing a consensus with private efforts as well. Republican Senator Arthur Watkins of Utah, one of the Senate's most fervent isolationists, publicly criticized bipartisan foreign policy and Vandenberg. The Michigan senator responded to Watkins's attack with a conciliatory letter that sought to emphasize, as Vandenberg wrote, their "*agreements* instead of our occasional *disagreements*." Vandenberg acknowledged Watkins' assertions that he, Vandenberg, had no authority to speak for the party and that a full debate of the issues was indispensable. However, the Michigan senator objected to Watkins's characterization that the Republicans "are supposed to take *anything* the Administration hands us." In contradicting Watkins, Vandenberg pointed to the MAP, where the administration significantly altered its bill to meet Republican objections. The Michigan senator assured Watkins that "we are very close to *common ground* regarding the *procedures* which should govern our Republican attitudes in foreign affairs."[16]

Despite Vandenberg's attempts to mollify the opponents of bipartisanship, their war fires were not easily doused. About a week after Vandenberg had spoken, Republican Senator Kenneth S. Wherry of Nebraska, another extreme nationalist, called his own press conference in rebuttal. In the sharpest attack on bipartisanship to date, Wherry announced his unwillingness to accept commitments "made by bipartisan big wigs." To make his reference to Vandenberg more pointed, the Nebraskan asserted: "Before any commitments are made by anyone, the whole Senate should take the matter under consideration." Wherry offered his own ideas on how bipartisanship should work. He believed the country should be "committed to no step by the State Department or the Congressional leaders . . . unless it was brought before the entire Senate in all its details." That would avoid the situation encountered in the past where, Wherry charged, the Senate rank and file had little alternative, except "to go along or seem to repudiate the position of his country."[17]

In January 1950, Taft Republicans had returned to Congress spoiling for a fight over "statism," when the Formosa issue was thrust into their arena like a hapless Christian. Several newspaper reports of secret administration conferences concerning Formosa generated an instant furor. On December 30, *New York Times* columnist James Reston reported the results of a National Security Council meeting on Formosa. During the conference, the Joint Chiefs of Staff concluded that although Formosa had some strategic value for the United States, occupying it was not worth the risk of war, given the state of America's defenses. Another newspaper story two days later elaborated on the decisions reached at the meeting. The NSC agreed that the United States should not occupy Formosa and should not recognize the Communist Chinese government. Several days later, a secret directive of December 1949 from the State Department to its foreign posts also hit the front page, probably leaked by MacArthur. The directive instructed American officials to minimize the strategic importance of Formosa to the United States, anticipating the fall of the island to the communists. Moreover, it directed American officials to emphasize that further aid to Chiang would not prevent the inevitable fall of Formosa, but would only open the United States to charges of imperialism.[18]

Republican reaction to the disclosures gave swift evidence of the aggressive partisanship that permeated much of the party. Ironically, the first blasts were sounded by two individuals who had shown relatively little interest in East Asia—Taft and ex-president Herbert C. Hoover. In a letter to Knowland, Hoover opposed recognition of the communist regime and favored support of the Nationalist Government. He added, "if necessary, [the United States should] give . . . naval protection to the possessions of Formosa, the Pescadores, and possibly Hainan Islands." The ex-president also suggested that Formosa could be administered by the United States as part of the American occupation of Japan, since a Japanese peace treaty had not been concluded.[19]

Several days later, Taft echoed Hoover's sentiments. The Ohioan favored taking "steps to see that the Communists do not cross over into Formosa" and advocated using "the Navy to keep them out if necesary." Taft believed that with the Nationalists' permission, the United States should establish a naval base on Formosa. Hoover and Taft had thus ventured further than even the China bloc in their attempt to support Chiang. Throughout 1949, the China bloc had advocated aid for the Nationalists as well as American military advisers, but they had rarely suggested the introduction of American combat units into the China situation.[20]

Subsequent speeches by Knowland and Smith revealed the differences within the Republican party on China policy. Smith and Knowland, while delighted to receive new support from Hoover and Taft, were embarrassed over their drastic naval approach. Knowland and Smith opposed recognition of the communists and advocated a shake-up of the Far East section of the State Department, "supervised aid" to Chiang, American military commands in the Orient united under one leader, and increased naval strength in the western Pacific. When asked during floor debates whether they supported the Hoover-Taft naval strategy, both Smith and Knowland demurred. Knowland asserted that he would place naval units "in the area" and would warn the communists that the United States would permit no more bloodshed. The Californian added that the warning should be issued through the United Nations. Smith favored "neutralizing" the island with a "peaceful occupation of nonmilitary personnel."[21]

Several days later, Republican Senator Styles Bridges of New Hampshire, another member of the China bloc, also delivered a major address on the Formosa question. The New Hampshire sen-

ator lauded the Hoover-Taft approach and criticized the administration for acting one way in Greece in 1947 and quite the opposite
in Formosa in 1950. Bridges reserved most of his venom, however,
for State Department officials, whom he labelled "isolationists" and
"appeasers." Democrat Tom Connally asked Bridges if he were
willing to send an American army to Formosa. Bridges retorted:
"As of today, at this minute, I am not in favor of sending an American army to China," but would send only supplies and "advisers."
Connally pressed further: Would Bridges favor using the United
States Navy to stop an invasion of Formosa? Bridges responded by
saying that he would have the Navy in the area and "ready to
act."[22]

The isolationists, who had traditionally restricted their support
for the China bloc to rhetoric, also contributed to the Formosa
controversy. Republican Senator William E. Jenner of Indiana, a
conservative isolationist, grilled Knowland on the floor of the Senate. Both parties, Jenner asserted, were equally to blame for what
he called the East Asian "disaster." Jenner charged that Republicans

have closed their eyes and have said, "We will cooperate with you [the
administration] in a bipartisan foreign policy in Europe, but if you do not
want to tell us what is going on in the Far East, it is all right, and when
you get ready to take us in on your program we will come in to 'bipartisan'
some more with you."

Jenner went on to argue that instead of spending billions for defense around the world, the government could more profitably spend
the money building America's strength at home.[23]

When confronted with Jenner's attack on bipartisanship and the
containment policy, Knowland stood his ground. The Californian
rebutted Jenner by proudly recounting the triumphs of American
policy in Europe and the Republican contributions to it. Then
Knowland moved to attack, using tactics perfected by Truman and
Vandenberg for quelling dissent. The Californian reminded Jenner
that "this nation can[not] return to isolationism any more than an
adult can return to childhood, no matter how pleasant our childhood recollections may be." Since there were few better ways to
discredit an opponent than to call him an "isolationist," Jenner's

retort that "isolation[ism] is about as extinct as the Pharaohs of Egypt," was inconsequential.[24]

In the Formosa conflict, as in so many others his party had faced, Vandenberg sought to discern a "middle way" to keep the party from flying apart. On January 5, Vandenberg released a statement on Formosa that adeptly spanned Republican thinking on the subject. He supported "every practical discouragement" to the Communist Chinese forces "short of active American military preparation." Vandenberg also scolded Truman for having arrived at "conclusions regarding Formosa ahead of a realistic consultation of the subject with the appropriate committees of Congress." Privately Vandenberg wrote that he wanted some self-determination for the Formosans and a greater role for the United Nations in administering the island, but was opposed to "any military action."[25]

Thus the Republican party seized on the Formosa issue with more enthusiasm than unity. In this election year the Taftites were in an aggressive mood, determined to prove that the politics of partisanship could win. Taft, who faced a challenging reelection fight, saw in Formosa an opportunity to oppose communism with relatively little risk of a large commitment, while it also allowed him to appear tougher on the communists than the administration. Ironically, Taft used many of the same arguments for aid to Chiang that others used against him in the Greek-Turkish aid fight. Taftites also charged that since the Democrats had not consulted with them on East Asian policy, they were free to condemn the "loss" of a "free" government to the communists. Taft and Hoover were the first to take advantage of the situation and, in so doing, they breathed life into the China bloc. Their solution, however, exacerbated splits within the party. Republicans were happy to attack Truman, but did not want to get involved in the Chinese civil war. Chen Chih-mai, an official with the Nationalist embassy, correctly noted that "there is *much confusion* among the Republicans, and presumably some Democrats, on the whole issue."[26]

Faced with the unintentional disclosure of its policy of standing back from Formosa and the onslaught of the Republicans, Truman and Acheson struck back. On January 5, both held press conferences to clarify the American position on Formosa. Truman stated that the United States had no "intention of utilizing its Armed Forces to interfere in the present situation" and that America would no longer provide the Nationalists with military aid. In an obvious reference to Taft and Hoover, Acheson expressed scorn concerning, as he put it, the "amateur military strategy indulged in regard to this matter of Formosa." Acheson emphasized that the Nationalists' difficulties did not stem from their lack of equipment, but from their lack of the will to resist.[27]

Believing that the Joint Chiefs of Staff (JCS) held a different view of Formosa's value, Vandenberg pressed Connally to call them to testify. At first Connally refused, but several days later the administration relented; it could hardly afford to alienate Vandenberg. On January 26 the chairman of the JCS, General Omar Bradley, revealed that since November 1948 the JCS had prepared five reports on the Formosa situation. Bradley summarized the contents of the first four reports as follows: "Formosa was strategically important [to American security], but it was not of such strategic importance that it warranted us using United States military forces to hold it." The JCS did not favor committing American troops "so long as [the] present disparity between United States military strength and global obligations existed." In its most recent report, the JCS had arrived at the same conclusion, but believed that a survey team should be sent to Formosa to accurately assess the island's defense requirements.[28]

The effect of the Truman-Acheson-Connally counterattack was to cow the more moderate supporters of Chiang, such as Smith and Knowland. In his November 29 report to the Senate Foreign Relations Committee, Smith had favored an American military presence in Formosa as part of the Japanese occupation, but by January 1950, Smith and Knowland had retreated. Now they spoke of "neutralizing" the island by sending in supplies, while the American Navy was only to be "in the area." When put on the spot by Connally about whether they favored "American boys dying" in the Chinese civil war, Smith and Knowland stepped back, leaving Taft and Hoover alone to defend the more aggressive approach.[29]

On January 11, Taft pressed the attack. The Ohioan reiterated his stand of a week before, stating that he never wanted to occupy Formosa, only to let it be known "that ships carrying [communist] troops will not be allowed to cross" from the mainland to Formosa.

The Ohioan then asserted that the administration's China policy contradicted the containment approach it employed in Europe. Why, the senator asked, was the administration now suddenly afraid of involvement in civil wars after having been up to its elbows in the Greek and Korean civil wars?[30]

The most unsettling aspects of the speech were in its references to the State Department. Taft argued that "the proper kind of sincere aid to the Nationalist Government a few years ago could have stopped Communism in China." The reason such aid was not provided, Taft concluded, was because "the State Department has been guided by a left-wing group who obviously have wanted to get rid of Chiang, and were willing at least to turn China over to the Communists for that purpose." The department's latest statements, Taft charged, represented the "bitter resentment of the State Department and its pro-Communist allies against any interference with its policy of liquidating the Nationalist Government."[31]

To date, that sort of argument had been confined to the more extreme elements of the China bloc such as Styles Bridges and Democratic Senator Patrick McCarran of Nevada. More recent China converts, such as H. Alexander Smith and William Knowland, avoided such rhetoric by emphasizing that the State Department policy was merely mistaken, not subversive. In the recent hearings Smith reasserted that attitude, despite his sharp disagreements with Acheson. Smith believed his party could either work for changes in East Asian policy within the bipartisan framework or attack the department vigorously in public. Smith still preferred bipartisanship, but the tide was running the other way and Taft was riding with it.[32]

The day after Taft's address, Acheson delivered what was to be known as one of his most famous and controversial foreign policy addresses. In it he defined the American defensive perimeter in the western Pacific without mention of either Korea or Formosa. Once the Korean War broke out, his opponents charged Acheson with having invited the attack by telling the communists in advance that he would not defend Korea. In the context of January 1950, however, his exclusion of Formosa was far more significant. The secretary explained that Asian peoples were emerging from the old patterns of imperialism and were seeking to establish themselves as modern states. The United States, he counseled, had to stay clear of the process to avoid being characterized as one of the imperialist powers; this was especially true in China. The Soviets and their Communist Chinese "stooges," Acheson believed, would thus be seen by the Chinese people as the true imperialists.[33]

The splits between the factions of the Republican party which were exacerbated by the Formosan situation were papered over by Republican National Chairman Guy Gabrielson's efforts to unite the party on a campaign statement for the congressional elections of 1950. At the beginning of January 1950, Gabrielson requested Senator Taft, in his role as chairman of the Senate Republican Policy Committee, to appoint a committee of senators and congressmen to sit with the National Committee to write the new statement. On January 3, the Republican Policy Committee met to consider Gabrielson's proposal. Taft questioned whether the National Committee was able to draft a statement to which all Republicans could adhere. The Ohioan preferred that the statement be made by the senators and congressmen after conferring with Gabrielson's committee, and that it have the assent of the entire Minority Conference. That permitted the bipartisan wing to have its say too.[34]

The Senate Republican Policy Committee concurred with Taft's wishes. The Ohioan immediately appointed a committee (over which he presided) to draft a statement of principles. In mid-January, a variety of senators sent their proposals to the committee. Drafts from some of the senators gave ample evidence that the intense partisan feelings prevalent on domestic issues had spilled over into foreign policy questions. Senator Karl E. Mundt of South Dakota, for instance, wanted part of the statement to read: "Many in this Administration tend to conceive of 'bipartisanship' in Foreign Policy as giving support and strength to programs largely conceived in the White House and the State Department without consultation with the Republican Party in the creation and formation of these programs."[35]

Vandenberg opposed such sentiments, but the Michigan senator declined to join the Taft committee. He feared his presence would make some of its members harder to deal with, and he wanted to avoid the charge that he was dominating the committee. The senator also preferred to see what the committee would devise in his absence. Vandenberg privately feared that the statement of principles would bear the kind of disastrous attack on bipartisanship that Mundt proposed. Vandenberg argued that if the party pursued the Mundt approach, it would unnecessarily arm Truman with a potent political weapon in the fall. Truman could argue that to vote Republican would be to vote for an executive-legislative stalemate in foreign affairs for two years, while the president finished his second term.[36]

Despite his recent outspoken opposition to the administration's Formosa policies, Taft worked closely with Vandenberg to hammer out a moderate statement of principles. In mid-January, Taft sent the Michigan senator a working draft of the foreign policy section. Vandenberg's most important addition was a section in which the party would support a "critical exploration of foreign policy . . . between the Executive and Members of both major parties in the Legislative Branch of Government in the initiation and development of a united American foreign policy."[37]

Vandenberg was delighted to learn that the drafting committee accepted most of his suggestions. The only major addition was a phrase that was tacked on the end of Vandenberg's contribution to read: "And we deplore the failure of the Administration in so many fields to give such cooperation or even adequate information to Congress." The Michigan senator had feared that the statement would be a general attack on "me too" bipartisan foreign policy, but it emerged as a lukewarm affirmation of bipartisanship. In a private chat with Acheson, Vandenberg described it as "very internationally minded" and said "that if ever there was a 'me too' document this was it."[38]

That was one of the last victories the bipartisan Republicans would enjoy for some time. The Formosa controversy had revealed serious splits within the party and had weakened the position of the bipartisan Republicans. It also gave Taftites a new strategy against the bipartisan coalition. Before the Formosa controversy, Vandenberg argued that support for bipartisanship was patriotic and politically profitable. In so doing, however, he blurred the two meanings that the phrase "bipartisan foreign policy" had assumed. On the one hand, it referred to an executive-legislative relationship where the administration was supposed to confer with responsible members of the opposition prior to making major decisions. If that were all the phrase meant, then Vandenberg should have stood shoulder to shoulder with Smith in expressing his anger over the lack of prior consultation in East Asian matters. That the Michigan senator muted his criticisms on China points to the second meaning that the phrase "bipartisan foreign policy" had assumed.

To Vandenberg and others, the phrase had come to mean not just the process but also the results. The results by 1949 included, of course, the containment policy in Europe. When defending bipartisanship, then, Vandenberg lauded the process in patriotic terms, hoping that patriotism would spill over into support for containment. Taft Republicans, heretofore frustrated by this tactic, now began to turn Vandenberg's logic on him when it came to East Asia. They attacked the lack of consultation on China, hoping it would unravel the containment tapestry. In the same month that the Formosa crisis unfolded, Alger Hiss was found guilty of perjury, showering new sparks into an already highly flammable political atmosphere. In February 1950, the Republicans, with the help of a little-known Republican senator, Joseph R. McCarthy of Wisconsin, made an assault on the administration that finally carried them over the bipartisan battlements.

5

McCarthyism and Bipartisanship, January–June 1950

The Formosa controversy was a harbinger of things to come. The wing of the Republican party led by Senator Robert A. Taft of Ohio had worked with the China bloc to prevent the fall of Formosa. They had failed to force Truman to intervene to save the island because their policy raised the possibility of war with the Chinese Communists, and because the bipartisan wing of the Republican party had supported the administration. The advocates of bipartisanship had won that round, but a more formidable assault was in the offing.

Although stymied on Formosa, the Taft Republicans' discontent over bipartisanship had not been alleviated. They had failed to nominate a presidential candidate in the past four general elections and yearned for a chance to lead the party. In 1950, after having endured what they believed to be a milquetoast-like campaign in 1948, the Taft Republicans were in an aggressively partisan frame of mind. Although they initially concentrated their political firepower on the Fair Deal, the Formosa issue demonstrated that foreign policy might be mined for political pay dirt too. Republican Senator Joseph R. McCarthy of Wisconsin provided an important ingredient that enabled Truman's critics to turn the tables on their foes. Previously cowed into silence by epithets such as "isolationists" and "saboteurs of bipartisanship," Taft Republicans now hurled some epithets of their own, claiming that Truman had "let" China fall because his administration harbored communists and communist sympathizers.

By 1949, Joe McCarthy was a little-known freshman senator who had been unsuccessful in capturing the limelight. In 1949, during the Malmedy Massacre hearings, for instance, McCarthy took the side of Nazi war criminals, who it was alleged had been tortured into confessing that they had murdered about 150 Americans during the Battle of the Bulge. In late 1949, however, McCarthy stumbled on an issue that guaranteed him a ready audience within his party and around the country. From McCarthy's point of view, it was a case of saying the right thing at the right time. Taft Republicans were eager to grasp at any straw to gain political advantage over the bipartisan coalition. Americans, unsure why the United States had lost so much influence in the world since 1945, were also susceptible to McCarthy's arguments.[1]

In a Lincoln Day address in 1950 at Wheeling, West Virginia, and subsequently in other cities across the country, McCarthy claimed that America had lost large numbers of people to communism because of "traitorous actions" by individuals in the State Department. McCarthy dramatically announced that he had a list of 205 names of individuals involved in a State Department spy ring. Although the number would vary in subsequent speeches between 205 and 57, the message was the same. On February 20, McCarthy made his charges on the Senate floor, reading into the *Record* the case files of eighty-one State Department employees whose loyalty was questionable. Those cases had already been reviewed and cleared by the State Department Loyalty Review Board several years before. McCarthy tantalizingly withheld names, referring to the cases by number only. He would give the names, he declared, only to an investigating committee.[2]

Republicans eagerly acceded to McCarthy's wishes to investigate the State Department, and they demanded that a committee be appointed with the power to subpoena the administration's loyalty files. Shortly thereafter, the Senate instructed the Foreign Relations Committee to investigate "whether persons who are disloyal to the United States are, or have been, employed by the Department of State." In late February 1950, Foreign Relations Committee Chairman Tom Connally of Texas appointed Maryland Democrat Millard Tydings to head the subcommittee.[3]

The Republicans on the subcommittee, Lodge and Hickenlooper, represented the two wings of their party. Hickenlooper was a Midwestern Taft Republican. He was born and educated in Iowa and entered Republican state politics in the 1930s, becoming governor in 1943 and United States senator in 1945. Like Taft, Hickenlooper supported efforts to trim Truman's domestic programs. On foreign policy, Hickenlooper was a cautious internationalist, having supported the British loans and the United Nations Treaty. Like Taft, however, Hickenlooper was happy to use McCarthy's charges to bludgeon the Democrats and the bipartisan Republicans. The Republicanism of Henry Cabot Lodge, Jr., was worlds apart from that of Hickenlooper. Lodge was a staunch defender of bipartisanship and a political lieutenant of Republican Senator Arthur H. Vandenberg of Michigan and New York Governor Thomas E. Dewey. In late 1948, Lodge had called Taft a "reactionary" and led an unsuccessful move to deny the Ohioan the chairmanship of the Senate Republican Policy Committee. As a Republican advocate of the administration's foreign policy, Lodge's political position was vulnerable to the kind of partisanship that McCarthy aroused.[4]

The Tydings subcommittee hearings settled into predictable patterns for its two Republican members. Hickenlooper, although not as extreme as McCarthy, was clearly sympathetic to the Wisconsin senator. On several occasions, Hickenlooper asked witnesses questions written for him by McCarthy, and he could be as prosecutorial as the Wisconsin senator in this interrogation. Lodge, realizing that the hearings were politically damaging to bipartisan Republicans, sought to defuse the situation. For instance, he suggested that the hearings be held in executive session to reduce sensationalism and protect the witnesses' rights. Within a month after the hearings began, Lodge concluded that the subcommittee was incapable of deciding if there were disloyal individuals in the State Department. He therefore introduced a resolution to refer the issue to a commission appointed by the House, the Senate, and the president, which would be given access to the FBI files. The commission would make its report in December, after the elections.[5]

In retrospect, the obvious tactic for the Democrats on the committee was to cooperate with Lodge, but they had other ideas. Lulled into a false sense of overconfidence, the Democrats opted for taking a hard line with McCarthy. Hence, Truman denied the subcommittee access to government personnel files for some time, and at one point called McCarthy a "Kremlin asset." That, of course, only fueled the fires of partisanship, driving a wedge between the Democrats and the bipartisan Republicans. Probably it was too much to expect the Democrats not to be outraged by McCarthy's charges and to strike back in kind. The Democrats reasoned that, with so little substance to his charges, McCarthy could be dispatched with one good punch.[6]

During the last two weeks of March and the first two weeks of April 1950, the situation intensified as several sensitive areas of the administration's foreign policy came under simultaneous attack. In the Tydings subcommittee, McCarthy created new sensations that renewed the pressure on Truman to turn over the FBI's confidential files. At the same time, the Taftites demanded drastic revisions in both the administration's East Asian policy and the nature of bipartisan consultations. Several Taftites also demanded Acheson's resignation. Through such turbulent political waters, Truman had to navigate the annual Marshall Plan appropriation. The Democrats responded to these crises in classic bipartisan fashion by appointing two prominent Republicans to the State Department and reorganizing the Senate Foreign Relations Committee. The Taft Republicans remained unimpressed and unintimidated.[7]

On March 21, McCarthy introduced some new excitement into the proceedings of the Tydings subcommittee by revealing the name of someone he called "one of the biggest Soviet espionage agents" in the State Department—Professor Owen Lattimore, who headed the School of International Relations at Johns Hopkins and was an expert on East Asia. McCarthy further asserted that he was willing to stake his whole claim that there were communists in the State Department on Lattimore's guilt. For proof, McCarthy demanded that the subcommittee subpoena Lattimore's FBI file, which, although he had never seen it, he was sure would sustain his case.[8]

McCarthy's charges exacerbated the splits within his own party. The day after his charges against Lattimore, the Senate Republican Policy Committee, chaired by Taft, decided against making the Lattimore controversy a matter of party policy, but Acheson's ouster was mentioned. Once outside the meeting, however, Taft intimated that he hoped McCarthy would continue, saying that "if one case didn't make it, [he should] . . . bring up another." By contrast, H. Alexander Smith, a bipartisan Republican, was disturbed by McCarthy's charges against his friend, Philip Jessup. On March 21, Smith pondered in his diary: "Should I have made a statement expressing my confidence in Jessup in light of my long experience with him? My trouble is with his Hiss and Lattimore connections. But I am sure of his complete loyalty and fine public service." Three days later, Smith delivered a speech in the Senate praising Jessup's "complete loyalty and patriotic devotion to his country."[9]

Certain that he finally had enough rope to hang McCarthy, Truman permitted the subcommittee to see a digest of Lattimore's FBI file. Truman was sure that would stop McCarthy. All the subcommittee members except Hickenlooper attended the FBI briefing on Lattimore's file. Tydings declared that it revealed that Lattimore was "in the clear." Hickenlooper later disagreed, while Lodge said the file did not prove the case one way or the other. McCarthy also insisted that the actual Lattimore file, not just an FBI digest, be made available.[10]

In the midst of McCarthy's charges, the administration introduced its annual appropriation for the Economic Cooperation Administration (ECA) in the House. Budget-minded Republicans vowed to save $500 million from the administration's proposed $3 billion request. The Taftites were determined to show that they could trim excesses from government spending. Such an issue prompted a response from the ailing Vandenberg. In a letter to ECA Administrator Paul G. Hoffman, whom Vandenberg had recommended for the job, the Michigan senator praised the ECA's accomplishments. Vandenberg applauded Hoffman for keeping the ECA in the proud tradition of an "unpartisan enterprise" in which it had begun. In an aside, he alluded to "the impact of communist aggression in the Far East," adding to Hoffman: "These are essential subjects for judicial Congressional survey in the same factual spirit which must continue to strive to put our country first in our considerations." H. Alexander Smith and Republican Senator William E. Knowland of California, supporters of bipartisanship and the ECA, were enthusiastic about the letter. Taft, in remarks to the press, emphasized those few segments relating to East Asia: "There is no question about the desirability of bringing in all viewpoints. There is certainly a need to resurvey the entire [foreign policy] situation, particularly in light of what happenend in the Far East."[11]

Truman penned a note to Vandenberg praising him for his letter
to Hoffman. The president fondly recalled the role bipartisanship
had played in the passage of such programs as the Marshall Plan,
the United Nations, and the Greek-Turkish aid bill. Truman lamented that "the approach of some Senators to the foreign policy
program, in an effort to find an issue for the coming campaign this
fall, is unfortunate." Truman reiterated the *China White Paper* position, asserting that the reasons for the fall of China lay with the
Chinese. Vandenberg replied: "There is much to be said for the
argument you present. Certainly we cannot fundamentally divide
at home in respect to foreign policy and expect to have much authority abroad." Vandenberg's letter and a lot of political spade-
work by the Democrats secured House approval of the ECA bill
several days later, with a cut of only $250 million instead of the
$500 million the Republicans had originally demanded. The next
day, the administration reported that it could support the House
bill. The bipartisan coalition had proven potent once again.[12]

In January 1950, a jury found Alger Hiss guilty of perjury in the
most celebrated "spy case" of the 1940s. Eighteen months earlier,
in the House Un-American Activities Committee, former communist Whittaker Chambers had first accused Hiss, a State Department official, of passing secret documents to the communists during the 1930s. Hiss subsequently sued Chambers for libel when
Chambers repeated his allegations outside the sanctuary of the
committee room. Citing statements Hiss had made during that trial,
the government then charged Hiss with perjury. Since the statute
of limitations had run out on the alleged espionage, many viewed
his perjury trial as a treason trial by another name. McCarthy and
the Taftites greeted the Hiss conviction as further proof of disloy-
alty within the State Department. Hiss represented much about
the Democrats that they had grown to hate and fear; he was Ivy-
League educated, had clerked for Supreme Court Justice Oliver
Wendell Holmes, was an ardent New Dealer, and had accompanied Roosevelt to the hated Yalta conference in 1945.[13]

While the political fallout from the case initially focused on
Acheson, it soon struck at the heart of bipartisanship itself. The
Taft Republicans seized on the arguments of the China bloc with a
special dimension provided by McCarthy. They argued that it was
misguided and probably treasonable policies by men, such as Jes-

sup and Lattimore, that had caused the fall of China, and not the Nationalists' internal weaknesses as the White Paper had charged. Taft's supporters also blasted Truman for never having practiced bipartisanship in his East Asian policy. If the president had done so, they implied, such disasters might have been averted.[14]

Acheson, the urbane secretary of state, had not won many friends on Capitol Hill in his first year in office. During his confirmation hearings the previous year, Acheson denied that Alger Hiss had worked for him in the State Department, but he insisted that Hiss was still a personal friend. In January 1950, Acheson still stubbornly maintained: "I do not intend to turn my back on Alger Hiss." Acheson's statements about Hiss, coinciding with the rise of McCarthyism, emboldened the secretary's critics. In March 1950, Republican Senator Styles Bridges of New Hampshire (one of only six who had voted against Acheson's confirmation) called on the secretary to resign. On March 25, Styles Bridges announced that during the next week he and several other senators would "go after" Acheson in speeches on the Senate floor. The speeches were to coincide with the appearances of Acheson and Jessup before the Senate Foreign Relations Committee. Bridges insisted that any new approach in East Asia had to begin with a "long overdue cleaning out of personnel in the [State] Department's Far Eastern Division."[15]

Democrats and bipartisan Republicans pleaded with Bridges not to go through with his speech. Truman even wrote a personal note to the New Hampshire senator regretting that he had joined the "wolf-hounds" in going after Acheson. The president argued that such attacks had "been most satisfactory . . . to the Politboro in Moscow." He implored Bridges "not under any circumstances, at this time, [to] upset the solid front here at home for our approach to the world situation." Bipartisan Republicans were equally appalled at what was happening. Republican Henry L. Stimson, who had been President Herbert C. Hoover's secretary of state and President Franklin D. Roosevelt's secretary of war, wrote a letter to the New York Times defending Acheson and Jessup's loyalty foursquare. Stimson asserted that "the formulation of foreign policy most urgently demands an adjournment of mere partisanship." H. Alexander Smith echoed those same themes in a speech on the Senate floor. Departing from his prepared text, Smith appealed to

Bridges not to go through with his anti-Acheson speech, which was scheduled for later the same day.[16]

Bridges would not be deflected. On March 27, Bridges stated that although Acheson had been confirmed a year ago with only six dissenting votes, the secretary could not muster a "corporal's guard" if the same vote were taken again. The New Hampshire senator charged that Acheson "had attempted to divert the attention of our people from the inadequacies of the State Department." Bridges concluded that "the wreckage of our diplomatic and military efforts is no accident. Stalin is not a superman. He had to have help from inside our ranks."[17]

Truman was furious. He had tried to be reasonable with Bridges and it had gotten him nowhere. In a March 30 press conference, Truman lashed out. The president began by proudly pointing to the achievements of bipartisanship. He blamed that policy's most recent setbacks on the Republicans' desperate attempts to find a political issue for the fall elections. Truman charged that some Republicans had even dug up "that old malodorous dead horse called 'isolationism' " and were "willing to sabotage the bipartisan foreign policy of the United States." The president asserted that in destroying bipartisanship, McCarthy and his colleagues had become "the greatest asset the Kremlin had." When pressed by reporters, Truman also named Republicans Kenneth S. Wherry of Nebraska and Styles Bridges as saboteurs of bipartisanship. In a confidential note to Acheson, he boasted, "I think we have these animals on the run. Privately I refer to McCarthy as a pathological liar, and Wherry as the blockheaded undertaker from Nebraska."[18]

The three senators wasted no time in exchanging caustic replies with Truman. McCarthy retorted that he liked "to plead guilty [to] sabotaging foreign policy in the Far East." Bridges reacted in a similar vein: "Truman charges that I sabotaged a bipartisan foreign policy which does not exist, for I am convinced that no Republican helped frame our China policy." Wherry sneered that Truman only wanted a bipartisan foreign policy to "beat the Republicans, not to beat the Russians." Taft chimed in, "The greatest Kremlin asset in our history has been the pro-Communist group in the State Department who surrendered to every demand of Russia at Yalta and Potsdam."[19]

Despite Truman's tough stance before the press, he was already making moves to placate the opposition. On March 27, the State Department announced a shift of personnel. Jessup would remain as ambassador-at-large, but W. Walter Butterworth would be reassigned from the sensitive position as assistant secretary of state for Far Eastern affairs to Acheson's special assistant for the Japanese Peace Treaty. Dean Rusk was appointed as Butterworth's replacement. As Rusk later recalled, "I was put in that job for two reasons: one was that I was willing to do it; and secondly I had no contact with the Far East and knew nothing about it. And that made me eminently qualified for the job in the then-existing political situation."[20]

In late March, Acheson, Butterworth, and Jessup met with the Senate Foreign Relations Committee to counter charges that the administration had not consulted Congress on its East Asian policy. H. Alexander Smith objected to the administration's attempts to abandon Formosa and recognize the communist regime. Acheson assured Smith that he saw "no immediate prospect" of recognition, but "we want to be flexible on it." Acheson argued that the primary aim of America's policy in China was to have a China controlled by individuals who were as independent of Moscow as possible. In order to achieve that, the secretary argued that the United States had to remain aloof from the Chinese civil war so as to allow the natural antagonisms between the Chinese and the Russians to develop. The only alternative was a massive American military intervention; the secretary asked rhetorically, "Do we want to assume that commitment? . . . Why should we reverse our entire objectives as regards China in order to fight the Chinese for an island that is not vital?"[21]

In late March 1950, Truman needed a dramatic gesture to demonstrate his commitment to bipartisanship. On March 29, he appointed Kentucky Republican John Sherman Cooper as a consultant to Acheson in the upcoming talks in London concerning the military organization for the North Atlantic Treaty. Cooper had served in the Senate during the Eightieth Congress and had represented the country as a delegate to the United Nations in 1949. While newspapers noted that the administration had consulted with Connally and Vandenberg on the appointment, in fact Vandenberg was notified at the last minute. Vandenberg did not object, but he did not believe Cooper's credentials were the strongest. The next day, Vandenberg told Dulles in a private chat that he would like to recommend him, but could not in view of the possibility that Dulles might run for the Senate in the fall. Dulles assured the Michigan senator that he considered playing a "responsible part" in foreign affairs more important than running for the Senate. The Michigan senator then penned a note to Acheson that endorsed Dulles and called him "my proxy in my own enforced absence from the firing line."[22]

Dulles was not, however, in the good graces of the Truman administration. In 1949, New York Governor Thomas E. Dewey appointed Dulles to fill out the term of Democratic Senator Robert Wagner, who had resigned. In the fall of 1949, Dulles stood for election against Democrat Herbert Lehman. In a particularly hard-fought campaign, where Dulles spent most of his time attacking the Truman administration for being "socialistic," foreign policy issues came up repeatedly. Truman was particularly delighted when Lehman won, since the president believed Dulles had taken unfair advantage of his position in the bipartisan relationship during the campaign. On March 26, Truman was still adamant that "under no circumstance would he consider appointing John Foster Dulles to this position [in the State Department] or to any other position at this time."[23]

Public service in foreign affairs had deep roots in Dulles's background. There were two secretaries of state in Dulles's immediate family—his uncle, Robert Lansing, who had served under President Woodrow Wilson, and his grandfather, John W. Foster, who had filled the same post under President Benjamin Harrison. Dulles viewed diplomacy firsthand when he accompanied Lansing to the Paris Peace Conference in 1919 through 1920. During the 1920 and 1930s, Dulles was a senior partner in the Wall Street law firm of Sullivan and Cromwell while working on a number of cases that involved foreign companies and international issues. Since 1945, Dulles had established a close relationship with Vandenberg that put him in the middle of Republican bipartisan consultations with the Democrats. As such, Dulles played a critical role in the origins of the United Nations and in the negotiations over the Berlin airlift. Had Dewey won the election of 1948, Dulles would have fulfilled his lifelong ambition to become secretary of state.[24]

After having lost the 1949 senatorial election, Dulles wrote a book about foreign affairs entitled *War or Peace*, which was published in mid-April 1950. Since he was no longer on the "inside," the book served as one of his few outlets for voicing his opinions on foreign relations. The book's praise of much of Truman's foreign policy was doubtless designed to demonstrate to the administration that despite the senatorial campaign, Dulles was still a dependable Republican. For instance, Dulles lauded the establishment of such programs as the Marshall Plan and the Military Assistance Program, being sure to note his contributions to them. In writing about the fall of China, Dulles noted that the administration was not "without fault" and that bipartisanship should have been extended to East Asia; this was standard Republican fare. However, in describing the reasons for the Nationalists' collapse, he kept remarkably close to the White Paper position. He even favored recognition of the Communist Chinese government and its admission to the United Nations, after it had "been tested over a reasonable period of time."[25]

With the news of the Cooper appointment, Dulles saw his opportunity to return to power. On the afternoon of March 29, he conferred with Vandenberg. After assuring the Michigan senator that he would renounce his senatorial campaign in favor of a State Department post, Dulles was whisked into Dean Rusk's office within an hour with Vandenberg's blessing. Dulles assured Rusk that if appointed he would not run for the Senate, but that he would have to make that decision soon and unlike his 1949 campaign he would not feel constrained to avoid foreign policy issues next time. Dulles then had a short meeting with Acheson. Two days later, Dulles sent the president a copy of *War or Peace* with a note explaining that he had "tried to do this in a non-partisan spirit." Dulles called the president's attention to page 137 where he expressed his appreciation for the president's having appointed him to the United Nations Delegation in 1948. Neither Truman, Acheson, nor Rusk had much affection for Dulles, but as Acheson later put it, "we had to preserve some sort of a semblance of bipartisanship." On April 4, Truman wrote to Dulles that he liked the book, especially in its kind references to bipartisanship.[26]

Even at the eleventh hour, Dulles managed to annoy Truman by insisting that he be called an "ambassador at large." Truman preferred the title "consultant." On April 6, the morning of his appointment with the president, Dulles had still not given up, claiming that Vandenberg, Dewey, and Smith agreed that any title other than "ambassador" meant that "the Republican Party was selling out awfully cheap." Truman relented, noting privately to Acheson that: "I don't think I have ever known a man with such a monumental ego." Dulles accepted the position the next day, stating, "It is time to rally from a frustrating confusion that has its roots in mistakes of the past rather than in the circumstances of the present." In subsequent questioning by reporters, Dulles left no mistake that the main source of the "frustrating confusion" was McCarthy.[27]

The bipartisan Republicans rejoiced in Dulles's appointment while they made plans to repair the damage done by McCarthy to their wing of the party. In an April 6 meeting with H. Alexander Smith, Vandenberg encouraged Smith "to lead the fight for bipartisan foreign policy" in Vandenberg's enforced absence from the Senate Foreign Relations Committee. Then Vandenberg wrote to Dulles, congratulating him on his ability to "play ball" with Truman. "I am very sure," the Michigan senator noted, "that the immediate results have been tremendous in recapturing a sense of sanity in our foreign relations at a moment when politics and hysteria were threatening disaster." Vandenberg hoped that the bipartisan Republicans had finally taken the initiative from McCarthy and the Taftites.[28]

Taft, however, was no longer so easily intimidated. The Ohioan's only comment on the Dulles matter was to repeat his statement of the previous week concerning the Cooper appointment. Then he icily asserted that bipartisanship was "not accomplished by the appointment of an individual Republican to executive office as a roving ambassador." Taft pointed out that bipartisanship had worked in the past because Vandenberg was a "responsible representative" of Congress, something Cooper and Dulles were not. "Bipartisan foreign policy," Taft concluded, "is being used by Mr. Truman as a slogan to condemn Republicans who disagree with Mr. Truman's unilateral foreign policy, secretly initiated and put into effect without any real consultation with Congress."[29]

Taft had touched on a key problem that the Republican party faced in the absence of Vandenberg. During the Eightieth Congress, Taft had remained in the background on foreign policy, deferring to Vandenberg. The Michigan senator had played a critical balancing act in his party. He had the confidence of Dewey and Dulles because of his strong support of Truman's European programs, while Taft trusted the Michigan senator as a fellow conservative on domestic issues. With Vandenberg on the sidelines, however, the Republican next in line of seniority on the Senate Foreign Relations Committee was Alexander Wiley of Wisconsin. Lacking Vandenberg's towering stature, Wiley could not command the respect needed to be the party's foreign policy spokesman. The resulting vacuum left Taft, H. Alexander Smith, Wiley, Bridges, Lodge, Wherry, and Millikin all vying for Vandenberg's mantle. Consequently, as Acheson scheduled a number of meetings with prominent Republicans, he found that members of the Foreign Relations Committee were "perturbed" about being overlooked. With Republicans in such a quandary as to their identity, it was little wonder that the administration had trouble figuring out with whom it should consult.[30]

In Vandenberg's absence, the Republicans were divided on how to carry on bipartisan consultations. Bipartisan Republicans favored keeping the executive-legislative dialogue within the bounds of the established committees in Congress. In a letter to Acheson, for instance, Vandenberg suggested that the administration confer with the four Republicans on the Senate Foreign Relations Committee and the four ranking Republicans on the House Foreign Affairs Committee. Moving in the direction suggested by Vandenberg, Connally announced that the Senate Foreign Relations Committee would establish subcommittees to facilitate communication with the State Department. Lodge applauded the new arrangement, declaring that "it could mean, if utilized to the fullest, that the senators from both parties would be in on the formulation of policy rather than being called upon to solve problems of policy after they have become almost insoluble." The Taftites objected to such an approach because no major representative from their group was on either committee. Taft proposed instead that the president consult the ranking Republicans on the Senate Foreign Relations Committee, as well as the Senate minority leadership, positions held for the most part by Taft and his followers.[31]

The administration, realizing that the days were gone when it could ignore or intimidate the Taftites, made a gesture in their

direction. On April 18, Truman and Acheson held a meeting with
Styles Bridges, the ranking Republican in the Senate in Vandenberg's absence, to discuss the whole gamut of foreign policy questions. Only a fortnight before, Truman had called Bridges a "Kremlin
asset," but little of that rancor was present now. At the conclusion
of the talk, all three agreed that such discussions were important
in maintaining bipartisanship and Truman promised he would have
more of them. True to his word, the president instructed his secretary of state to set up a meeting on the upcoming London Conference with senior Republicans in the Senate after talking to the
Foreign Relations Committee.[32]

The next day, Bridges reported the details of the meeting to the
Senate Republican Policy Committee. The committee endorsed
Bridges's statement that Republicans were willing to consult with
the administration. Bridges, of course, was delighted at the attention he had received and recommended that in the future the president should regularly consult with the following Republicans: Taft,
as chairman of the Policy Committee; Millikin, as chairman of the
conference; Wherry, as floor leader; Bridges, as the ranking Republican on the Armed Services and Appropriations Committee;
and Wiley, as the ranking Republican on the Foreign Relations
Committee. Taft seconded Bridges's recommendations. Republican Senator Owen Brewster of Maine noted perceptively that the
Senate Republicans could not "recreate" another Vandenberg.[33]

The new partisan tone of the Republican party could also be
seen as the Tydings's subcommittee attempted to wrap up its find-
ings. In mid-July, Tydings presented the subcommittee's report to
the full Foreign Relations Committee. The Republicans on the
subcommittee, Lodge and Hickenlooper, claimed that it had not
completed its work, having become "devoted to trying Senator
McCarthy rather than trying the issues for which this subcommittee was set up." They asked the full committee to print their minority reports, but Tydings hotly disagreed. He noted that Hickenlooper had been given his chance but had never turned in a
report, while Lodge wanted to have his report printed separately
from that of the majority. Lodge added, "The chickens will come
home to roost in this kind of attitude." Connally finally got Tydings
to relax his objections to Lodge and Hickenlooper. The committee

voted to "receive" the majority report and "transmit it to the Senate without comment."[34]

Two days later, the majority report encountered a fiercely partisan reception on the Senate floor. Wherry and Taft immediately pounced on it, agreeing with Lodge and Hickenlooper that the subcommittee had not finished its job. In two parliamentary maneuvers, Wherry challenged whether the report had the endorsement of the Foreign Relations Committee and moved that it be returned to the committee so that it could either carry out the intent of the resolution or appoint a bipartisan commission that would. The Nebraska senator was defeated in both attempts in straight-party-line votes of forty-five to thirty-seven and forty-five to thirty-five.[35]

The first six months of 1950 had witnessed a marked change in the bipartisan foreign policy. The fall of China and the impending downfall of Formosa brought an avalanche of criticism down upon the administration. The Taftites claimed that the Democrats, either through gross incompetence or treasonable activites, had allowed the most populous country on earth to fall to the communists. Further, they accused Truman of appeasing the communists in refusing to come to Chiang's aid. While the administration had consulted with Republicans on European matters, the Taftites were quick to point out that in East Asian policy there had been no bipartisanship. In short, Truman's critics charged that while the president had locked the front door against communism in Europe, it had left the back door wide open in Asia.

A year before, such a problem would have been handled without much difficulty. Truman and Vandenberg would have worked out a "middle way" which would have pleased the Democrats and most Republicans. In the winter of 1949–1950, however, Vandenberg was too ill to lend his considerable talents to the cause, so Truman met the crisis by relying on the old bipartisan formula. He appointed two bipartisan Republicans to the State Department— Cooper to accompany Acheson to London, and Dulles to work on East Asian policy. Vandenberg did what he could, writing a public letter to support ECA and several private letters to bolster the morale of the bipartisan Republicans. Acheson stepped up consultations with the Senate Foreign Relations Committee, holding a meeting late in March to discuss East Asian policy. Finally, Truman lashed out publicly at McCarthy, Bridges, and Wherry, accusing them of resurrecting "isolationism" and being "Kremlin assets."

The bipartisan Republicans did not miss their cues either. They lent vocal support for each of the administration's moves and added several touches of their own. The position of the bipartisan Republicans, after all, was vulnerable to foreign policy issues that divided senators on the basis of party. Their whole approach was predicated on the notion that Republicans should consider the merits of foreign policy over partisan considerations. Their support of the consultative subcommittees of the Foreign Relations Committee reinforced the older notion that bipartisanship should be confined to the State Department and the committee. Bipartisan Republicans also worked to restrain the impact of McCarthyism on their party. Lodge, for instance, proposed placing the whole loyalty controversy before a bipartisan commission that would not issue its report until after the 1950 elections.

Unfortunately, the old formulas did not work anymore. The Taft Republicans, in an aggressively partisan mood, were determined to capture control of their party in the elections of 1950 and 1952. Once cowed by jibes from Truman that they were "isolationists" and "saboteurs" of bipartisanship, they now retorted that the administration's foreign policy had failed in Asia because of security leaks in the State Department. When the administration brought in Dulles and Cooper, the Taft Republicans objected to the president's selection of Republicans who already agreed with the administration policy in order to call that policy "bipartisan." When Acheson consulted with the Foreign Relations Committee and the committee later reorganized, Taft Republicans complained that those liaisons were not bipartisan either. The Taft Republicans demanded that they be consulted too. So, as Vandenberg lay dying, like a great ship going down, he created a vortex at the center of the bipartisan foreign policy, pulling the smaller ships into its middle.

6

Bipartisanship and the Korean War, June–November 1950

The Korean War gave the Republicans more than their fair share of political difficulties. Since most Republicans had criticized the administration for its weak foreign policy in East Asia, they were quick to applaud President Harry S Truman's decision to intervene in Korea. They were unhappy, however, about losing the political initiative on an issue that has been as promising as East Asian policy in an election year, and unwilling to allow voters to forget that the administration had reversed itself in East Asia. China bloc and bipartisan Republicans had few reservations about the intervention, but reminded the president that they had recommended strong measures for some time.

Those Republicans who followed the lead of Senator Robert A. Taft of Ohio, however, had the most trouble handling the war. Politically they were committed to a strong Asian policy, but as nationalists they were leery of any "entangling" ventures that might increase America's commitments abroad and thus augment the president's powers. The Taft Republicans adopted a "yes, but" approach to the war, reluctantly voting for war appropriations and increases in presidential authority, while vociferously blasting Truman for his past errors.

The immediate background to the Korean War lay in decisions made during World War II. During the war, the Allies agreed to divide the Korean peninsula temporarily between the Americans and the Soviets at the thirty-eighth parallel in order to accept the surrender of Japanese troops. It was hoped that once the Japanese were removed, Korea would soon become an independent nation. Six months after Japan's defeat, however, the distrust that had grown between the Soviets and Americans made reunification of the peninsula impossible. Since the emerging North and South Korean regimes each claimed to be the legitimate ruler of all Korea, border skirmishes and strident rhetoric became commonplace. In June 1950, the North Koreans (probably with the acquiescence of the Soviets) launched a major attack to bring the whole peninsula under their control.[1]

On June 25, Truman and his advisors quickly assembled in Washington to determine the American response to the situation. The same day, the United Nations Security Council passed a resolution calling for a cease-fire and the withdrawal of North Korean units from South Korea. After listening to Acheson's summary of the alternatives and the conclusions of the Joint Chiefs of Staff on the Soviets' war-making potential in East Asia, Truman ordered that supplies be dispatched to Korea, a survey team be sent to reconnoiter developments, and plans be formulated to knock out "all Soviet air bases in the Far East." By the next day, with South Korean forces in dire straits, Acheson suggested that American air and naval units be given authority to attack North Koreans operating south of the thirty-eighth parallel and that the fleet be sent to protect Formosa. Truman readily acceded. The same day, the secretary detailed the situation to Democratic Senator Tom Connally of Texas, Republican Senator Alexander Wiley of Wisconsin, and Democratic Representative John Kee of West Virginia, who was Chairman of the House Foreign Affairs Committee; a full briefing of congressional leaders was conducted the following day.[2]

In the two days between the initial attack and Truman's call to arms on June 27, Republican factions gave early indications of the kinds of criticism they would voice later. China-bloc veterans, such as Republican Senators Styles Bridges of New Hampshire and William F. Knowland of California, feared that Truman would once again vacillate in the face of communist aggression in East Asia. Bridges urged strong action that would "tell the world we will not equivocate, appease, or hesitate." Knowland echoed those same sentiments, asking if the administration was going to "sit back and twiddle [its] thumbs and do nothing." Neither senator, however, had any recommendations of his own, making only vague references to sending more military aid.[3]

Later that same day, Republican Senator Eugene Millikin of Colorado outlined the preliminary Taftite position on Korea. Acting as a spokesman for the Senate Republican Policy Committee, Millikin reported that the committee was "unanimous that the incident should not be used as a provocation for war." Since he believed the United States had a moral commitment to the South Koreans, Millikin recommended that the president provide them with more supplies. The Colorado senator concluded that the crisis was the result of the administration's vacillating policies and poor intelligence about the communists' intentions. Republican Senator Kenneth S. Wherry of Nebraska had a similar reaction: "You couldn't expect anything else with the Chinese policy we've got of waiting until the dust settles."[4]

On June 27, Truman and his principal advisors conferred with a congressional delegation to explain the situation and to announce their decision to intervene with American air and naval forces.[5] Acheson summarized the most recent developments, and Truman then read the statement he would release to the press after the meeting. Subsequent questioning revealed overwhelming support among the congressmen. Most of them asked about the political climate in the United Nations, but none challenged Truman's decision. Expressing the group's consensus, Connally declared that the attack was "the clearest test case that the United Nations has ever faced." That afternoon, Senate Majority Leader Scott Lucas of Illinois read Truman's statement on the floor of the Senate. In it Truman announced that American naval and air units would provide "cover and support" for the South Koreans, the Seventh Fleet would "prevent any attack on Formosa," and more supplies would be sent to French forces in Indochina.[6]

Speeches by Republicans revealed their overwhelming support for Truman's actions by all but the isolationists. The *New York Times* reported that after the statement had been read, the senators "rose to their feet and cheered." H. Alexander Smith, for instance, called Truman's action "a real stand in the Far East comparable to the stand we have taken in the Atlantic area," while Lodge hoped that Truman "would not shrink from using the Army."

Even such bitter opponents of the president as Styles Bridges, for example, concluded: "It was the only realistic step we could have taken," and added that "by these steps we have finally recognized the implications of Communist aggression in the Orient as well as in Europe." Former president Herbert Hoover declared: "Like others I have opposed many of our foreign policies, but now is not the time to argue origins, mistakes, responsibilities, or consequences." New York Governor Thomas E. Dewey, Truman's opponent in 1948, asserted that the president's actions "should be supported by a United America." Republican Senator Arthur H. Vandenberg of Michigan termed Truman's move as "courageous and indispensable," but reminded the president that he, Vandenberg, had "heretofore disagreed with our official attitude toward many phases of the Korean situation."[7]

The only voices of dissent came from Republican Senators James Kem of Missouri, Arthur Watkins of Utah, and George Malone of Nevada, who represented the hard core of isolationism in the Senate. Kem interrupted Lucas's reading of Truman's statement to ask if the president had "arrogated to himself the authority of declaring war." The Missouri senator also demanded to know who was responsible for selecting the congressional delegation that was briefed by Truman: "Were they the supporters of the so-called bipartisan foreign policy, or were any representatives drawn from the so-called critics of that policy?" Kem was silenced when Lucas pointed out that Bridges and Wiley had been included. Watkins and Malone were also troubled by the constitutional question, and each recited the familiar litany of past administration mistakes in East Asia as an explanation for the Korean situation.[8]

A full development of the position of the Taftites awaited Taft himself. On June 28, after having sat quietly for several days mulling over the issues, Taft delivered a major address on the floor of the Senate. In recounting the events of the preceding week, Taft concluded that the North Korean attack was "an outrageous act of aggression [that] in all probability was instigated by the Soviet Union." He commended the president for acting forthrightly; this was something, Taft averred, that the administration had done too little of in the past when it came to East Asia.[9]

Taft's criticisms of the administration fell into two main categories—that past policy had invited the communist attack, and that the president had failed to seek formal congressional approval for his actions. The Ohioan charged that the whole history of America's East Asian policy since World War II was noted for its appeasement of the communists. Administration policy statements such as Acheson's National Press Club speech, Taft maintained, made it clear to the communists that they could seize either Korea or Formosa without interference from the United States. Since the administration had now reversed that bankrupt policy, Taft urged Acheson to resign. The Ohio senator also questioned whether the president had "the right to precipitate any open warfare" without congressional approval. He encouraged Truman to submit a joint resolution to Congress authorizing his Korean involvement, adding, "I would vote in favor of it."[10]

Taft and his followers were troubled by the war. They had scored points against the administration throughout the first half of 1950, charging that it had been insufficiently aware of communist aggression in East Asia. The administration's turnabout in the Korean War pleased them, but Taft and many of his colleagues were on the verge of an election. Taft wrote: "The only way we can beat the Democrats is to go after them for their mistakes. We were making some progress in this when the war came and forced a change in policy. There is no alternative except to support the war, but certainly we can point out that it has resulted from a bungling of the Democratic administration." Another source of discontent lay in their fear of any accretions of presidential power or foreign commitments that the war might bring. Consequently, although the Taftites reluctantly voted for war appropriations and executive war powers, they missed few opportunities to denigrate the administration's handling of the war.[11]

Despite the introduction of small contingents of American forces, the South Koreans were still losing badly. On June 30, the president called another meeting of cabinet officers and congressmen to announce that he had ordered American troops in Korea and that American forces were permitted to operate north of the thirty-eighth parallel. As in the June 27 meeting, the majority of the congressmen's questions demonstrated their overwhelming support for Truman's actions. The only note of discord came from Wherry, who asked the president if he was going to advise the Senate before committing American forces in Korea. Truman responded that he was acting in an emergency under his powers as Commander-in-Chief: "If there is any necessity for Congressional action . . . I will come to you [that is, Congress]. But I hope we can get those bandits in Korea suppressed without that."[12]

In early July, the administration briefly debated the possibility of introducing a joint resolution, but rejected the idea. On July 3, in a cabinet-level meeting, Dean Acheson circulated his drafts of a joint resolution and a presidential message to Congress. Acheson's draft resolution stuck to the common denominators, concentrating on the president's actions only in Korea, and not in Formosa or Indochina. Senator Lucas, the only congressman present, believed that the president had acted properly, but that "the resolution itself was satisfactory and that it could pass, " although he did not think it desirable. Ultimately, administration leaders agreed with the chairman of the Joint Chiefs of Staff, General Omar Bradley, that the resolution would open up a "long debate in Congress on matters which now seem to be taken for granted."[13]

It is probable, given the reaction of key Republicans in those first few weeks, that if a carefully managed liaison with the right Republican senators had been cultivated, a resolution could have passed. That sort of liaison had worked in the Berlin crisis of 1948. The administration later complained that it was "too busy," as George Elsey, one of Truman's advisors wrote, "thinking of military action and United Nations action to try to cover up their tracks with congressional resolutions. The President's motivation was to stop the aggression, not to prepare for future political skirmishes." Instead, the State Department formulated a memorandum that listed eighty-five cases where past presidents had used American forces abroad without congressional sanction. Such thinking followed the pattern of the administration's past performance in the area of congressional relations and East Asian policy. After having acted unilaterally on East Asian matters for years, the administration would soon pay the price.[14]

In mid-July, the administration decided that the situation in Korea made it imperative to push for its larger, new strategy for containing communism worldwide. In September 1949, American officials were forced to reevaluate the country's military strategy after learning that the Soviets had detonated their first nuclear weapon. In January 1950, Truman ordered the development of the more powerful hydrogen bomb and instructed State and Defense Department officials to present recommendations concerning the impact of the Soviet bomb on American foreign policy. In April 1950, the results of their deliberations were finalized in National Security Council Paper Number 68 (NSC 68), which was later initialed by the president. The authors of NSC 68 believed the Soviets were determined to spread communism to the entire world; that they would exploit any weak spot in the West's defenses; and that the United States would have to play a major role in stopping communist probes wherever they appeared. The paper recommended that the United States increase its annual defense spending more than threefold to prepare to meet the expected Soviet initiatives. Defense spending on such a scale, however, was not forthcoming from Congress before the Korean War.[15]

In a Cabinet meeting on July 14, Acheson and Defense Department officials were more convinced than ever that the Soviets would create troublesome situations throughout the world. Acheson recommended that the president ask for more troops, money, and authority to confront the world situation; Truman agreed. On July 19, the president took his case to Congress. After dramatically recounting the situation of the last week of June, Truman concluded, "The fateful events of the 1930s, when aggression unopposed bred more aggression and eventually war, were fresh in our memory." He wanted an increase in appropriations to cover the war, as well as a general increase of $10 billion in defense appropriations to meet other potential threats. On the domestic front, the president favored establishing wage and price controls, allocating strategic materials, and increasing taxes. Truman ended his message with the exhortation: "The free world has made it clear, through the United Nations, that lawless aggression will be met with force. This is the significance of Korea—and it is a significance whose importance cannot be overestimated."[16]

Congress greeted the president's statement with enthusiasm. Connally applauded Truman's call for controls for the economy and increases in military spending. Even Wherry echoed the same sentiments, assuring Truman that Congress would give a "full measure of support for those recommendations of the President that will aid our cause." Taft admitted that while Republicans did not plan to "withold any money needed for the armed forces," he believed that the "powers requested were somewhat more than necessary." In a letter to Truman, Dulles reported that after having spoken with several "leading Republicans," the consensus was that "subject to scrutiny of detail, your proposals will have Republican support."[17]

With an election in the offing and the politics of partisanship threatening to overwhelm them, the defenders of bipartisanship again tried to establish a "middle way." In the absence of Vandenberg, H. Alexander Smith and Henry Cabot Lodge, Jr., led the bipartisan Republicans. By mid-July, Smith got John Foster Dulles, Republican ambassador-at-large, to address a gathering of Republican senators, which included Taft and Smith. The senators asked Dulles a variety of questions about Korea, centering on the contributions other nations had made to the war effort. Smith noted in his diary that the meeting had been "a great success" and hoped it would "lay the foundation for the development of a real Republican approach to a foreign policy which can be used with the Democrats to make a real Bipartisan-*American* foreign policy." Two days later, Taft, Smith, and Dulles met with the rest of the Republican senators. Smith confided that "there was a real hot discussion. We are getting into an atmosphere of working together or at least thinking together. We must unite America."[18]

Early in July, Smith believed that the party would be well served by developing "a Republican White Paper re Far Eastern policy . . . so that the Democrats will not claim that *they* (rather than the Republicans) saw the issues." Smith penned an outline of a proposed Republican policy statement that included strong support for the war. Nevertheless, he admonished his colleagues, "We are still left with the responsibility which no opposition party can ignore to hold the Administration to strict accountability for the causes as well as for the conduct of the war." Smith hoped that the Republicans in the Senate Foreign Relations and House Foreign Affairs Committees would prepare the statement, and that other Republicans would then endorse it.[19]

Two days later, the Republicans held several meetings to hammer out the details of the statement. Major participants included the Republican members of the Senate Foreign Relations and House Foreign Affairs Committees, as well as representatives from the Republican National Committee. They agreed that the National

Committee would publish a Republican White Paper that would be, as Smith put it, "a chronological sequence of events or statements from various persons showing without argument the breakdown in our foreign policy in the Far East and especially those events leading up to the Korean crisis." At the same time, the congressional Republicans would prepare a "statement of Republican policy," emphasizing that the Republicans, although critical of the administration's handling of Korea, favored a foreign policy along the lines of the Vandenberg resolution of 1948. Since the Vandenberg resolution advocated collective security arrangements within the framework of the United Nations, this was a way of heading off charges that they were isolationists.[20]

Through the course of the intraparty negotiations, Smith and Lodge kept in touch with the ailing Vandenberg. Although the Michigan senator could not play a leading role, his advice was, nonetheless, important. When told about the idea of a Republican statement, Vandenberg counseled: "If we could wholeheartedly unite on a meaningful statement, it would be grand. But I doubt whether this is possible." Vandenberg favored the release of only a "Summary of Facts," that "should be allowed to speak for itself as a compendium of facts for the consultation of those who want it as a basis for their own interpretation." Above all, the Michigan senator stressed that they should "be extraordinarily careful not to create the public impression that we are more interested in 'nailing Democrats' than we are in 'winning the victory.'" Therefore, he cautioned, they must "'unite for victory' and make our postmortems 'subordinate to this end.'"[21]

Taftites gave ample evidence to substantiate Vandenberg's fears. The Republican Minority Leaders of the Senate and House, Taft and Joseph Martin of Massachusetts, stated that the Republicans supported Truman's actions in Korea. However, they continued,

The disastrous policies in Asia were initiated and pursued by the Truman administration over the last five years without consultation with Republican members of Congress. Similarly, the Truman administration did not consult with Republicans—nor even Congress—in its decision when Korea was invaded, nor has it done so in the days since.

In the beginning of August, Republican National Chairman Guy Gabrielson struck the same themes while keynoting a party strategy conference. In a radio broadcast about a week later, Wherry demonstrated that he, too, was more interested in "nailing Democrats." The Nebraskan charged that the administration had blundered in not anticipating the attack and that Acheson should resign, since his policy of "letting the dust settle" had been repudiated.[22]

Despite such strong partisan crosscurrents, the bipartisan Republicans forged ahead. By August 8, House Republicans decided to write their own statement, so Senators Lodge, Smith, Wiley, and Hickenlooper, the minority members of the Foreign Relations Committee, prepared their draft. They all agreed that the statement had to stress "positive accomplishments," as well as "mistakes." Vandenberg and Dulles advised from afar that, as Smith phrased it, they keep "the statement on a rather conservative plane . . . letting the facts speak more or less for themselves, and without using exaggerated adjectives or using the attack method directly so much as the attack by inference." Lodge, who had always been more oriented toward Europe, wanted the statement to mention blunders in European policy too. The only note of discord came from Hickenlooper, who wanted several sentences criticizing the Tydings subcommittee; the others rejected that proposal.[23]

The next day, Smith sent a copy of the statement to Vandenberg for his comments. Smith mentioned that he had discussed it with Taft, Millikin, and Wherry, and that "they all feel that [the] procedure of our issuing it in this form is O.K. Bob Taft is the only one who has actually seen the report and made one or two suggestions which we have incorporated. He seems to think it is pretty good." Vandenberg's office authorized Smith and his colleagues to say that he saw the text and was "in general agreement with the viewpoint."[24]

On August 14, the long-awaited statement was released. It began on a familiar theme: "The major tragedy of our time was the failure and refusal of American leadership in 1945 to recognize the true aims and methods of the rulers of Soviet Russia." It went on to list six blunders made in 1945, including the Yalta and Potsdam agreements, the partition of Germany, and the loss of Eastern Europe and parts of Asia to the Soviets. By 1947, the statement contended, there was "a growing understanding of Soviet intentions" that coincided with a flowering of "bipartisan cooperation." Such bipartisanship never included East Asia. For the future, the Republicans urged Americans to support Truman in Korea, to increase arms shipments to friendly countries, and to "join together through the United Nations to establish peace in a free world." It was signed by Lodge, Smith, Hickenlooper, and Wiley.[25]

The four Republicans believed that they had carved out a middle-ground position between Truman's July 19 message and Taft's June 28 speech. Like Taft and Wherry, the minority party members of the Foreign Relations Committee believed that the administration's errors accounted in part for the North Korean attack, but unlike Taft and Wherry, they pledged unshakable support for the war effort with none of Taft's constitutional trepidations. In addition, although the senators were critical of Truman, their tone was always temperate, for instance, they never came close to calling for Acheson's resignation, as Wherry and Taft had done. The major difference between the four Republicans and Truman, aside from attempts to point out the president's shortcomings, was that the Republicans placed the war in a much broader context. To the four Republicans, Korea was the product of an inaccurate assessment, dating back to 1945, of Soviet intentions, not just in East Asia but worldwide. Their recommendations were equally broad in scope; they insisted that the administration regain the initiative in the Cold War. The day after the statement's release, Smith was ecstatic: "The reaction among our Senate Republicans was very favorable."[26]

The Democrats denigrated the statement, charging that it was politically motivated. The president's advisors agreed privately that Truman "should attempt to minimize the statement . . . and should do nothing which would be viewed as an effort by him to break up the bipartisan policy." Truman described the statement as "demagogic" among his White House friends. The president also angrily telephoned Dulles, accusing him of having written it: Dulles pled innocent. Senate Democrats were even less restrained. Tom Connally, for instance, growled that it was "a plain and palpabl[y] political statement . . . patently intended to influence the coming election." If the Republicans really wanted international peace, the Texan snapped, they should work "to have unity at home, instead of quarrelsome and pettifogging attacks." Democratic Senator Brien McMahon of Connecticut added, "The record shows that half of

the Republican party has vigorously opposed [Vandenberg's] patriotic efforts to secure legislative enactments necessary to the success of the Greek-Turkish, ECA, and Atlantic Pact policies."
McMahon especially damned Wherry, whom he characterized as
having "doggedly fought almost every administration effort intended to keep Europe out of the hands of the Communists."[27]

Wherry retorted in kind: "Instead of trying to whitewash the
Administration and blame others for its blunders, [McMahon] should
cooperate with [me] and other senators to try to get rid of the
alien-minded radicals and moral perverts in the Truman Administration." Acheson, of course, was first on Wherry's list. In his Press
Club speeches, Wherry charged, Acheson "invited" the North Korean attack by excluding Korea from the American defensive perimeter. Thus, although the statement formulated by the four Republicans was designed to give a balanced account of the war and
chart a positive course for Republicans, it predictably was engulfed
in a sea of partisan politics by Democrats and Republicans.[28]

With the elections approaching, the two parties drafted infor-
mational guides for their candidates. The Democrats reminded their
candidates that the "party still adheres to the principles of a bipartisan foreign policy. . . . The indictment for the Korea[n] situation rests on the isolationist bloc in Congress, not on a political
party." The Republicans released the Republican White Paper that
Smith had initiated, entitled *Bipartisan Foreign Policy*. The first
words of the pamphlet were: "The area of bipartisan foreign policy
is clearly defined. Asia, including China and Korea, has been ex-
cluded." Following Vandenberg's advice, the balance of the publication consisted of quotations from prominent Republicans that
demonstrated that the party had anticipated the problems of East
Asia but had been ignored. In general, however, the pamphlet
avoided campaign hyperbole.[29]

The bipartisan Republicans believed that the party could gain
strength in 1950 without sacrificing bipartisanship. In an article in
the *New York Times*, Lodge lectured his Republican colleagues on
the obligations of the "loyal opposition." He scorned "some Republicans who say that we of the opposition should always oppose
the Democrats no matter what they do, that to fail constantly to
oppose them labels one as a 'me too' Republican." Lodge was equally
critical of those Democrats who "define bipartisanship as meaning

that the minority must never under any circumstances whatever criticize the majority." Instead he encouraged the Republicans to "support the Administration when it is right and to oppose it when it is wrong." He added that, in order to "make constructive suggestions," Republicans should "appraise the past solely as a help in avoiding mistakes for the future."[30]

The pressures of campaigning and the existing political atmosphere made a mockery of Lodge's sentiments. Democratic leaders followed the path laid out in their campaign literature. Averell Harriman, for instance, noted that Taft had opposed the two programs that the Kremlin had attacked the most: the Marshall Plan and the North Atlantic Treaty. Harriman concluded that "if Congress had adopted his positions, Communist objectives would have been thereby furthered." David Lloyd of the White House staff advised Truman to concentrate his attack on the "isolationists . . . without even mentioning the word 'Republican.'" Lloyd argued that Truman needed to point out that "isolationists [have attacked] the bipatisan foreign policy . . . [and] have tried to make the people believe that the Korean War was a tragic mistake." Truman followed this advice, announcing in one speech that "isolationism is one of the chief issues in this election."[31]

Republicans also ignored Lodge. Wherry set the tone in his comments on the Republican White Paper, saying that "the [paper's] forward ought to be strengthened. It should be made more positive, more assertive in putting the responsibility for the war in Korea where it belongs." He again asked for Acheson's resignation. Bridges exclaimed: "Our predicament [that is, Korea] is the result of many errors. It is the result of many appeasements. It is the result, in many cases, I fear, of outright treason. . . . Incompetents, traitors, fools, perverts, knaves, and scoundrels have contributed to our plight." Taft also fixed the blame on a State Department that "told the American people that the Chinese Communists were just agrarian reformers, kind of Chinese New Dealers, and that a New Dealer ought to love them." Even such bipartisan stalwarts as Senators Smith, Ralph Flanders of Vermont, and Irving Ives of New York, declared on election eve that the administration's policy had been "dominated by a small willful group in the State Department intent upon appeasing the Chinese Communist revolution. . . . We are challenged to turn these years of destruction into new years of hope and fulfillment. A Republican vote means a vote for a united American foreign policy."[32]

The Republicans had strayed so far from Lodge's ideal that Vandenberg was unable to make a statement in support of Republican candidates on the eve of the election. In a letter to Senator Owen Brewster of Maine, chairman of the Republican Senatorial Campaign Committee, Vandenberg explained that he "had no right to speak for Republican policy in [the] next Congress." The Michigan senator believed that "Wherry has more official right to do so than have I" and Wherry favored Acheson's resignation. "Meanwhile, many G. O. P. candidates," Vandenberg continued, "have tied themselves to the termination of what they erroneously construe as 'bipartisan foreign policy.' " Vandenberg concluded: "I cannot ignore these facts if I attempt any statement for the party. I think it would be [a] disservice to many Republican candidates for me to try to make any general statement under the circumstances and several candidates have said as much to me."[33]

The Republicans scored victories in the elections of 1950, gaining twenty-eight seats in the House and five seats in the Senate. This election was not as successful for the Republicans, however, as the previous three off-year congressional elections: Republicans gained seventy-one House and six Senate seats in 1938, forty-five House and nine Senate seats in 1942, and fifty-five House and twelve Senate seats in 1946. Nonetheless, many Republicans, particularly the Taftites, regarded the election returns as a vindication of the politics of partisanship. After all, Democratic Senators Millard Tydings of Maryland (who had taken on McCarthy) and Majority Leader Scott Lucas of Illinois were both defeated in campaigns that appeared to be related to foreign policy issues. Wherry declared that the election results constituted a vote of no confidence for Acheson.[34]

In late November, on the verge of the Chinese entry into the Korean War, the Taftites had strengthened their position in the party. They had preached that it was good politics to attack the administration's foreign policy blunders and believed that the election returns had sustained them. Bipartisan Republicans, such as Lodge and Smith (who also wanted to set the record straight on Korea) urged Republicans to exercise restraint in attacking the administration. They were scarcely heard in late 1950. The politics of partisanship burned brightly. Events in the rugged terrain of Manchuria, where Chinese Communist units massed for an attack, and in Brussels, where a North Atlantic pact force was born, combined to produce two tremendous political battles in 1951 that proved deadly to bipartisanship.

7

The Great Debate of 1951

Once a generation during this century, the American people have questioned basic assumptions about the relations of the United States with the rest of the world. During the great debate of 1917–1919, Americans had to determine whether their country should enter the "Great War" and, once the war was over, whether the United States should participate in the League of Nations. In 1939, with the outbreak of World War II in Europe, the question of American involvement in European affairs was again intensely debated. The new wisdom that emerged after Pearl Harbor held that international organizations and collective security arrangements in which the United States played an active role were crucial to protecting and promoting the country's national interest, and that American security depended on opposing the expansion of aggressor states. The implications and specific policies that grew out of those assumptions during the 1940s and 1950s became the crux of the explosive debates of the 1960s, which centered on the Vietnam conflict.

While the debate of 1951 was not on the same scale as those more momentous conflicts, it did define an emerging Cold War strategy. Unlike the "great debates" of the first half of the century, the dissenters in 1951 did not question the administration's central assumptions, which held that the Soviets were dangerous, that they must not be permitted to expand, and that the United States should play some role in stopping them. Crucial to the challengers—most of whom were fiscal conservatives who since the 1930s had had a deep distrust of the presidency and shrank from the idea of an America that was more politically active in world affairs—was the means by which the United States could pursue these goals most effectively. Their answer was: as frugally as possible while retaining the greatest freedom of action for the country and carefully guarding against accretions of presidential power. In most respects, the great debate of 1951 represents the last hurrah of the noninterventionists of 1939–41. In one way, however, 1951 foreshadowed the 1960s. In both instances, the dissenters sought formal legislation (Senate Resolution 8 in 1951 and the War Powers Act in the 1970s) to protect Congress from an unbridled executive. The debate nonetheless was the most formidable challenge experienced by President Harry S Truman's European containment strategy. Out of it emerged a clear consensus behind an American military presence in Europe that has continued virtually unchanged to the present.

When viewed in the context of the political battles between the parties, and particularly among Senate Republicans, the debate represented a new departure for those Republicans who followed the leadership of Senator Robert A. Taft of Ohio. Whenever they had criticized the administration's European programs, the Taftites were silenced by the bipartisan coalitions' charges that they were "isolationists" who disrupted the bipartisan foreign policy. During the great debate of 1951, the Taftites for the first time effectively applied to Truman's European strategy the aggressive tactics they had utilized during the previous year attacking East Asian policies. While they did not change the president's plans, their charges about his imperious behavior struck a responsive chord among the public, and even among some Democrats.[1]

Fresh with electoral victory, the Taftites' new confidence became evident in their renewed demand for Dean Acheson's resignation. A week after the election, when asked about Truman's plans to place American troops into a North Atlantic pact army, Taft noted that while he was "in favor of aid to the Western European countries . . . [the] whole problem ought to be thoroughly re-examined by the new Congress." A week later, Acheson ridiculed Taft by declaring that there were no more "isolationists," just "re-examinists," whom he compared to farmers who pulled up their crops in the morning to see how they had done during the night. Republican Senator Eugene Millikin of Colorado snapped that "a re-examinist is like a farmer who goes out every morning and pulls out all the weeds to see how they have grown overnight. . . . Bad foreign policy weeds—Acheson jackassery weeds!"[2]

Meanwhile, events in distant Korea served to exacerbate the already explosive political situation in the Senate. After a stunning victory in September at Inchon, General Douglas MacArthur proceeded to mop up the demoralized North Korean units. As United Nations forces came closer to China, the Chinese Communists bided their time and then, during the last week of November, they struck MacArthur's forces with awesome blows, which sent the Americans reeling back in a confused retreat.

The Chinese attack made the Taftites more vocal; they charged that this was further evidence of the bankruptcy of Acheson's East Asian policies. In such an atmosphere, Senator Irving Ives, normally a supporter of bipartisanship, introduced a resolution in the Senate Republican Policy Committee that would make Acheson's resignation a matter of party policy. Ives's proposal was passed in slightly altered form by a staggering twenty-three to five. Dissenting were Senators Margaret Chase Smith, Wayne Morse, George Aiken, William Langer of North Dakota, and H. Alexander Smith. Smith of New Jersey characterized the action as excessively "partisan" at a time of "grave danger." Aiken, too, lamented that "it is extremely unfortunate that a presidential campaign and what may be the opening stages of World War III had to get underway at the same time!" Several days later, however, Truman reaffirmed his faith in Acheson.[3]

In the face of a military setback in Korea, the administration pressed for the immediate implementation of its European strategy. The initial North Korean attack of June 1950 had lent a sense of urgency to Truman's plans to develop an American-led, North Atlantic pact–armed force. In late November, before an executive session meeting with the Senate Foreign Relations Committee, Acheson argued that in Korea the Soviets had demonstrated how ruthless and aggressive they could be. The secretary concluded that the situation demanded "strong and firm measures . . . which call for very considerable stepping up in the military preparation of the United States and the North Atlantic countries with the clear knowledge that anything can happen." The president asked Congress for an additional appropriation of $16.8 billion for the armed forces in order to meet the situation.[4]

On December 13, Truman invited an impressive list of congressional leaders to the White House for a briefing on the world situation and to discuss declaring a national emergency. When the president went around the room to solicit the opinion of each senator and congressman present, only Taft and Wherry criticized him. Taft believed that Truman ought to spell out his plans on how much larger the military would be, the taxes it would incur, and the additional powers he needed. The Ohioan concluded: "I'm generally against a declaration of national emergency without knowing the details of what is involved." Truman retorted that a declaration would rouse the country, hearten America's allies, and give him important discretionary powers to act quickly in an emergency. Republican Senator Millikin, however, gave ample evidence that Truman had carried the day. Millikin, normally an ally of Taft, agreed that a declaration should be issued and that "we ought to make ourselves as strong as possible as fast as possible," while the others shouted "aye, aye!" During the next week, the president made his declaration and began drafting plans to impose wartime controls and initiate universal military training. He also announced that the North Atlantic Council had agreed to establish a European army with an American contingent, and that General Dwight D. Eisenhower would command the new army.[5]

In the midst of the furor over Acheson and the declaration of a national emergency, ex-president Herbert C. Hoover and former ambassador Joseph P. Kennedy delivered crucial speeches that challenged Truman's global strategy. Journalists later pointed to the speeches as having touched off the "great debate." Hoover argued that the administration's policy of committing ground forces to the Eurasian continent, such as in Korea and Europe, was expensive and played into the communists' strength. The ex-president compared the populations of the communist and the noncommunist countries and concluded that "to commit the spare ground forces of the non-Communist nations into a land war against this communist land mass would be a war without victory." Instead, he asserted that America should concentrate on preserving "for the world this Western Hemisphere Gibraltar of Western Civilization" by relying on air and sea power in alliance with Britain, Japan, the

Philippines, and Formosa. Hoover also cautioned that before any more aid was extended to the Europeans, they should show "they have the spiritual strength and unity to avail themselves of their own resources." Hoover concluded that his policies were "not isolationism. They are the opposite. They would avoid the rash involvement of our military forces in hopeless campaigns," such as in Korea, from which he hinted America should withdraw.[6]

The administration wasted no time in replying to Hoover's address. Acheson, who had just returned from Brussels, criticized Hoover's ideas without mentioning him by name. If the United States followed the Hoover approach, Acheson argued, the Soviets could easily conquer Europe, thereby seriously menacing American security. The secretary advocated building mutual strength instead of "sitting quivering in the storm cellar waiting for whatever fate others may wish to prepare for us." Truman was more blunt, characterizing Hoover's position as "isolationism . . . nothing else."[7]

The administration tried to buttress its case further when State Department press officer Lincoln White implied that an upcoming speech by John Foster Dulles would be a reply to the Hoover address. Dulles was furious, since he had worked hard to attain a position of power by remaining in the good graces of all the Republicans. Earlier in the month, Dulles had arrived at an understanding with Taft, and he wrote the Ohioan to reassure him that the State Department release altered nothing, adding, "The State Department publicity people pulled this one on me." Dulles also penned a note to Hoover explaining: "I am sorry that my talk tomorrow night before the United National association is being featured as a 'reply' to you. . . . The point of view I shall express may be somewhat different from yours but I agree with much that you said and I hope and expect that you will agree with much that I say." In his speech, Dulles recounted the successes of recent American foreign policy, citing the founding of the United Nations, the end of the colonial system, and the extension of vast sums of money. Many of America's setbacks resulted, Dulles asserted, from "not creating enough military strength in being." He concluded by extolling the virtues of collective security and the development of air, sea, atomic, and ground strength.[8]

As the Eighty-second Congress convened in early January 1951, the forum of the debate shifted to the Senate, where Taft and

Wherry's speeches became rallying points for the critics. Like Hoover, Taft feared that a massive transfer of troops to the Continent was strategically unsound and would constitute an unacceptable economic drain on America. Taft argued that the basis of American foreign relations was "to maintain the liberty of our people . . . [and] not to reform the entire world or spread sweetness and light and economic prosperity to peoples who have lived and worked out their own salvation for centuries." He was not so adamant like Hoover and Wherry, and made it clear from the start that he would not oppose sending a small contingent to Europe and forming an alliance with nations such as Australia, New Zealand, the Philippines, Formosa, Britain, France, and Holland. The Ohioan bristled, however, at the cavalier attitude the administration assumed on whether the president needed congressional approval before he dispatched the troops and he feared that the vast wartime powers that Truman had requested might turn America into a "garrison state." In addition, with his own presidential ambitions, Taft could scarcely ignore so volatile an issue. He corrected reporters who asked him if he had decided to move in on foreign policy, replying that foreign policy had "moved in" on him.[9]

In several speeches in early January, Taft pointed out that in the past the administration had labelled any criticism of its foreign policy as isolationist and disruptive of national unity, and as "sabotaging" bipartisanship. Taft characterized such tactics as an attempt to "cover up the past faults and failures of the Administration." The proposition of sending troops to Europe was being handled, he asserted, the way the Marshall Plan and North Atlantic Treaty had been, with the administration creating such a groundswell of support that it became impossible for anyone to oppose it without being called an "isolationist."[10]

Taft argued that the United States was not legally obligated to send troops, and that the president had no authority to dispatch them without congressional approval. He effectively cited statements made by Acheson and Democratic Senator Tom Connally of Texas, chairman of the Foreign Relations Committee, during the debates over the North Atlantic Treaty and Military Assistance Program in 1949 which categorically assured the Senate that those measures would not commit the United States by sending any troops to Europe. If the president wanted to send troops under the provisions of Article 3 of the North Atlantic Treaty, Taft maintained, he must first obtain congressional authority as he had done with the Military Assistance Program of 1949. On January 8, Wherry formalized the debate by introducing Senate Resolution 8: "Resolved, that it is the sense of the Senate that no ground forces of the United States should be assigned on duty in the European area for the purpose of the North Atlantic Treaty pending the formulation of a policy with respect thereto by the Congress."[11]

The administration wasted no time counterattacking. On the strategic question, Truman defended the Europeans, noting that they were "building bigger armies than our own." In his State of the Union address, he tried to rally support for his program of mobilization and a closer cooperation with the North Atlantic pact. Truman also insisted that as commander-in-chief he had the power to send American armed forces anywhere, but that he would consult Congress beforehand. The president, however, made it clear that he was not compelled to consult, but added, "I am polite, and I usually always consult them . . . I don't ask their permission; I just consult them."[12]

As always, the bipartisan Republicans, led by Lodge and H. Alexander Smith with Vandenberg in the background, worked for compromise. They supported Truman's plans for placing American ground forces in Europe, but the constitutional question concerned them because, with Truman and Taft taking such unyielding stances, the situation excited the kind of partisan animosities that made their position more vulnerable. The bipartisan Republicans, therefore, worked to avoid the issue by stressing the need for national unity during a foreign policy crisis. They were, however, irritated that Truman had not tried to obtain advance congressional authorization. Vandenberg cautioned his colleagues:

We may not like Truman but he is the only President we are going to have for the next two years. Truman may not like this Congress but it is the only Congress he is going to have for the next two years. Unless they get together on a rational united basis we shall have no foreign policy at all during the two most critical years that the Republic has yet faced.[13]

In January, following Vandenberg's lead, Lodge delivered a speech in the Senate designed to smooth over differences within his party.

The Massachusetts senator emphasized how closely his views paralleled those of Senator Taft, listing sixteen points, as he put it, of "substantial—though not unanimous—agreement" between them. "They certainly do not justify the impression," Lodge continued, "either here or abroad, that the Senate is split right down the middle with globalists on one side and retreatists on the other." Taft and Wherry, however, remained unconvinced by Lodge's honeyed words. Taft asked Lodge if he thought the president had the power to send troops anywhere. "I prefer," Lodge responded, "to discuss the question on the basis of common sense and wisdom, and what is involved in this question, rather than to get into a legal question. I am not a lawyer." Wherry wanted to know if Lodge thought Truman could send troops to Europe before Congress had been consulted. Lodge replied: "I hope very much that some system can be devised which will call for congressional understanding and approval for whatever is done. . . . I do not believe that we should undertake to determine troop and plane and ship movements here in the Capitol." [14]

Several weeks after the debate began, a number of pressures developed to force Senate Democrats to take Wherry's resolution more seriously. On January 8, Vandenberg issued a brief statement from his sickbed, declaring that "both Congress and the President should prayerfully cooperate in this plea for essential unity." Within several days, venerated Democratic Senator Walter George of Georgia, a senior member of the Senate who commanded great respect from both sides of the aisle, echoed Vandenberg's sentiments in a statement of his own: "Regardless of the President's authority to commit troops to combat in foreign areas without the consent of Congress, we will not obtain national unity that is essential until the President advises the people he will submit the question to Congress before finally acting." Public opinion polls also revealed that while Americans supported sending the troops by more than two to one, they also believed, by about the same margin, that Congress should play a more positive role in the decision. Truman and Acheson, however, tenaciously clung to their position that, while consulting Congress might be useful, it was not mandatory prior to the transfer of troops. [15]

On January 23, Wherry's somewhat modified resolution was referred to the combined Foreign Relations and Armed Services

Committees. Two days later, during the first meeting of the committees, it became apparent that, although sending the troops aroused little controversy, the president's position on the constitutional problem did. Republicans Lodge and Smith argued that, although the president probably had the power to dispatch troops, as Smith put it,

what the President needs and the country needs is the confidence of the country, public opinion behind everything we do. . . . We have never done it before [that is, used Article 3 of the North Atlantic Treaty to send troops], and I think it would be wise for the President to consider the feelings of Congress and not make it appear as though he is going to do it without discussion.[16]

While the issues were being aired in public hearings, Vandenberg, gaunt and weakened by cancer, once again groped for a compromise behind the scenes. In late January, the Michigan senator initiated a correspondence with Wherry to attempt to get the Nebraska senator to define his resolution more narrowly. Vandenberg asked if he was correct in interpreting the resolution to mean that Wherry was not challenging the president's power to send troops abroad, only his prerogative to do so in advance of an emergency under Article 3 of the North Atlantic Treaty. The Michigan senator also stressed the need for national unity. Wherry affirmed Vandenberg's evaluation of Senate Resolution 8, but noted that "when sound global policy emerges we shall have national unity." In other letters to Wherry and others, Vandenberg outlined a substitute for the Wherry proposal that included a reaffirmation of the North Atlantic Treaty commitment, a recognition that the president's power to station troops abroad "involves 150 years of indecisive debate," and a provision that urged "the President to seek advance Congressional approval for the deployment of American troops abroad whenever long range planning is *not incompatible with our public interest in national security.*"[17]

Meanwhile, the combined committees assigned to discuss Senate Resolution 8 worked on alternatives. In mid-February, Lodge introduced a substitute to Wherry's proposal in the form of a joint resolution which stipulated that the major American "defense effort should be through the United States Air Force and the United

States Navy," and that any troops sent should represent "a minor fraction of the total armed forces created." Lodge's resolution provided that before any troops were sent under Article 3 of the treaty, the joint chiefs of staff had to certify that it was "essential to the security of the United States," and that other countries were making a "definite and dependable commitment" to their defense. Lodge also expressed confidence in the "ability and integrity" of Eisenhower, and voiced approval of sending a "limited number of United States troops to Europe." By offering his substitute in the form of a joint resolution, it meant that the measure required passage in both houses and the president's signature, and that it had the force of law. His proposal attracted the support of the Republicans on the committee as well as Democrats George of Georgia and Harry F. Byrd of Virginia.[18]

In March, the administration introduced its own proposal through Democratic Senators Richard Russell of Georgia and Tom Connally. Connally and Russell preferred a simple Senate resolution (which was just an expression of the Senate's opinion) to a joint resolution to allow them to maintain the constitutional position that Congress could not compel action. Their resolution recommended that the president "consult" with the appropriate military and congressional leaders, but only required that he satisfy himself as to whether any troop movements were in the national interest. Finally, the president would be required to submit semiannual reports to Congress on his implementations of the North Atlantic Treaty.[19]

By early March, H. Alexander Smith, who was sometimes called a "poor man's Vandenberg," had played a relatively low-key role in the debate and was often overshadowed by Lodge. The New Jersey senator's efforts had focused on private discussions and letters to the principals in the debate. During the combined committee's discussion over the form of the resolution, however, Smith offered an important compromise. To meet Connally's objection that a joint resolution would become so entangled in lengthy debate that it would impair Eisenhower's effectiveness, Smith proposed that two resolutions be reported. One would be a joint resolution dealing with the matter of consultation, and the other would be a simple resolution giving the Senate's approval of the initial dispatch of troops.[20]

Smith's idea gained favor with the Republicans as well as Democrats George and Byrd. They agreed that the two resolutions would inspire unity, express approval of the European army, and provide a mechanism for consultation. During a particularly testy moment in the committee debate, Knowland succinctly stated the bipartisan Republicans' case:

Might I just make this plea to the moderate members of this committee. It is entirely possible that you have the votes to insist upon a simple resolution, but there are a great many of us sitting on this side of the aisle, who have consistently supported the foreign policy of this government and have followed the leadership of Senator Vandenberg. . . . I do not believe that the cause of General Eisenhower in Europe . . . will be served by a narrow margin of victory in this committee which will bring a badly divided committee onto the floor. . . . I submit, gentlemen, that this issue runs very deep. It runs as deep in some quarters as the fight on the packing of the Supreme Court of the United States.

George eloquently reinforced his Republican colleague's position, arguing that Congress had "a strong moral obligation . . . to implement the North Atlantic Treaty . . . not by one House merely but by both Houses."[21]

Despite the pleas of Knowland and George, the votes on most of the amendments were extremely close. Some of Lodge's proposals were incorporated into the Connally-Russell resolution by a margin of only one or two votes, with the Republicans, plus Democrats Byrd and George, voting together. The issue of the two resolutions evoked a particularly sharp debate between Lodge and Russell, the latter arguing that a joint resolution would "put the President on the spot." Bending to political realities, Lodge agreed to a simple and concurrent resolution, which, unlike a joint resolution, did not have the force of law.[22]

The resolution that emerged was an uneven blend of Connally and Lodge's proposals.[23] Sections 1, 2, 3, and 7 were taken practically verbatim from the Connally-Russell proposal, while Lodge and Smith played a large role in composing sections 4, 5, and 6. The result was that some of the same topics were covered twice with a different emphasis. On the delicate constitutional question, for instance, section 3 noted that the president *"should consult"* with the secretary of defense, the joint chiefs of staff, Eisenhower, and the appropriate House and Senate committees "before taking action to send [further] units of ground troops to Europe under Article 3 of the North Atlantic Treaty." Smith's section 6, however, clung more closely to the spirit of Wherry's initial resolution by providing that "it is the sense of the Senate that . . . *congressional approval* should be obtained of any policy requiring the assignment of [further] American troops abroad when such assignment is in implementation of Article 3 of the North Atlantic Treaty." There was little difference between Lodge and Connally, however, in their endorsement of the appointment of Eisenhower and the assignment of the six initial divisions.[24]

In late March and early April, during the final round of floor debates, most of the challenges to the resolution focused on the constitutional problem, while the strategic concerns raised by Hoover, Taft, and Wherry played a much smaller role. The greatest controversies arose over whether the issue should be presented in the form of a joint resolution, and the manner in which section 6 should be strengthened. With the exception of the latter issue, an overwhelming number of the Democrats voted against all the amendments, and in the end supported the simple resolution (Senate Resolution 99) while opposing the concurrent resolution (Senate Concurrent Resolution 18). The voting pattern of the bipartisan Republicans mirrored that of the Democrats, except that they voted in favor of an amendment introduced by Republican Senator Joseph R. McCarthy of Wisconsin and supported Senate Concurrent Resolution 18. The Taft Republicans, however, experienced defeat on nearly every challenge they made to the resolutions, and in the end either voted against the resolutions or supported them without enthusiasm.[25]

Two quite different combinations of senators took turns trying to revise Smith's constitutional compromise (section 6). It was an indication that, try as he may, Smith was not Vandenberg. Lodge criticized it as being "so extremely ambiguous that it is an invitation to any executive to interpret the ambiguity precisely to suit his own plans at the moment." A list of seven Democrats and five bipartisan Republicans, led by Lodge and Ives, introduced a substitute for section 6 that demonstrated their pique at the administration's failure to consult the standing congressional committees on so important a decision. Their amendment provided that if a majority of the Senate Committees on Armed Services and Foreign Relations, or a majority of the same committees in the House, believed that "any proposed policy pertaining to the implementation of Article 3 of the North Atlantic Treaty is a new policy . . . such new policy . . . should be submitted to the Senate and the House for their consideration and approval." It also approved sending the initial six divisions of troops.[26]

The amendment was defeated thirty-five to fifty-seven by a coalition of Taftites and Democrats. Many of the Taftites opposed it because it institutionalized the bipartisan Republicans' definition of executive-legislative consultations, that is, consultations between the State Department and the established committees. Taft and Wherry had argued for at least a year that true bipartisanship had to include the Senate Republican leadership, of which they were prominent members. Many of the Taftites also voted against the amendment because it supported sending the troops. Numerous administration Democrats opposed the amendment because it was more precise in what it expected the president to do than was section 6.[27]

The Taftites and a small band of southern Democrats then advanced their modification to section 6, which was introduced by Democrat McClellan of Arkansas. It stated: "But it is the sense of the Senate that no troops in addition to four such divisions shall be sent to Western Europe in implementation of the North Atlantic Treaty without further congressional approval." The amendment was far less flexible than the Lodge-Ives proposal, since it required congressional approval for any troop transfer, not just a "new policy" as interpreted by certain congressional committees. Smith of New Jersey characterized the amendment as "too restrictive," since it provided that the president "cannot send another soldier without congressional approval."[28]

The McClellan amendment was as close to the original Wherry proposal as the Taftites ever got during the final round of floor debates. Karl Mundt bluntly stated their case: "If we blindly surrender our authority to the Chief Executive . . . we shall be surrendering the constitutional authority which we have as Senators of the United States." The proposal passed on its second vote by a slender forty-nine to forty-three margin. A phalanx of Taftites was

joined by four bipartisan Republicans and twelve Southern Democrats in support of the McClellan amendment. In opposition were
thirty-five Democrats and eight bipartisan Republicans, including
Smith of New Jersey, Lodge, James Duff of Pennsylvania, Flanders, Aiken, Saltonstall, Tobey, and Ives.[29]

The fiercest battle, however, came over a motion by Republican
Senator John W. Bricker of Ohio to recommit the resolution to the
committee with instructions that it restructure the measure as either
a bill or a joint resolution. Bricker chastised his colleagues for
agreeing passively to a concurrent resolution, which expressed only
the sense of Congress and had no force of law. "In my judgment,"
Bricker asserted,

this resolution is a sham. It is a fraud. It is a hoax on the American people
to adopt a concurrent or simple resolution. The people expect us to do
something positive. . . . But if we adopt such a resolution as this, it will
have no more effect than if we were to write a letter to the President of
the United States and say—"This is our desire."[30]

Bipartisan Republicans who had served on the committees, such
as Smith, Saltonstall, and Lodge, apologetically tried to acquaint
Bricker with political reality. All three noted that they had vigorously supported a joint resolution in committee but had been beaten.
Lodge explained that "if the Senator [Bricker] knew as much about
the situation inside those two committees as I do, he would realize
that if the matter ever gets back into those two committees it will
never come out." McClellan feared that even if the joint resolution
passed, it "will surely be vetoed and then we will have nothing."
This time all the Democrats stood together with twelve bipartisan
Republicans to defeat the motion fifty-six to thirty-one.[31]

The final round of floor debates demonstrated that a large number of senators agreed with sending the troops. On three votes
where the critics had an opportunity to express opposition to Truman's strategy, they could muster only twenty-four, twenty-nine,
and twenty-one votes. Events had played an important role in their
defeat. The Communist Chinese attack in Korea gave substance to
Truman's charge that the communists were dangerous and might
precipitate World War III at any moment. Americans agreed that

it was better to send troops to Europe to defend it than to retake it from an invading army, as they had done just seven years before at Normandy. Had the issue remained strictly on those grounds, Senate Resolution 8 would have been only a tempest in a teapot, but the constitutional issue complicated matters, adding considerable strength to Wherry's side.[32]

The Taft-Hoover-Wherry coalition scored heavily by pointing to the dangers of an unbridled executive who had failed to consult Congress on so important a decision. The Taftites, determined to reorient American life away from "statism," were alarmed by Truman's simultaneous decisions to introduce universal military training, send troops to Europe, mobilize the economy, and institute the Fair Deal. The "creeping socialism" they had inveighed against now seemed poised at the doors of the republic. Powerful partisan pressures to the contrary, numerous conservative Southern Democrats, who held similar fears, broke party ranks to join them, for instance, in suppport of the McClellan amendment.[33]

Bipartisan Republicans were in a quandary. As strong advocates of the Democrats' foreign policy, they had urged their fellow Republicans to eschew partisanship and judge foreign policy matters in a nonpartisan fashion for the good of the country and the party. Their point of view had received sharp blows from the Taftites since Dewey's loss in 1948 and the advent of McCarthyism. While the bipartisan Republicans heartily concurred with the dispatch of the troops, Truman's manner irritated them too. They did not wish to force a constitutional showdown, but they did expect Truman to include them in the decision-making process as he had during the height of bipartisan cooperation in 1948 and 1949. Many of them sought unsuccessfully to institutionalize that process with the Ives-Lodge amendment.[34]

What emerged from the "debate" was a reaffirmation of the administration's European policy and an indecisive admonition to consult Congress. The vote on the concurrent resolution, after all, was a slender forty-five to forty-one. Since the size of American forces in Europe has remained relatively unchanged since 1951, the constitutional requirement (section 6) remains untested. Ironically, Taft's constitutional ideas were revived in the late 1960s and early 1970s by liberal Democratic senators who wanted to restrain conservative Republican President Richard Nixon's actions in Southeast Asia. Those ideas were ultimately incorporated into the War Powers Resolution of 1973.[35]

Politically, the debate was important because it demonstrated that the aggressiveness the Taftites had displayed in attacking Truman's East Asian policies had emboldened them on European policy too. While unable to reverse Truman's ground troops decision in 1951, the Taftites' ideas played an important role in the 1950s, for instance, in the fight over the Bricker Amendment. The debate became the first round of a double-barreled assault in 1951 on the administration's European and East Asian strategies. Only a week after the debate ended, Truman fired General Douglas MacArthur, precipitating a "great debate" on East Asian policy that had been brewing for at least two years.

8

MacArthur and the Demise of the Old Bipartisanship

During 1951, the ideas of the China bloc became Republican party doctrine for all but a few bipartisan Republicans. The Chinese entry into the Korean War galvanized the GOP as few other issues had into a nearly party-line position against President Harry S Truman's limited-war strategy. Republicans believed that General Douglas MacArthur's more aggressive tactics would end the war quickly without appeasement. When the general was relieved in April for openy criticizing the administration, Republicans flocked under his banner, using the incident to initiate an investigation of the administration's entire East Asian policy back to 1945. The minority report signed by most of the Republicans on the investigating committees demonstrated how widespread China bloc attitudes had become throughout the party. The bipartisan coalition of 1947–1950 had reached its nadir.

The history of the Korean conflict from September to December 1950 swung from brilliant victory to ignominious defeat for the United Nations. In September, General MacArthur's forces surprised the communists by landing behind their lines at Inchon, which caused their position to collapse. Within a month, United Nations forces had cleared virtually all South Korea of North Korean troops and stood poised at the thirty-eighth parallel, ready to move north. After some hesitation because of objections from America's allies, Truman agreed that MacArthur should proceed carefully up the peninsula. As United Nations forces neared the Chinese border, however, the Chinese Communist officials warned them against coming too close. In early November, there were scattered reports that small numbers of Chinese Communist soldiers had joined their North Korean comrades. Because MacArthur and the administration failed to take sufficient heed, the massive Chinese Communist attack of late November surprised and shocked nearly all Americans. At a time when Truman was ready to wrap up the Korean War and return his attention to Western Europe, the new war in Korea disrupted things. Early on, the president and his advisors decided that, despite the initial military setbacks, they would not leave Korea unless forced out, and they would confine the war to the Korean peninsula.[1]

MacArthur held another view of the situation. The general argued that since the administration had initially entered Korea to punish North Korean aggression, it should do the same to the Chinese. Korea, the general argued, was where the communists had thrown down the gauntlet, and the United States had to respond strongly or pay a heavy price later for appeasing them. Specifically, MacArthur favored a blockade of China's ports, the bombing of supply centers in Manchuria, the use of troops that Chiang Kai-shek had offered in Korea, and the landing of Chinese Nationalist forces on the Chinese mainland as well.[2]

The war brought Taft Republicans and the China bloc together in opposition to Truman's limited war. The Taft Republicans, who were never very comfortable with foreign commitments, were appalled at the specter of a larger war. By January 1951, many of them advocated withdrawal while paradoxically supporting the MacArthur formula. Undoubtedly, the Taft Republicans believed that MacArthur's solution offered the quickest way to end the war, and they hoped to capitalize politically by being associated with the charismatic general. The China-bloc senators, long critical of the administration for not taking stronger measures against communism in East Asia, wholeheartedly embraced MacArthur's recommendations. Although there were important differences between the Taft Republicans and the China bloc that later emerged in the debates on the Japanese Peace Treaty, those differences were ignored for the time being. Meanwhile, the once-powerful voices of those bipartisan Republicans who were oriented toward Europe were now barely audible.[3]

China-bloc Republicans such as Smith and Knowland were among the first to take a definite position on the new war. In a December 4 speech, Knowland proudly pointed to his record of unflinching support of Republican Senator Arthur H. Vandenberg of Michigan on European programs, and asked rhetorically: "But are we to take the position that human freedom is less worth supporting in Asia than it is in Europe?" Knowland also questioned why Truman moved to punish North Korea's aggression but was reticent to apply the same logic to China. "Is aggression any less dangerous to peace," he asked, "because it was committed by a large power? Of course not." Knowland advocated the MacArthur program for ending the war, adding that "the hands of our combat commanders in Korea should be untied." Smith gave his hearty concurrence.[4]

The Taft Republicans' early response to the new war revealed the contradictions that had plagued them for some time. For almost a year, since the Formosa crisis of early 1950, they had advocated a tougher stand in East Asia and had encouraged Republican Senator Joseph R. McCarthy of Wisconsin in his attacks on administration policies. At the same time, the Taft Republicans were cautious about accepting elaborate commitments abroad, fearful of the concomitant rise in presidential power, taxes, and government controls. The consistent elements in their thinking were their opposition to Truman for political reasons and their desire to end the war quickly in order to return to their chief domestic concern, combating statism. Those same motives inspired contradictory behavior in them, however. Consequently, their position on the war varied from guarded enthusiasm in June, to criticism in August, back to enthusiasm again in September after the Inchon landing. After Inchon, and especially during the new war, the Taft Republicans alternately either embraced MacArthur's quick victory strategy or advocated withdrawal from Korea.[5]

In early January 1951, with United Nations forces barely hanging on in Korea, the Taft Republicans switched from advocating the use of "all the force at our command" to recommending withdrawal. Although ex-president Herbert Hoover expressed the idea first in his December 20, 1950, speech, it awaited Robert Taft to make a full presentation of his group's thinking on the new war. The Ohioan questioned the legitimacy of the United Nations' initial decision of June 1950, since the Security Council had acted without the concurrence of all five permanent members. At a time when he was attacking Truman for sending troops to Europe, Taft reiterated the constitutional qualms he had expressed the previous July. Taft favored withdrawing American troops from Korea, while at the same time claiming he supported the MacArthur program since he advocated the use of air and sea power against the Chinese as well as the use of the Nationalists in Korea and against the mainland.[6]

By February and March 1951, when it became obvious that the United Nations would not be forced out of Korea, the Taft Republicans advocated a somewhat schizophrenic policy. They argued that if the administration would not "untie" MacArthur's hands, then the United States should withdraw from Korea. Taft Republicans also cited the behavior of America's allies as another reason for withdrawal, noting that they had not contributed many troops to Korea and favored a compromise to end the war. The British, for instance, advocated peace talks between the United States, Britain, the Soviet Union, and the Communist Chinese on such problems as the Korean War, the status of Formosa, and the admission of the Communist Chinese to the United Nations. Such proposals were anathema to the Republicans who claimed that they smacked of "appeasement."[7]

During the same period in early January 1951, when United Nations' forces were doing poorly, the China bloc took a different tack than the Taft Republicans. On January 11, Knowland, like Wherry, delivered a long tirade against America's European allies and called for implementing MacArthur's program. The Californian, however, had no doubts about the wisdom of Truman's original decision of June 1950, let alone its constitutionality, and he also opposed withdrawal. However, as was evidenced in an exchange with Republican Senator Homer E. Capehart of Indiana, a Taft Republican, it never caused a ripple of discontent between Knowland and Taft's groups. Capehart stated that "we ought to get our Army out of Korea or we ought to be given permission to go into China proper and fight the enemy with every weapon at our command." Knowland did not object even though his emphasis was on winning the war, not withdrawal. Other Taft Republicans questioned Knowland too, but none quarreled with him despite differences in their approaches. There was, after all, plenty upon which to agree: that America's allies and the United Nations were inadequate, that Communist China must be punished, that MacArthur and Chiang should be unleashed, and that Acheson should be banished.[8]

Bereft of the support of Smith and Knowland, the Europe-oriented bipartisan Republicans, such as Senators Henry Cabot Lodge, Jr., and Leverett Saltonstall of Massachusetts, Charles Tobey of New Hampshire, and Irving Ives of New York, were a forlorn group. They had little to say about the new war, although some of them did participate in the attack on Acheson in December 1950. They were unenthusiastic about MacArthur's proposals that might bring on a larger war in an area they considered of lesser importance. In the highly charged political atmosphere surrounding the limited war strategy, however, they could say little in support of the Democrats. Bipartisan Republicans instead concentrated their efforts on the troops to Europe issue.[9]

By March and April 1951, the Korean War had settled down to a stalemate at the thirty-eighth parallel, while attention of the Senate was fixed on the great debate. After having voted in early April on sending troops to Europe, the Senate paused to catch its breath. The crisis that had begun five months before with Hoover's speech and had been perpetuated by acrimonious debate which generated hours of mind-numbing testimony, had finally come to an end. In less than a week, however, the political atmosphere again burned white hot, this time over the dismissal of General Douglas MacArthur.

MacArthur was one of the more sharply etched figures in recent American history, inspiring either great adulation or disgust among his contemporaries. Surely there was much to admire. The general graduated from West Point with one of the finest academic records in the history of the academy, and rose rapidly through the ranks to the highest position in the Army, chief of staff, before he was fifty. Then he commanded the huge operation against the Japanese during World War II and presided over their occupation beginning in 1945. Nonetheless, MacArthur had a deep streak of vanity that made it difficult for him to admit errors. His memoirs, for instance, are laced with comparisons of his exploits to those of the great soldiers of history such as Napolean and Caesar. The general often blamed others if something went wrong in his area of responsibility, such as when he was surprised by the Japanese in 1941 and by the Communist Chinese in 1950. Even a MacArthur sympathizer such as Herbert Hoover complained that the general had a "St. James [version of the Bible] vocabulary with a Napoleonic bent." Hoover added, however, that he was "one of the greatest military leaders of all time."[10]

By the fall of 1950, bolstered by the adulation of Republican senators who were enthusiastic over his strong stand on Formosa and his brilliant victory at Inchon, MacArthur's self-confidence had never been higher. After Inchon, as MacArthur pressed northward to mop up the remnants of the North Korean army, he paid little attention to the gradual introduction of Chinese Communist units. In late November, the Chinese struck in a terrific attack that split MacArthur's forces and compelled them to retreat through snow-clogged passes. Significantly, the general claimed that his troops had not been defeated but that the withdrawal was all part of his plan to "spring the Red Chinese trap and then draw back suddenly to avoid its jaws." Several days later, the general hinted that had he been permitted to conduct air reconnaissance over China, he would not have been surprised by the attack. By late December, he submitted his four recommendations for ending the war, including a naval blockade, bombing in Manchuria, and the use of Nationalist Chinese troops against the mainland and in Korea.[11]

The Joint Chiefs of Staff passed MacArthur's recommendations onto the National Security Council; they cautioned the general to clear any future public statements with Washington. That order was aimed at avoiding another incident such as had happened in August 1950, when the general sent a letter to the Veterans of Foreign Wars (VFW) that embarrassed Truman by contradicting his Formosa policy. By March and April 1951, with the war settling down to a stalemate near the thirty-eighth parallel, MacArthur could no longer contain himself. During an inspection in early March, he called for a stronger policy. In mid-March, despite being informed that delicate negotiations over a cease-fire were in progress, the general issued an ultimatum to the Chinese Communist commander to withdraw from Korea or face "an expansion of our military operations into . . . coastal areas and interior bases." The coup de grace occurred several weeks later when House Minority Leader Joseph Martin of Massachusetts read a letter into the *Congressional Record* that he had received from MacArthur.

In it MacArthur stressed the importance of waging more than a "limited war" in Korea: "If we lose the war to Communism in Asia the fall of Europe is inevitable, win it and Europe will most probably avoid war and yet preserve peace. . . . There is no substitute for victory."[12]

Truman and his advisors had had enough of MacArthur's opposition to their Korean War strategy. The president had decided to relieve MacArthur after he had delivered his battlefield ultimatum, but the Martin letter was released before he had a chance to act. On April 11, Truman relieved the general of all of his commands, explaining that "by fighting a limited war in Korea, we have prevented aggression from succeeding, and bringing on a general war." General MacArthur "did not agree with that policy." Because of delays in transmitting the news to MacArthur, the general first learned about it from his wife, who heard it on the radio. Truman described the situation to Eisenhower in terms more characteristic of the salty Missourian: "I was sorry to have to reach a parting of the ways with the big man in Asia, but he asked for it and I had to give it to him."[13]

News of MacArthur's dismissal electrified the nation. Mail coming into congressional offices was both voluminous and opinionated in favor of the general. On April 14, the Republican Congressional Committee reported that the mail sent to Republican congressmen ran 1,000 to 1 against Truman's action. Gallop polls taken in early May showed public disapproval of the president's decision by three to one. By mid-May, the public had calmed down to about two to one. A reading of a sample of the type of mail received revealed genuine anger over the president's decision and the insulting manner in which it was carried out. Most feared that the action signaled a willingness on the part of the president to "appease" the communists. Many questioned the integrity of the president, and wondered if there was "another Alger Hiss in the Blair House." Nearly all demanded action from their representatives, ranging from official protest to investigation, to outright impeachment of at least Truman and possibly Acheson as well.[14]

The Republican hierarchy was also outraged over the dismissal. On April 11, there was a flurry of meetings between Dulles, Taft, H. Alexander Smith, Knowland, Wherry, and Martin. It was widely reported that Joe Martin, who was a personal friend of MacArthur, made several telephone calls to the general during that week. Martin announced that the Republican leadership had agreed that a major investigation was needed into "the conduct of foreign and military policy," that MacArthur should "be invited to return" to give his views, and that "the question of possible impeachments was discussed." Wherry immediately introduced a resolution claiming that because MacArthur had "unsurpassed knowledge of political and military conditions in Korea and Asia generally," Congress should invite him to address the joint Houses of Congress.[15]

Meanwhile, Joe Martin and the Republican National Committee worked feverishly to wring the maximum political advantage out of the controversy and give the general a chance to present his case. The same morning that the general was fired, Martin telephoned MacArthur to see if he would agree to address a joint session of Congress; his aide replied immediately that MacArthur would be delighted. Above all, the National Committee stressed that MacArthur must appear to be above politics. Bonner Fellers, a retired Air Force general who worked for the committee, confided to Hoover that no member of the committee would be on hand to greet MacArthur in San Francisco. Nonetheless, Fellers's correspondence reveals that as early as April 15, four days after the dismissal, the committee had developed a detailed itinerary for MacArthur that included exact times of arrival in different cities and the names of the hotels where the MacArthur entourage would stay.[16]

MacArthur did not disappoint his backers. On April 18, his airplane, the *Bataan*, touched down at San Francisco where he was greeted by Joe Martin, Kenneth Wherry, Secretary of Defense George Marshall, various local dignitaries, and tumultuous crowds. The next day, the general delivered his most well-known address before Congress with a style that few of his contemporaries could match. In sonorous, well-paced tones, MacArthur argued his case for a policy that took greater account of Asia and adopted a more aggressive strategy to end the Korean War. The general tried to portray the debate over the Korean War as one between military and civilian leaders, asserting that the Joint Chiefs of Staff "fully shared" his views. MacArthur dramatically ended his speech by reminding his listeners that his career had begun over fifty years before at West Point. Like the soldier of a popular barracks ballad of that day, however, he was now going to "just fade away, an old soldier who had tried to do his duty as God gave him the light to see that duty. Good bye." In a letter to a constituent, Taft stated the obvious: "I cannot help but feel that the whole episode was to the advantage of the Republicans."[17]

Ironically, on April 18, the same day that MacArthur's plane landed in San Francisco amidst a rising chorus of partisan rhetoric, Arthur Vandenberg died after months of illness. As Vandenberg passed away, the policy of bipartisanship for which he had labored so hard was also at its lowest ebb. Although a few bipartisan Republicans at first expressed themselves on the MacArthur controversy, they were soon cowed into silence. On April 11, Republican Senators Duff and Leverett Saltonstall of Massachusetts applauded Truman's action as the only reasonable course against the general. Several days later, Paul Hoffman, who in 1948 had been Vandenberg's hand-picked candidate to head the Economic Cooperation Administration, implored his colleagues: "I do believe that we must rise above partisanship, that the vote of every Senator and Representative should register his individual convictions as an American, rather than as a Republican or Democrat." Several days later, however, the newspapers reported that some of General Dwight E. Eisenhower's Republican senatorial supporters, who did not want to be named, were in a gloomy mood over the MacArthur incident. They were convinced that Eisenhower had to lead the party in 1952 to salvage bipartisanship and a Europe-first foreign policy. Their voices were inaudible as the two parties girded themselves for a partisan struggle.[18]

The Taftites and China-bloc Republicans demanded a broad investigation of the dismissal and on East Asian policy in general; they also wanted it to be conducted to the greatest extent possible in public hearings. The Democrats proposed that an investigation be conducted by a joint committee composed of the Foreign Relations and Armed Services Committees, the same committees that meditated the great debate. The Senate Republican Policy Committee, headed by Taft, insisted that the investigation be conducted by a twenty-four man committee drawn equally from both parties, but the Democrats' approach won out. In the first meeting of the joint committee, Republican Senator Bourke Hickenlooper of Iowa proposed that there be public sessions on public matters and executive sessions on secret matters. The Democrats rejected the plan by a fourteen to nine vote with only one Republican, Charles Tobey of New Hampshire (a supporter of bipartisanship), crossing party lines. The next day, Taft Republicans carried their fight to the floor, where the Democrats at first filibustered and then called for a vote to adjourn that carried by a slender forty-three to forty-one margin. Several days later, the Democrats again barely beat back Hickenlooper's proposal, forty-one to thirty-seven; even Republicans such as Lodge, Saltonstall, Alexander Wiley of Wisconsin, Wayne Morse of Oregon, Tobey, and Irving Ives of New York voted against them. The hearings were held, therefore, behind closed doors, while the transcripts were given to an admiral who deleted the sensitive portions before releasing them to the press.[19]

In May the hearings finally began, with MacArthur as its first witness. The general argued that in ignoring the vast potentialities of Asia, administration officials had become "the 'isolationists' of the present time." The Democrats had relegated MacArthur's campaign against the Japanese during World War II to a second-rate status, and now, the general pointed out, they were sending troops to Europe while there was a shooting war going on in Korea. He added, "I believe we should defend every place from Communism. I believe we can. I believe we are able to. I have confidence in us. . . . I don't admit that we can't hold communism wherever it shows its head." MacArthur, of course, reserved most of his criticisms for the inconsistent manner in which the Korean War was being waged. When North Korea initially attacked, the general argued, it was America's duty to punish it, something he had accomplished at Inchon. When the Chinese Communists entered the war, MacArthur believed America's response had to be the same, and he maintained that his recommendations of December 30 would accomplish that. His solution (a naval blockade of Communist China, bombing Manchuria, and using the Nationalist Chinese in Korea and against the mainland), as opposed to Truman's war of attrition, offered "the best chance that is possible of ending this war in the quickest time and with the least cost in blood." In any case, MacArthur assured the senators that if his plan did not work (a possibility that he did not concede) "no man in his proper senses would advocate throwing our troops in on the Chinese mainland."[20]

George Marshall, Omar Bradley, Dean Acheson, and the members of the Joint Chiefs of Staff (JCS) presented the administration's rebuttal. Marshall and Bradley asserted that MacArthur had flirted with insubordination in his public criticisms of the limited war strategy. Marshall argued that if MacArthur had had such sharp disagreements with the administration, he should have resigned. Although the JCS admitted that they had agreed with some of MacArthur's recommendations such as sending more aid to Formosa, they believed that MacArthur's plans risked a general war at a time when America's military establishment could not handle it. Bradley stated that the position of the JCS was that a larger war in East Asia would be "the wrong war, at the wrong place, at the wrong time, and with the wrong enemy." Bradley and the administration argued that it was foolish to get involved in a major effort in Korea when the truly strategic prizes, Western Europe and Japan, required so much more attention.[21]

Those Republicans who had long criticized the Truman-Acheson East Asian policy finally had their chance to interrogate Marshall and Acheson on events as far back as 1945. Knowland, for instance, grilled Marshall about the Marshall mission to China in 1946, where Marshall attempted to arrange a coalition government between the Nationalists and Communists. Marshall pointed out that at the time, MacArthur approved of the mission and that Chiang had originated the idea. Other questions centered on the charge that the administration came close to recognizing the Communist Chinese government in early 1950 to appease the British. Acheson firmly denied that the State Department had even "considered" recognition, which was false; he also denied that he had worked to dissuade the British from recognition, which was true.[22]

The behavior of the twelve Republicans on the combined committees revealed how different factions of the party responded to the MacArthur incident. The China bloc, led by Knowland, H. Alexander Smith, and Styles Bridges of New Hampshire, combined forces with such Taft Republicans as Hickenlooper, Harry Cain of Washington, and Owen Brewster of Maine, and with two nominally bipartisan Republicans, Ralph Flanders of Vermont and

Wiley, to support MacArthur. Although there were important differences between those groups in their reaction to MacArthur, their overwhelming solidarity made the differences negligible for the duration of the hearings. The bipartisan Republicans who were oriented toward Europe, such as Lodge, Saltonstall, Tobey, and Morse, were silenced by the partisan nature of the dispute and the surge of popular sympathy for the general. The politics of partisanship in foreign policy were in command.

Since MacArthur's views coincided most closely with those of the China bloc, their leaders gave the general every opportunity to defend himself in the hearings. Knowland, for instance, asked the general a series of questions about the VFW letter, the Wake Island Conference, and the reaction of the JCS on his recommendations, to allow MacArthur to demonstrate that he had followed orders and that his military superiors had supported his plans. Smith asked the general about the extent of his jurisdiction in Korea prior to June 1950 to permit him to refute charges that he had been at fault for the surprise attack. MacArthur responded that he did not have "an ounce of responsibility" for the peninsula prior to the attack since it was then under the purview of the State Department.[23]

Although Smith was outraged over MacArthur's dismissal and its possible impact on the Japanese Peace Treaty, the New Jersey senator preached moderation to his Republican colleagues because of his long affiliation with bipartisanship. "I am concerned," he wrote to a constituent, "that this [the hearings] may take a partisan turn and end in sort of a political cat and dog fight." A sense of alienation had developed among those Republicans who had voted with the Democrats on sending troops to Europe. In mid-May, when the MacArthur hearings were at their peak, Smith met with those Republicans who had voted against the McClellan amendment on the restrictions on troop strength in Europe, including Lodge, Duff, Ives, Saltonstall, and George Aiken and Ralph Flanders of Vermont. Smith confided in his diary that the consensus of the gathering was that "we should keep our little group together even though we have been written out of the Republican Party by General [sic] McCormick of the *Chicago Tribune* and we should try as much as possible to unite on policies in which we all believe."[24]

Much of the confusion and contradiction in Taft's statements on

Korea sprung from his aversion to foreign commitments on the one hand, and his political attraction to the charismatic General MacArthur on the other. The Ohioan argued that "the best defense of the free world for all nations, if a war with Russia shall arrive" was the free enterprise system. Taft explained that "in time of peace there is a definite limit to what we can do. In time of war there is a definite limit. We must not undertake a project like Korea and risk disastrous defeat." In the midst of the hearings, Taft assumed the ambivalent position of advocating the MacArthur program for Korea while proposing that the defense appropriations be pared by 500,000 men and $20 billion. MacArthur, on the other hand, expressed confidence in being able to defend every area against communism. Even during the great flush of excitement over MacArthur, Taft still admitted that he believed the initial decision to aid South Korea had been a mistake and that Truman had acted in an unconstitutional manner in committing American troops without congressional consent.[25]

MacArthur and his China-bloc compatriots were rarely troubled by such thoughts. The only criticism the general had over the initial decision was that Truman should have consulted him before making the commitment, but he emphatically supported the intervention, saying it lit "a lamp of hope throughout Asia." In an exchange with Lyndon Johnson, MacArthur took a slap at the constitutional position that Taft had advanced during the controversy over sending troops to Europe. Congress, the general lectured, should pay the "closest attention" to professional military men in the disposition of troops.[26]

Nonetheless, those differences were ignored by both the Taft Republicans and the China bloc in their warm and eager embrace of each other. Taft and his disciples were appalled by MacArthur's dismissal and the administration's limited war strategy, portraying it as part of a "disastrous" East Asian policy begun at Yalta. Taft also argued that the Republicans would not win the next election "unless we point out the utter failure and incapacity of the present Administration to conduct foreign policy and cite the loss of China and the Korean war as typical examples of their [sic] very dangerous control. We certainly can't win on domestic policy, because every domestic policy depends entirely on foreign policy." Hickenlooper, Cain, and Brewster's questioning of the general, therefore, was sympathetic, while their encounters with administration witnesses were testy. Hickenlooper, for instance, pressed Marshall as to the differences between the Berlin crisis of 1948 and the Korea situation. Why, the Iowa senator asked, was the United States willing to risk war in Berlin and not in Korea?[27]

At the conclusion of the hearings, eight of the twelve Republicans who had served on the combined committees, including Knowland, Smith, Bridges, Hickenlooper, Cain, Brewster, Wiley, and Flanders, submitted a report. Lodge, Morse, Tobey, and Saltonstall did not sign it, preferring to file their views separately. The report of the eight demonstrated how the ideas of the China bloc had permeated the Republican party. The eight charged that the administration's record in East Asia represented "the most desolate failure in the history of our foreign policy. . . . The upshot has been catastrophe." It detailed the "calamitous" events that led the United States from a position of great influence in East Asia in 1945 to the sorry state of affairs in 1951. "For this ruinous collapse," the eight Republicans solemnly noted, "the administration in general and the State Department in particular has a direct and dreadful responsibility." On the Korean War, they denounced Truman for having made the commitment without congressional consultation but sidestepped the question of whether the president's decision was correct.[28]

Republicans Knowland and Hickenlooper, and Democrats Brien McMahon and Tom Connally of Texas generated the sparks in the hearings, while the Europe-oriented bipartisan Republicans, who were once so pivotal, were reduced to an uncomfortable silence. Three of the four who did not sign the report, Lodge, Saltonstall, and Tobey, were extremely circumspect in their behavior on the committee. Lodge and Saltonstall were very careful not to attack MacArthur, but in their reports and questioning they demonstrated that they did not approve of the general's stand. Saltonstall's cross examination of MacArthur, for instance, simply elicited information with none of the speech making that had highlighted the presentations of Knowland and Hickenlooper. Saltonstall's report also eschewed controversy, concluding that: "MacArthur had a positive policy, which, if successful, would end the fighting with a prompt victory. The administration's victory, as I see it, can win only by the wearing down of the Chinese Communists." Lodge, only slightly more challenging, asked MacArthur at one point what he would do if Chiang landed on the mainland and got into trouble. When the general assured Lodge that such a problem would not arise, the matter was dropped. In his report, Lodge argued that since bombing in Manchuria was a "technical military" decision, he could not pass judgment on it.[29]

The only Republican on the combined committees who attacked MacArthur directly was Wayne Morse. Even Morse began his questioning of the general by saying that he only wanted to give him a chance to make his views known, and did not wish to be "argumentative." However, he went on to probe MacArthur in areas where his case was weakest, such as the general's estimate of Soviet intentions and his responsibilities in Korea prior to the attack. In his report, Morse charged the eight Republicans with having produced a "very highly partisan and biased report," the bulk of which, Morse asserted, was "irrelevant" to whether MacArthur should have been relieved. Morse believed that the general's "recall was necessitated by his own misconduct."[30]

The old bipartisan approach of 1947–1949 had reached its nadir. That coalition had been forged out of the crises of postwar Europe and had focused its energies on containing the Soviets in Europe militarily while reviving the European economy. Politically, the administration had forged a powerful alliance with important members of the GOP in order to carry out its containment strategy. A part of the coalition was the China bloc, which supported containment in Europe but argued in vain that it need to be extended to East Asia too. The bipartisan coalition enforced the consensus of 1947–48 by accusing its critics of being isolationists and disrupters of bipartisanship. By 1951, the Taftites, who in 1948 and 1949 had had misgivings about the efficacy of containment and little interest in East Asia, had for political reasons come to parrot the China bloc's program. The rise of McCarthyism, the new war in Korea, and the firing of General MacArthur, however, brought these two unlikely groups together in opposition to the Truman administration. Nevertheless, a new bipartisan coalition was in the offing.

9

Dulles, Eisenhower, and the New Bipartisanship

Even as the bipartisanship of Vandenberg's day was being battered during 1950 and 1951, the seeds of a new bipartisan coalition were being sown. Principal actors in forging this new coalition were John Foster Dulles and Dwight D. Eisenhower. During 1951, Dulles was the Truman administration's principal negotiator for the Japanese Peace Treaty and the Pacific security treaties. This gave Dulles a unique opportunity to expand the containment policy to East Asia, something that pleased the China bloc. In developing the treaty system, Dulles astutely took cognizance of the objections the Taftites had advanced during the North Atlantic Treaty deliberations. Eisenhower and Dulles carefully weaved these same groups together in their successful fight for the presidency in 1952.

Since McCarthy's accusations of early 1950, the administration had been under steady attack for its East Asian policies; this escalated dramatically after the Chinese intervention in December 1950, and culminated in the MacArthur hearings. By 1951, those political pressures, coupled with Truman's concern over the Soviet Union's aggressiveness in East Asia, moved the administration in directions long advocated by the China bloc. In early 1951, Truman reversed his policy of aloofness toward the Formosa regime and collaborated closely with the Republicans in negotiating a Japanese Peace Treaty. In the treaty, the administration for the first time extended bipartisanship in a major way to an East Asian problem, and the results were reminiscent of the successes of 1948 and 1949. Once again, a coalition of bipartisan Republicans and Democrats, now joined by the China block, quelled the more extreme Taft Republicans by labeling them "isolationists" and "appeasers"; the result was an advance for the containment policy.

The man who played the greatest role in the Japanese Peace Treaty was John Foster Dulles, who was the ambassador-at-large assigned to the project in May 1950, a month after he had joined the administration. With the onset of the Korean War, Truman wanted to complete a peace treaty with Japan and establish a security system for the Orient that would strengthen America's position in East Asia. Dulles commenced multilateral negotiations with the Philippines, Australia, New Zealand, Japan, Britain, and France concerning such thorny issues as which China, if any, would be invited to attend the peace conference, and how Soviet participation would be circumscribed. By the summer of 1951, Dulles had devised a magnanimous treaty for Japan as well as three bilateral security treaties between the United States and the Philippines, Japan, and Australia-New Zealand to establish a barrier to communist expansion in East Asia. The peace conference was scheduled for September 1951 in San Francisco.[1]

Politically, the most important aspect of Dulles's negotiations lay in his constant contacts with Vandenberg and H. Alexander Smith. The correspondence between the three Republicans revealed an active collaboration on the details of the treaties. Upon learning of MacArthur's dismissal, for instance, Dulles immediately conferred with the Republican Senate leadership to determine its views on how that action impacted on the treaties. To insure senatorial support, Dulles and Acheson invited Senators H. Alexander Smith and John Sparkman (Democrat of Alabama), the ranking members of the Subcommittee on Far Eastern Affairs of the Foreign Relations Committee, along with Wiley and Bridges, to San Francisco. The bipartisan manner in which the treaties were conducted satisfied long-held criticisms by H. Alexander Smith and Knowland; they had maintained that the administration, in its eagerness to contain communism in Europe, had ignored East Asia.[2]

In the aftermath of the San Francisco peace conference, the Republicans indicated the positions they would later develop during the ratification debates in January 1952. The conference featured a nationally televised speech by a stern Dean Acheson who upraided the Soviet- and other communist-bloc delegates, and culminated with forty-eight countries signing the peace treaty. Knowland and Smith were radiant. Smith reported that Dulles had done "excellent work" and that Acheson's management of the conference had been "commendable and brilliant." Knowland lectured his colleagues on the responsibilities of the opposition to criticize mistakes, but also, as in this case, to support truly bipartisan ventures. In tones that recalled the older bipartisanship, Knowland reminded the critics: "I do not believe this Nation can return to isolationism any more than an adult can return to childhood, regardless of how pleasant the recollections may be."[3]

Only a few senators rose in rebuttal. Republican Senator George W. Malone of Nevada, a staunch isolationist, complained: "We had broken bipartisan control in [the Senate], but a few members of the Senate, including [Senator Connally] seem to want to bring it back." Malone also rankled at Knowland's bandying about "the silly charge of isolationism. . . . Unless one favors the Japanese Peace Treaty," Malone declared, "which carries with it the recognition by the Japanese of Communist China, unless he favors the reckless and wanton expenditure of the taxpayers' money . . . without debate, he is called an isolationist."[4]

During the hearings begun in January 1952, Dulles, Knowland, Smith, and the Democrats stressed that the treaties did not injure the Nationalist Chinese and avoided the constitutional pitfalls of the North Atlantic Treaty. The peace treaty and the security system were, then, a Republican-style alliance system for East Asia. The three major problems that the treaties' advocates sought to overcome were the fears that Japan might recognize Communist China, that the peace treaty might be interpreted as affirming Soviet territorial gains acquired at Yalta, and that the collective security agreements infringed on the war-making powers of Congress. As Smith noted in his diary: "We must guard against the isolationist Republicans trying to put conditions on ratification."[5]

There was a genuine concern among a large number of senators that Japan's traditional reliance on the mainland for raw materials would eventually force it to recognize the Chinese Communist regime. In September 1951, Knowland circulated a letter to the president, which was signed by fifty-six senators from both parties and which opposed American recognition of the Communist Chinese. The letter also argued that Japanese recognition would be "adverse to the best interests of the people of both Japan and the United States." Knowland later revealed that he had secured the signatures in only twenty-four hours and could easily have gotten many more. After negotiating the problem with the Japanese, Dulles was assured by Japanese Premier Shigeru Yoshida that "the Japanese government had no intention to conclude a bilateral treaty with the Communist regime of China."[6]

The language of the security pacts was carefully phrased to avoid it appearing as a "North Atlantic Treaty" for the Pacific. Three separate, bilateral treaties were contemplated with the Philippines, Australia-New Zealand, and Japan, rather than having a "treaty organization." Furthermore, the language of the collective security sections was not as binding or as specific as in the North Atlantic Treaty, stating only that the parties "would act to meet the common danger in accordance with its constitutional processes." The North Atlantic Treaty, of course, included the "use of armed force" as an appropriate response. Dulles explained that the phraseology of the Pacific treaties resembled "the Monroe Doctrine language rather than the North Atlantic Treaty language . . . [which] if repeated, would renew the debate . . . as to whether it involved any shift in the relative responsibilities of the Executive and the Congress."[7]

Finally, the bipartisan Republicans and Democrats sought to blunt any criticism that the peace treaty legitimatized the Yalta accords. According to the treaty, the Japanese ceded, among other things, the Kurile Islands and the southern half of Sakhaline Island, territories the Soviets had acquired at Yalta. Advocates of the treaty pointed out that since it never mentioned to whom those territories were ceded, the treaty was mute on the question of Yalta's legitimacy. Nevertheless, the Foreign Relations Committee unanimously passed a declaration specifically stating that nothing in the treaty had any bearing on Yalta. The bipartisan coalition had done well in anticipating major criticisms.[8]

The treaties then went before the entire Senate, where their supporters skillfully employed the techniques of the old bipartisanship to counter the threat of reservations. Connally and Wiley (the ranking members of the Foreign Relations Committee) as well as Knowland and Smith, made speeches praising, as Wiley said, the "fine bipartisan and cooperative manner in which it [the adminis-tration] negotiated the treaties." They pointed out how the lan-guage of the treaties resembled the Monroe Doctrine and empha-sized that the treaties would be carried out "in accordance with our constitutional processes." Connally contrasted the Japanese Peace Treaty favorably with the vindictiveness of the Treaty of Versailles of 1919, assuring his collegues that magnanimity would sow the seeds of a truly lasting peace.[9]

Republican Senators William E. Jenner of Indiana and Margaret Chase Smith of Maine introduced a series of reservations to the treaties. Smith, normally a bipartisan Republican, explained that she cosponsored the reservations to assert greater congressional authority over foreign affairs; in practice, however, she said little in the debates and in the end voted for ratification. Jenner fought hardest for the reservations, contending that the treaties were the opposite of MacArthur's ideals, which, Jenner asserted, were "a continuation of our historic policy of free intercourse between sov-ereign nations. The policy that flowered into the Monroe Doctrine and the Open Door." The Dulles treaties, Jenner argued, were in the ominous tradition of the "Institute for Pacific Relations and some of the figures in the shadows that guided their hands."

The reservations he proposed were a blend of isolationist and China-bloc concerns. The first, repeated in each of the four trea-ties, stated that nothing in them would in any way impair the sov-ereignty of any of the parties. Jenner proposed another reservation providing that the president could not dispatch troops to Japan except when approved by an "act or joint resolution specifically referring to such arrangements." That, of course, resurrected the issues that had dominated the great debate of the previous year. Jenner also introduced three reservations to protect Nationalist China. He insisted that a more strongly worded version of the For-eign Relations Committee's declaration relating to Yalta be in-serted into the peace treaty. Also, since Jenner did not trust the Yoshida letter, he wanted a section added specifying that "China" meant the Nationalist regime, which he defined as exercising sov-ereignty over China, Formosa, and Manchuria. Jenner hoped that such a section would thwart any attempt by the Communist Chinese to lay claim to the reparations that Japan owed to "China." Finally, in a conscious throwback to the Stimson Doctrine, Jenner proposed that the United States not recognize any situation in China that impaired American rights.[10]

The administration wisely left the task of refuting the Jenner-Smith reservations to Knowland. Knowland challenged Jenner's assertion that the treaties were contrary to MacArthur's ideals, revealing that in recent talks he had had with the general, MacArthur had approved of the treaties. Knowland argued that the alliances were the opposite of the "dust settles" policies of the past. Observing that the Soviets had fought the peace treaty at every turn in San Francisco, Knowland concluded: "I think it would cause great comfort in the Kremlin, if the United States at this time were to refuse to ratify the treaty." Knowland brushed off those reservations which related to American sovereignty, noting that any treaty, by definition, involved the surrender of some sovereignty. Regarding Jenner's reservations about Yalta, the Californian argued that the Foreign Relations Committee's declaration made it unnecessary. Knowland also pointed out that the territorial definitions of "China" in the treaties were written by the Nationalist Chinese themselves. The Californian, therefore, urged prompt ratification, observing that, "I do not believe the American people would stand for a Far Eastern Munich at this time."[11]

Knowland's performance was a tour de force, coming from a man who had been the leader in promoting Chiang's interests in the Senate since the days when it had been less fashionable. The best Jenner could do in rebuttal was to argue weakly that Knowland had misread the Soviets' behavior at the conference: "When the Communists are against something they use knives not theatricals, as they used in San Francisco." Republican Senator Everett M. Dirksen of Illinois, who supported Jenner, called for postponement while unsuccessfully trying to associate the treaty with the unpopularity of the limited war strategy.[12]

On March 20, 1952, when the votes had been counted, the new bipartisan coalition won a resounding victory, striking down all the reservations by hefty two-to-one margins and securing ratification by sixty-six to ten. The number of senators voting for the Jenner-Smith reservations fluctuated between twenty-five and twenty-nine, and included the core of the most isolationist Taft Republicans and several Southern Democrats. Voting against the reservations were

the overwhelming majority of Democrats, joined by such biparti-
san Republicans as Flanders and, usually, Aiken of Vermont, Morse
of Oregon, Ives of New York, Wiley of Wisconsin, Saltonstall of
Massachusetts, H. Alexander Smith of New Jersey, Knowland of
California, and Tobey of New Hampshire, as well as a few Taft
Republicans such as Eugene Millikin of Colorado and sometimes
Karl Mundt of South Dakota. In the end, only ten senators voted
against ratification: Dirksen of Illinois, Jenner of Indiana, Henry
Dworshak and Herman Welker of Idaho, Zales Ecton of Montana,
Kem of Missouri, Malone of Nevada, McCarthy of Wisconsin, Pat
McCarran of Nevada, and Milton Young of North Dakota. With
the exception of McCarthy, whose ideology was always difficult to
discern, they represented the most isolationist senators. With the
issue carefully stripped of anything that might produce a partisan
squabble, the isolationists could muster only about the same number as they did at the time of the North Atlantic Treaty debates of
1949.[13]

As the smoke cleared from the congressional elections of 1950
and senators prepared for the great debates of 1951, professional
politicians turned their thoughts toward the presidential election
of 1952. Numerous Republican senators, particularly Taft and Lodge,
played prominent roles in the presidential contest. The initial
question in the Democrats' minds was whether President Harry S
Truman wanted to seek reelection; for Republicans, however, it
was not that simple. The two wings of the party girded themselves
again for another round in the struggle for party leadership that
dated back to 1940. The Taftites, convinced that America and the
party were at a crossroads, naturally lined up behind the candidacy
of Robert A. Taft. The bipartisan Republicans, realizing they could
not renominate two-time presidential loser, Governor Thomas E.
Dewey of New York, hoped to convince Eisenhower to contest
Taft's candidacy. Since most Republicans agreed that the Democrats were profligate in their domestic policy and the Democratic
party was rife with corruption, the major differences that developed between Taft and Eisenhower were on foreign policy and
whether Taft could win in November. One of the keys to the election and his subsequent presidency was Eisenhower's ability to
smooth over the rifts within the GOP.[14]

By 1951, foreign policy had assumed a much larger role in Taft's thinking, partly because of his presidential ambitions and partly because the death of Vandenberg had left a void in the GOP on foreign affairs. As the campaign season approached, Taft developed his thinking in a book, *A Foreign Policy for Americans*. The book gave the Ohioan a chance to summarize the approach he had developed over the past four years and to introduce some new themes as well. Typically, his tone was openly partisan. Recounting the "disasters" in American foreign policy, Taft noted that the first step in reversing the precipitous decline in America's prestige since 1945 was to turn the Democrats out of office. Striking major themes in the nationalist repertoire, he averred that the country needed to return to George Washington's policy of the "free hand" that "would leave us free to interfere or not interfere according to whether we consider the case of sufficiently vital interest to the liberty of this country." Taft also argued that instead of spending billions on foreign aid, the United States should lead the world "by example." "The trouble," he explained, "with those who advocate this policy [of spending large amounts abroad] is that they really do not confine themselves to moral leadership. They are inspired with the same kind of New Deal planned-control of ideas abroad as recent administrations have desired to enforce at home."[15]

Taft's solution to America's foreign-policy woes stemmed from his belief that while the Soviet Union was dangerous, America's resources were limited. Therefore, the Ohioan favored increases in air, sea, and atomic power over expensive long-term commitments of ground forces. While he agreed that some economic and arms aid should be distributed, he made it clear that he would be more frugal than the Democrats had been. Taft added a new element to his thinking that would soon be called "liberation." He advocated conducting "world-wide propaganda on behalf of liberty," sending "secret agents" into communist satellite countries, and establishing an agency to make contact with "those forces and individuals fighting for freedom throughout the Communist world."[16]

Taft's chief opponent for the nomination became Eisenhower. Possessing little of the flash and bravura of generals such as George Patton and Douglas MacArthur, Eisenhower's strength lay in his ability to reconcile competing groups. During World War II, Eisenhower utilized that talent to hold the Allies together during the North African, Italian, and D-Day campaigns. Eisenhower was a general with a common touch, whose greatest skill may have been his ability to appear devoid of political skills. His political philosophy, especially on domestic issues, was amorphous; indeed, having been prominently mentioned as a possibility for the Democratic presidential nomination in 1948, there was confusion as to his political affiliation on the eve of the 1952 primaries.[17]

By 1951, the bipartisan Republicans who were oriented toward Europe had fallen on hard times with the loss of Vandenberg and the rise of Taft, McCarthy, and the China bloc in 1951. They realized that their old hero, Tom Dewey, was anathema to too many Republicans, so they hoped to persuade the popular Eisenhower to fight Taft for the nomination. In June 1950, in the midst of the Tydings committee hearings on McCarthy's charges, Lodge paid the general a visit. Eisenhower was then president of Columbia University where he had established friendships with some of the powers of Eastern Republicanism such as William Robinson of the *New York Herald Tribune*. The senator got down to business. If "the isolationist elements in the Republican party got so strong that the party would be faced with a definite turn in the wrong direction," he would urge the general to run for president. That would be especially true, he added, if Taft won his 1950 reelection bid. Eisenhower replied: "It would be the bitterest day of my life if I ever had to become involved in party politics. . . . It would be just like a man who has been a Catholic up until the age of 50 suddenly becoming a Protestant. . . . But I think a man who definitely has a public duty to perform and doesn't perform it is in the same category with Benedict Arnold."[18]

In the autumn of 1950, Eisenhower was chosen by Truman to head the army of the new North Atlantic pact. In February 1951, Truman asked Eisenhower to return to the United States to testify during the great debate. While he was in Washington, the general held a secret meeting with Taft at the Pentagon. Eisenhower hoped to assure himself that the government "would be solid in support of NATO . . . [and] to kill off any further speculation about me as a candidate for the Presidency." Therefore, he drafted a statement that "was so strong that, if made public, any political future for me thereafter would be impossible." During their conference, Eisenhower asked Taft, "Would you, and your associates in the Congress, agree that collective security is necessary for us in Western

Europe—and will you support this idea as a bipartisan policy?" Taft was coy in his reply, however, noting that he did not yet know whether he would vote for two, four, or six divisions of troops. Eisenhower later remembered that "this aroused my fears that isolationism was stronger in the Congress than I had previously suspected." The general immediately tore up the statement, commenting that "It would be silly for me to throw away whatever political influence I might possess to help keep us on the right track."[19]

Despite his fears about Taft's isolationist impulses, Eisenhower refused to run openly for the nomination during 1951. Throughout the autumn of 1951, Taft, sensing Eisenhower's distaste for a political fight, tried to reassure the general that he was "safe" on foreign policy. In October, for instance, the senator penned a note to Charles White of Republic Steel, who passed it on to the general. Taft supported the "completion of the arming of Western Europe . . . [and] the maintenance of six divisions abroad and even some reasonable additions." *New York Times* correspondent C. L. Sulzberger remembered Eisenhower as saying, however, that "a promise from Taft on this subject didn't strike him as being worth very much." As the New Hampshire primary approached, Taft carefully focused most of his foreign policy attacks on Truman. The senator explained that his foreign policy differences with Eisenhower were "of degree rather than of principle."[20]

Despite his nonparticipation, in early March Eisenhower's forces scored a stunning upset in the New Hampshire primary. A week later in Minnesota, favorite son Harold Stassen won the primary, but the real news lay in the vigorous write-in campaigns that Eisenhower and Taft forces waged for second place; the general won by a four-to-one margin. These victories convinced Eisenhower to come home well before the convention. After the reverses, Taft adopted a more aggressive campaigning style that featured foreign policy themes for the upcoming Ohio and Wisconsin primaries. Taft stressed the ideas he had developed in his book, while showing lukewarm support for McCarthy, especially in Wisconsin.[21]

With the primaries heating up and Eisenhower due home in June, John Foster Dulles entered the scene in the role of conciliator. In March 1952, after spending two years in the State Department as the chief negotiator of the Japanese Peace Treaty and bilateral security pacts, Dulles left government service. He was eager to take part in Republican politics to insure his own selection as secretary of state in the next Republican administration and to make sure the party did not drift back into isolationism. In March, Dulles summarized his thinking in a memorandum that was published two months later at greater length in a *Life Magazine* article entitled "A Policy of Boldness." [22]

The article provided Republicans with a way of attacking Truman's foreign policy without moving in the nationalist direction outlined in Taft's book. Dulles criticized containment as a "static" strategy that simply blocked Soviet political and military moves without taking the initiative. He complained that "ours are treadmill policies which, at best, might perhaps keep us in the same place until we drop exhausted." Dulles commented that such a policy menaced America with bankruptcy and militarism. He also criticized the isolationists "who would turn their backs on all the world's problems and wrap the United States in some magically 'impregnable' isolation." [23]

Dulles believed that the best way to handle the Soviet threat was embodied in the phrases "instant retaliation" and "liberation." Since the Soviet empire had a twenty-thousand-mile border and could muster six to seven million soldiers, Dulles believed it was impossible to build a wall around them (that is, to attempt containment). Instead, he advocated creating regional centers of power backed by the nuclear arsenal of the United States to *"retaliate instantly against an aggression by Red armies."* Dulles also recommended taking the initiative in the Cold War by using *"ideas as weapons"* to encourage the liberation of peoples under communist control. Specifically, he hoped the United States would make it known that *"it wants and expects liberation to occur,"* by developing "freedom programs for each captive nation," increasing Voice of America broadcasts, and ending diplomatic recognition of "puppet governments." He added, however, that "We do not want a series of bloody uprisings and reprisals." [24]

The article wedded Taft's aggressive tone to the internationalists' goals. Unlike Taft's book, the Dulles piece did not rehearse the familiar Republican harangue against the Democrats' mistakes back to Yalta. At one point he praised the administration, commenting that "I can testify from personal knowledge, that the President and

Secretary of State really want bipartisanship and congressional co-operation in foreign policy." His clear concern about communism worldwide was also in tune with the thinking of bipartisan Republicans and the China bloc. Taft Republicans could take comfort in his insistence that America could not contain communism everywhere, particularly under the Democrats' military strategy with its heavy reliance on costly ground units. The talk of "liberation" also fit the Taft Republicans' penchant for using rhetorical militancy without having to assume more commitments.[25]

In April, Dulles sent a draft of his forthcoming article along with a memorandum on Formosa to Eisenhower. Eisenhower complimented him on his approach but posed a question: "What should we do if Soviet political aggression, as in Czechoslovakia, successively chips away exposed portions of the free world? . . . To my mind, this is the case where the theory of 'retaliation' falls down." Dulles agreed that "you put your finger on a weak point in my presentation." At the beginning of May, Dulles had a very friendly meeting with Eisenhower in Paris, where he came away solidly in support of the general.[26]

In mid-May, Dulles received a call from Taft. Before he met the senator, Dulles conferred with Eisenhower's campaign managers. "We agreed," Dulles told Eisenhower,

that we should if possible, try to shape the discussions so as to promote the foreign policy plank in the Republican platform which would avoid an open battle between the so-called "isolationist" wing the so-called "internationalist" wing and also avoid the possible risk of a plank being adopted on which it would be difficult for you to run.

Dulles found that Taft's thinking ran along parallel lines. The senator, Dulles reported, made a "bid for my support or at least 'neutrality' saying that he believed that we could work together on foreign policy," but Dulles informed him he was about to announce for Eisenhower. The Ohioan then asked Dulles to "prepare a draft" foreign policy plank on behalf of Eisenhower and the senator, noting that "it would be tragic if the Party were rent asunder [at the convention], particularly as Taft said he felt that my recent speeches and writings had developed a large area of possible agreement." Taft shrewdly added that if Dulles took on the job, he should "avoid publicly seeking support for" Eisenhower.[27]

In June, Taft continued to emphasize that he was in tune with the major elements in Republican foreign policy thinking. In a press conference held while Eisenhower was making his way across the Atlantic, Taft cited Dulles's *Life* article and recent speeches to show that he and Dulles shared a similar approach: "He feels as I do that control of the air, and the ability to strike when Russia makes a move threatening our security, must be the key to our military policy, that our present program of containing Russia throughout the world is far beyond our economic capacity." Later in the month, Taft commented that "Eisenhower possibly puts more emphasis on Europe than I do but it is a difference in methods, not in principle."[28]

In the midst of the electoral battle, Dulles labored to produce a foreign-policy plank that would be acceptable to the major candidates. His initial drafts paralleled his "Policy of Boldness" article. Dulles wrote that the Democrats "looked on, at first acquiescent, then worried, and [were] now panicky" at the rise of Soviet power. Underscoring "liberation," he noted that "Freedom, operating as a positive force throughout the free world, will set up strains and stresses within the already over-extended Soviet world which will make its leaders impotent to pursue their present aggressive purposes." Dulles, however, carefully skirted such controversial items as whether Truman's initial decision in Korea was correct and constitutional, and whether the United States should rely more heavily on ground or air power. Dulles wrote that the party favored bipartisanship, cooperation with other "free nations in accordance with the principle of enlightened self-interest; respect scrupulously [for] our United Nations and other collective security relationships."[29]

While Colorado Senator Eugene Millikin and other Taft Republicans on the platform committee got along quite well with Dulles, they demanded more "fire and brimstone" in the platform. They added scathing attacks on the administration's policies at Yalta, Teheran, and Potsdam, and on "the surrender of Manchuria," and the "no hope for victory" strategy in Korea. Millikin also included a sentence calling for the removal of "loafers, incompetents, and unnecessary employees" from the State Department. The section that caused the greatest difficulty, however, was the one that promised to create a "force of such retaliatory striking power as to deter sudden attack or promptly and decisively defeat it." The phrase leaned toward Taft's air-power concepts.[30]

Several days earlier, Eisenhower had insisted that at a minimum the platform must support "collective security measures for the free world. . . . Exclusive reliance upon a mere power of retaliation is not a complete answer to the broad Soviet threat." When Eisenhower read the Millikin draft, therefore, he stormed: "I'll be damned if I run on that!" Dulles then persuaded Millikin to delete the phrase "retaliatory striking" from the text. In its final form, the foreign policy plank represented a compromise. It contained plenty of sharp criticisms of the Democrats and an emphasis on fiscal conservatism that appealed to the Taft Republicans, while there were also sections applauding the fruits of bipartisanship and collective security.[31]

After a bitter convention fight that featured a challenge to the seating of several state delegations, the general captured the nomination on the first ballot. Eisenhower won not so much for the ideas he represented as for his tremendous personal popularity. While the general's backers did include such "Eastern internationalists" as Dewey, Lodge, Duff, and Ives, Eisenhower also drew important support from Frank Carlson and Harry Darby (both orthodox Midwestern conservatives) as well as Governor John Fine of Pennsylvania, who had called MacArthur "the greatest living American." As Eisenhower demonstrated once he got into office, there were few differences between him and Taft on domestic issues. On foreign policy, the two were further apart, but they were able to agree on a common platform. In 1952, most Republicans feared another defeat might spell the dissolution of the party, so they desperately wanted a winner. Taft's losses in the New Hampshire and Minnesota primaries, and his narrow victory in South Dakota, where he should have won handily, convinced many Republicans that the Ohioan could not beat the Democrats in November.[32]

While foreign policy was an important factor in the Republican nomination, it had little impact on the Democrats. In March 1952, Truman surprised his audience at a Jefferson-Jackson Day dinner by announcing his decision to retire at the end of his term. Senator

Estes Kefauver, a liberal Tennessean, led the field of contenders by convention time with Senator Richard Russell of Georgia and Averell Harriman of New York holding important blocs of votes. Truman, however, favored Illinois Governor Adlai E. Stevenson, whose eloquent opening speech at the convention propelled him into the nomination. In dramatic addresses by Eleanor Roosevelt and other Democrats, the convention's speakers defended Truman's Korean War policies. The urbane, sophisticated, and witty Stevenson provided a sharp contrast to the folksy, smiling Eisenhower and his heavy-handed running mate, Senator Richard M. Nixon of California.[33]

Later that summer, foreign policy issues played an important role in the presidential campaign in uniting the Republicans and in providing the measure of victory over the Democrats. In mid-August, in a pitch to voters of Eastern European descent and others frustrated by containment, Dulles and Eisenhower revived the "liberation" theme. Eisenhower declared that the United States will "never desist in our aid to every man and woman of those shackled lands who seek refuge with us, any man who keeps burning among his people the flame of freedom or who is dedicated to the liberation of his fellows." When the Democrats struck back, claiming that "liberation" threatened war, Eisenhower backed off. Originally devised as a more aggressive policy than containment and as a possible way of cutting into the traditionally Democratic ethnic vote, "liberation" became a political liability that was quietly dropped.[34]

One of Eisenhower's greatest problems in the campaign was to draw the Taftites actively and enthusiastically into the picture. Taft and his disciples left the Chicago convention bitterly disappointed. The general nonetheless tried to enlist their support from the start. He appointed Senator Karl Mundt of South Dakota, a Taftite, as codirector of the Republican Speaker's Bureau, and he personally conferred with Dirksen and former Senator C. Wayland Brooks of Illinois. In mid-July, Eisenhower also telegraphed Taft directly, asking if they could confer. Taft agreed to meet the general in early September only after having been given assurances that any joint statement issued by him and the general be checked so it would not appear that he had sold out his principles.[35]

Eisenhower's backers were at first unenthusiastic about a meet-

ing on Taft's terms, but they ultimately agreed. On the morning
of September 12, the two rivals had a short, amiable conference at
Morningside Heights in New York City, where Taft showed Eisenhower his prepared statement of endorsement; with a few minor
modifications the general accepted it. Taft then went across the
street to read it before the press. The Ohioan admitted that he had
been concerned about Eisenhower, since some of the general's
supporters had urged him to "approve New Deal policies, and purge
everyone who has fought hard for Republican principles against
Truman and Acheson and the rest of the left wingers. I have felt
confident that General Eisenhower had no such intention." Taft
declared that the "one great fundamental issue" between the parties was "the issue of liberty against the creeping Socialism in every
domestic field. . . . I cannot say," he added, "that I agree with
all of General Eisenhower's views on foreign policy . . . but I think
it is fair to say that our differences are differences of degree."[36]

The long-awaited meeting gave both men what they wanted, but
at a price. Taft, the defeated candidate, must have been pleased
to dictate terms to the man who had beaten him. He received
assurances from Eisenhower on nearly everything he had mentioned in an earlier premeeting "memorandum." To achieve that,
however, Taft probably realized that he would have to describe his
differences with the general on foreign policy as only "differences
of degree;" the senator also said nothing about the Korean War.
Eisenhower was roundly criticized by the Eastern press for what
it called his "Surrender at Morningside Heights," since he had
accepted Taft's whole domestic program. As his later performance
in office would demonstrate, however, the general was already in
accord with much of Taft's thinking on domestic policy anyway.[37]

The manner in which Eisenhower handled McCarthy and Jenner also demonstrated the lengths to which the general would go
to mollify the Taftites. Jenner, who was up for reelection, was among
the most vitriolic of the isolationists. He had voted against nearly
every collective security measure, and had personally attacked Eisenhower's mentor, General George Marshall. In early September, when the general's campaign swung through Indiana, Jenner
shared the platform with Eisenhower for an evening. After a rousing speech, the general urged his listeners to vote a straight Republican ticket, but he never mentioned Jenner by name. None-

theless, at the conclusion of the speech, the Indiana senator rushed up to Eisenhower and embraced him. The general, red-faced, quickly exited by a back door.[38]

In October, a sterner test awaited in Wisconsin where Joe McCarthy was running for reelection. The senator had also impugned the loyalty and integrity of George Marshall. As the Eisenhower campaign train sped through Illinois on its way to Wisconsin, McCarthy dropped in on the general to demand that he delete any reference to Marshall in his Wisconsin speeches. Eisenhower flatly refused. The next day, however, Wisconsin Governor Walter Kohler finally persuaded Sherman Adams and Eisenhower to abide by McCarthy's request for the sake of the party. Although the general made several speeches in Wisconsin without mentioning his mentor, the next week in Utah and New Jersey he included George Marshall's name in a list of patriotic Americans. Eisenhower had paid a high price for party unity and the Eastern press reminded him of it.[39]

In November, Eisenhower won a tremendous victory with the largest turnout at the polls in American history to that date, capturing every state except the "Solid South," Kentucky, and West Virginia. The general's coattails, however, were not wide; the Republicans controlled both Houses of Congress, but their margin in the Senate was only one vote. Americans apparently believed that the GOP, branded as the party of isolationism and the Great Depression, could only be trusted with a man who seemed above politics to guide them. The general was also the beneficiary of public frustration over revelations of corruption and communists in the government, as well as the seemingly endless struggle in Korea.[40]

During 1951 and 1952, Eisenhower and Dulles pulled the Republican party back together. With the decline of Vandenberg and the rise of McCarthyism, the GOP threatened to self-destruct; the party needed someone who could show them the "middle way." Those bipartisan Republicans who were more enamored of Europe and ignored East Asia were in dire straits, barely holding their own during the great debate of 1951 and becoming virtually inaudible during the MacArthur controversy. The China bloc rose in influence from 1950 through 1952. Their basic point that containment had to include to East Asia seemed to be sustained by the events. The Taftites faced the period 1950 through 1952 with more passion and confusion than leadership. For political reasons, the Taftites attacked the administration for being "soft on commu- nism," but were inconsistent in their support for the Korean War. As fiscal conservatives, their militancy was circumscribed by their pocketbooks, and as nationalists it was circumscribed by their mis- trust of "entangling alliances." Dulles and Eisenhower, with assis- tance from China-bloc members such as Knowland and Smith, pulled the pieces back together, borrowing many of their tactics from the old bipartisan book. By election day in 1952, only the most isola- tionist Republicans were dissatisfied with the direction their party was going; this was the same situation they had confronted in 1948.

Conclusions

This book began with the assertion that to study the impact of foreign policy on the politics of this era through the prism of bipartisanship might reveal some interesting insights into critical questions relating to the history of the Cold War. That a Cold War consensus developed in the late 1940s and 1950s, and came under attack in the 1960s, is common knowledge. The major outlines of the consensus were that the goals of international communism in general, and the Soviet Union in particular, were anathema to the United States. It also presumed that the United States must play a major role in containing the communists. Those convinced of the efficacy of the consensus often tended to doubt the intentions and sometimes the patriotism of their opponents. The principle lessons they drew from recent history were never to repeat the appeasement of Munich and the partisanship that surrounded the defeat of the Treaty of Versailles.

While the origins and early development of the Cold War consensus predate the scope of this work, the evidence discussed here clearly shows the crystallization and expansion of that consensus during these years among an important group of the elite: the Senate Republicans. It was, for instance, quite apparent during the debates on the North Atlantic Treaty in 1949 and the great debate of 1951, that most of the administration's opponents (all but the isolationists) were in agreement with most of its assumptions: that the Soviet Union was a dangerous power that menaced central Europe and that the United States had to play an important role in opposing it. The principal differences between Truman and the Taftites were in the cost of the enterprise, the increase in presidential power, the appropriate strategy for opposing the Soviets, and the extent to which the United States should be committed in advance to taking action.

An important theme this work develops is the change that this period wrought on the Republican party and foreign policy. In the period between the wars, the GOP was the home of some of the most famous isolationists in American history. By 1948, their numbers were greatly diminished and their tone had changed from the brash confidence of the 1930s to defensiveness. Growing up alongside the isolationists were the nationalists, who shared some of the same assumptions about American foreign policy but modified their views to meet the new world situation. Like the isolationists, the nationalists were leery of foreign commitments and increases in presidential power.

The years 1950 through 1952 became a crucible for Republicans when the force of events (particularly the Korean War) and the exigencies of politics drove the nationalists in new directions. Having accepted the administration's assumption that increases in the power of international communism were detrimental to the United States, for political reasons they sought to portray themselves as being more militant towards the communists than the administration. Exploiting the situation in East Asia appeared to pay handsome returns to Republicans in the elections of 1950. By mid-1951, this stance practically became party doctrine and, by 1952, a new bipartisan consensus emerged that included East Asia and sounded more militant than that of the Democrats. In so doing, however, the Taftites moved their wing of the GOP in universalist, anticommunist directions. Where Robert Taft had been an isolationist before Pearl Harbor and a nationalist in the late 1940s and early 1950s, his protégés, William Knowland and Barry Goldwater, were at the cutting edge in attempting to oppose communism anywhere in the world.

This is not to say that the nationalist-isolationist point of view disappeared during the early 1950s. Taft's vacillations over the Korean War attest to the alternating pulls of his nationalist proclivities and politics. While the war was going well in the autumn of 1950, Taft was behind it, but he expressed reservations about the president's authority to dispatch troops and the need for such expansive wartime powers. During the dark days of early 1951 when the Chinese Communists were doing well, Taft vacillated between pulling out of Korea and adopting MacArthur's more militant approach. The nationalists' distrust of executive power also surfaced later in the Bricker amendment controversy of the 1950s.

The central theme of this work has been an exploration of the essential nature of bipartisan foreign policy. Was it simply a bludgeon to use against its opponents, or was it, as its proponents argued, patriotic and, incidentally, politically profitable, too? Unquestionably, the bipartisan coalition used terms such as "isolationist" and "disrupters of bipartisan foreign policy" to silence its opposition. In powerful floor presentations, Vandenberg and his Democratic colleagues inveighed against the follies of isolationism and the lessons that a generation of Americans had learned from the 1930s. Truman frequently called his opponents isolationists and in fact made that an important part of his campaign effort in the off-year elections of 1950. In the face of such attacks, the nationalists' plea that "isolationism is about as dead as the Pharaohs of Egypt" fell flatly.

Did the bipartisan foreign policy stifle the development of a more meaningful exploration of alternatives to the Cold War consensus? With the Left in increasing disrepute during the late 1940s and early 1950s, the best avenue from which alternatives could have been advanced was from the Taftites. With their fiscal concern for balancing ends and means, the Taftites could have presented an alternative to the universalist anticommunism that dominated the 1950s and 1960s and which helped set the stage for the Vietnam debacle. Taft and his colleagues provided an interesting critique on the evolving Cold War consensus. The Ohioan, for instance, questioned the right of the president to make sweeping commitments that in effect circumvented the war-making powers of Congress without congressional approval, such as the introduction of troops into Korea in 1950 and into Europe in 1951. In addition, his suggestion that the United States employ an air-sea-atomic defense against the Eurasian land-mass was probably more closely in line with America's resources than the spiralling "pactomania" of the 1950s.

Nevertheless, the Taftites were beset by too many problems to be a source of reasonable alternatives. Convinced that the bipartisan Republicans were leading their party into political oblivion, the Taftites grasped at any straw to gain a political advantage against the bipartisan coalition. Indeed, rather than serving as a brake on the evolving Cold War, their reliance on an aggressively partisan approach helped propel America even more quickly down that road.

Was there any way the United States might have been spared the excesses of McCarthyism? While McCarthyism was born of a number of factors, politically it was propelled by the marriage of the Taftites to the goals of the China bloc. The best hope for the administration to have headed off such a combination would have been to develop a relationship with like-minded Republicans on its East Asian policy. Truman and Acheson did attempt this several times during 1949 and 1950; they even brought John Foster Dulles into the government in mid-1950. However, their hearts were just not in it. Acheson loathed stroking the vain Vandenberg and had little interest in East Asia. In any case when they needed Vandenberg the most in 1950 and 1951, he lay dying. The tragedy is that the GOP could not invent another Vandenberg to take his place.

Abbreviations in Notes

AHV   Arthur H. Vandenberg Papers, Bentley Historical Collections, University of Michigan, Ann Arbor, Michigan.

CR   U.S. Congress, *Congressional Record.*

DDE   Dwight D. Eisenhower Papers, Dwight D. Eisenhower Presidential Library, Abilene, Kansas.

DGA   Dean G. Acheson Papers, Harry S Truman Presidential Library, Independence, Missouri.

FRUS   U.S. Department of State, *Foreign Relations of the United States* (Washington, D.C.: Government Printing Office).

HAS   H. Alexander Smith Papers, Seeley G. Mudd Manuscript Library, Princeton University, Princeton, New Jersey.

HCH   Herbert C. Hoover Papers, Herbert C. Hoover Presidential Library, West Branch, Iowa.

HST   Harry S Truman Papers, Harry S Truman Presidential Library, Independence, Missouri.

JFD   John Foster Dulles Papers, Seeley G. Mudd Manuscript Library, Princeton University, Princeton, New Jersey.

NA   National Archives, Washington, D.C.

NYT   *New York Times.*

Public Papers   U.S. President, *Public Papers of the Presidents of the United States* (Washington, D.C.: Office of the Federal Register, National Archives and Records Service, 1953–).

RAT   Robert A. Taft Papers, Library of Congress, Washington, D.C.

Notes to Chapters

INTRODUCTION

1. General works include H. Bradford Westerfield, *Foreign Policy and Party Politics: Pearl Harbor to Korea* (New Haven, Conn.: Yale University Press, 1955); Norman A. Graebner, *The New Isolationism: A Study in Politics and Foreign Policy since 1950* (New York: The Ronald Press, 1956); Malcolm Jewett, "The Role of Political Parties in the Formation of Foreign Policy in the Senate, 1947–1956" (Ph.D. dissertation, State University of Pennsylvania, Philadelphia, 1958); Richard Grimmet, "Who Were the Senate Isolationists?" *Pacific Historical Review* 42 (November 1973): 479–98; Cecil Crabb, *Bipartisan Foreign Policy: Myth or Reality?* (Evanston, Ill.: Row, Peterson Co., 1975); Gary W. Reichard, *The Reaffirmation of Republicanism: Eisenhower and the Eighty-third Congress* (Knoxville: University of Tennessee Press, 1975); Justus Doenecke, *Not to the Swift: The Old Isolationists in the Cold War Era* (Lewisburg, Pa.: Bucknell University Press, 1979); Michael Miles, *The Odyssey of the American Right* (New York: Oxford University Press, 1980); Susan Hartmann, *Truman and the Eightieth Congress* (Columbia: University of Missouri Press, 1971); and Alonzo Hamby, *Beyond the New Deal: Harry S Truman and American Liberalism* (New York: Columbia University Press, 1973).

2. Vandenberg press statement, December 21, 1949, Committee on Foreign Relations, 81st Cong., Records of the U.S. Senate (Record Group 46), NA.

3. Two statistical studies have used roll-call analysis to delineate the differences among Republican senators of this period. After examining votes of those Republican senators in the 82nd Congress who returned to the

83rd Congress, Reichard in *The Reaffirmation of Republicanism*, 241–50, concludes that of those Republican senators who returned to the 83rd Congress, twenty-two were "nationalists," ten were "internationalists," and five were "uncommitted." In a study on Senate isolationists, 1947–1956, Grimmett ("Who Were the Senate Isolationists?" pp. 484–85, 487) calculates that there were about twenty Republican "isolationists" in the Senate for the years 1948–1949.

CHAPTER 1

1. For literature on the origins of bipartisanship during the Roosevelt years, see Richard F. Darilek, *A Loyal Opposition in Time of War: The Republican Party and the Politics of Foreign Policy From Pearl Harbor to Yalta* (Westport, Conn.: Greenwood Press, 1976); Arthur H. Vandenberg, Jr., ed., *The Private Papers of Senator Arthur H. Vandenberg* (Boston: Houghton Mifflin, 1952), chapters 1–8.

2. For the intraparty struggles of 1940, see Robert A. Divine, *Foreign Policy and U.S. Presidential Elections, 1940–1948* (New York: New Viewpoints, 1974), chapters 1–2; for the Vandenberg quotation, see March 11, 1943, *CR* 89: 1848; for Vandenberg's earlier life, see C. David Tompkins, *Senator Arthur H. Vandenberg: The Evolution of a Modern Republican, 1884–1945* (East Lansing: Michigan State University Press, 1970).

3. Dean Acheson, *Present at the Creation: My Years in the State Department* (New York: W. W. Norton, 1969), pp. 217–25; Richard M. Freeland, *The Truman Doctrine and the Origins of McCarthyism: Foreign Policy, Domestic Politics, and Internal Security, 1946–1948* (New York: Alfred Knopf, 1972), pp. 70–81; Bruce Kuniholm, *The Origins of the Cold War in the Near East: Great Power Conflict and Diplomacy in Iran, Turkey, and Greece* (Princeton, N.J.: Princeton University Press, 1980).

4. Present were Democratic Senators Barkley and Connally, and Republican Senators Vandenberg and Styles Bridges of New Hampshire, Democratic Representatives Sol Bloom of New York and Sam Rayburn of Texas, and Republican Representatives Charles Eaton of New Jersey and Joseph Martin of Massachusetts. Joseph M. Jones, *The Fifteen Weeks: February 21–June 5, 1947* (New York: Harcourt, Brace, 1955) pp. 138–42.

5. Vandenberg, Jr., *Vandenberg*, pp. 338–39; Acheson, *Present at the Creation*, p. 219; March 12, 1947, *CR* 93: 1980–1981; Jones, *The Fifteen Weeks*, pp. 168–69.

6. Acheson, *Present at the Creation*, pp. 223–24; Vandenberg, Jr., *Vandenberg*, pp. 343–50; that was particularly true of Vandenberg's insis-

tence that the Rio and North Atlantic Treaties conform strictly to the regional defense provisions of the United Nations Charter.

7. May 13, 1947, *CR* 93, 5142–44, A 3248; Acheson, *Present at the
Creation*, pp. 227–29, 232–35. For a lengthy discussion of the problems
of postwar Europe, see John Gimbel, *The Origins of the Marshall Plan*
(Stanford, Calif.: Stanford University Press, 1976).

8. Vandenberg, Jr., *Vandenberg, pp. 376–77; Acheson, Present at the
Creation*, pp. 230, 235; Freeland, *The Truman Doctrine and the Origins
of McCarthyism*, pp. 264–65.

9. Present were Republican Senators Zales Ecton of Montana, William
Knowland of California, Homer E. Capehart of Indiana, Wayland Brooks
of Illinois, George W. Malone of Nevada, and Henry Dworshak of Idaho.
Frank McNaughton report, January 17, 1948, Frank McNaughton Papers,
Harry S Truman Presidential Library, Independence, Mo.

10. James T. Patterson, *Mr. Republican: A Biography of Robert A. Taft*
(Boston: Houghton Mifflin, 1972), pp. 340–41, 384–88; Vandenberg, Jr.,
Vandenberg, pp. 318–19. For a further discussion of opposition to the
Marshall Plan, see Joan Lee Bryniarsky, "Against the Tide: Senate Op-
position to the Internationalist Foreign Policy of Presidents Franklin D.
Roosevelt and Harry S Truman, 1943–1949" (Ph.D. dissertation, Univer-
sity of Maryland, College Park, 1972), chapters 6–7. For Hoover's role,
see Hoover memorandum, February 28, 1948, public statements series
#3604, Hoover to Herter, March 13, 1948; plus memorandum, Hoover
to Herter, October 30, 1947, Hoover to Herter, February 28, 1948, HCH;
Hoover to Vandenberg, January 18, 1948, Public Statements series #3051,
HCH; University of Chicago Round Table radio broadcast, January 18,
1948, RAT.

11. Vandenberg, Jr., *Vandenberg*, pp. 377–78, 385–86; *Congressional
Quarterly Almanac* 4 (1948): 172–73; Bryniarsky, "Against the Tide," p. 201.

12. Vandenberg to Carl Sanders, January 2, 1948, AHV; *Vandenberg,
Jr., Vandenberg*, pp. 392–93; *Congressional Quarterly Almanac*, 4 (1948):
173; U.S. Congress, Senate, 80th Cong., 2nd sess., March 13, 1948, *Journal of the Senate*, pp. 146–47.

13. Freeland, *The Truman Doctrine and the Origins of McCarthyism*,
pp. 269–72; Truman speech before Congress, March 17, 1948, in *Public
Papers, Harry S Truman, 1948*, pp. 182–86.

14. See Divine, *Foreign Policy and U.S. Presidential Elections, 1940–
1948*, pp. 188–89.

15. Vandenberg to Dulles, June 4, 1948, AHV; see also Vandenberg
diary, June 20–25, 1945, in Vandenberg, Jr., *Vandenberg*, p. 428; Dulles's draft for Republican platform, May 28, 1948, JFD; Dulles's draft,
June 6, 1948, AHV; see Vandenberg, Jr., *Vandenberg*, pp. 429–30, where

he compared the final version to Vandenberg's drafts; Kirk H. Porter and Donald B. Johnson, eds., *National Party Platforms, 1840–1956* (Urbana: University of Illinois Press, 1956), pp. 453–54.

16. For the Democratic platform, see Porter and Johnson, *National Party Platforms*, pp. 430–32; Truman speech, July 14, 1948, as cited in *Public Papers, Truman, 1948*, p. 407.

17. Dulles to Vandenberg, July 14, 1948; Dulles memorandum of conversation with Marshall and Lovett, July 19, 1948, JFD.

18. *NYT*, July 2, 1948, pp. 1, 10; Divine, *Foreign Policy and U.S. Presidential Elections, 1940–1948*, pp. 223–26; Vandenberg to Dulles, July 2, 1948, in Vandenberg, Jr., *Vandenberg*, p. 447; Vandenberg, Jr., *Vandenberg*, pp. 446–47, 450–52; Dulles to Ferdinand Mayer, September 7, 1948, JFD.

19. For instance, see Divine, *Foreign Policy and U.S. Presidential Elections, 1940–48*, chapter 7; H. Bradford Westerfield, *Foreign Policy and Party Politics: Pearl Harbor to Korea* (New Haven, Conn.: Yale University Press, 1955), chapter 14.

20. Vandenberg to Dulles, August 9, 1948, AHV (emphasis in original).

CHAPTER 2

1. The senators in the meeting included Smith, Leverett Saltonstall of Massachusetts, and Raymond Baldwin of Connecticut. Smith diary, November 11, 1948, HAS.

2. The thirteen senators were Irving Ives of New York, Wayne Morse of Oregon, Smith of New Jersey, George Aiken and Ralph Flanders of Vermont, Baldwin of Connecticut, Saltonstall and Lodge of Massachusetts, Milton Young of North Dakota, Charles Tobey of New Hampshire, Chan Gurney of South Dakota, William Knowland of California, and Edward Thye of Minnesota. *NYT*, December 31, 1948, p. 3; Lodge, "Does the Republican Party Have a Future?" *Saturday Evening Post* 221 (January 22, 1949): 23, 81–82; Smith diary, December 30, 1948, HAS; Arthur H. Vandenberg, Jr., ed., *The Private Papers of Senator Arthur H. Vandenberg* (Boston: Houghton Mifflin, 1952), p. 467.

3. Vandenberg to Dulles, November 13, 1948, JFD (emphasis in original); McNaughton report, November 17, 1948, Frank McNaughton Papers, Harry S Truman Presidential Library, Independence, Mo.; Vandenberg to Dewey, December 6, 1948, AHV.

4. "Meet the Press" interview, January 21, 1949, RAT; James T. Patterson, *Mr. Republican: A Biography of Robert A. Taft* (Boston: Houghton Mifflin, 1972), pp. 421, 424.

5. McNaughton report, December 18, 1948, McNaughton Papers; Lodge to Taft, December 20, 1948, RAT.

6. *NYT*, December 28, 1948, pp. 1, 5.

7. *NYT*, December 31, 1948, pp. 1, 3; Smith diary, December 30, 1948, HAS; for a fuller explanation of Smith's role, see William Leary, "Smith of New Jersey: A Biography of H. Alexander Smith, United States Senator from New Jersey, 1944–1959" (Ph.D. dissertation, Princeton University, Princeton, N.J., 1966), pp. 128–31; for the Taft–Vandenberg relationship during the Eightieth Congress, see Vandenberg, Jr., *Vandenberg*, pp. 318–19; Patterson, *Taft*, pp. 340–41; for Vandenberg's views on the revolt, see Vandenberg, Jr., *Vandenberg*, pp. 466–67 and Vandenberg to Lodge, December 23, 1948, AHV.

8. *NYT*, January 4, 1949, pp. 1, 2.

9. For a description of Vandenberg's demeanor, see McNaughton report, January 7, 1949, McNaughton Papers; for Vandenberg's comments, see January 5, 1949, *CR* 95: 61.

10. January 5, 1949, *CR* 95: 62–63; see also Vandenberg, Jr., *Vandenberg*, p. 468; Vandenberg to Stassen, January 24, 1949, AHV; *NYT*, January 6, 1949, 7, 20; McNaughton to Elson, January 7, 1949, McNaughton Papers.

11. Eban Ayers diary, February 12, 1949, Eban Ayers Papers, Truman Library; for Connally's role in the Foreign Relations Committee fight, see McNaughton to Elson, January 7, 1949, McNaughton Papers; Lewis Gould, "Tom Connally," in John A. Garraty, ed., *Dictionary of American Biography, Supplement 7, 1961–1965* (New York: Charles Scribner's Sons, 1981), pp. 136–39.

12. Marshall to Vandenberg, July 7, 1950; Vandenberg to Marshall, July 10, 1950, AHV.

13. For more information on Acheson's background, see David McLellan, *Dean Acheson: The State Department Years* (New York: Dodd, 1976), chapters 1–8; Acheson to Mary Acheson Bundy, June 7, 1945, in Dean Acheson, *Present at the Creation: My Years in the State Department* (New York: W. W. Norton, 1969), pp. 108, 318; Gaddis Smith, *Dean Acheson* (New York: Cooper Square, 1972).

14. Acheson, *Present at the Creation*, p. 317; Acheson, July 2, 1953, Princeton Seminar, DGA; Vandenberg to Clyde Reed, January 12, 1949, in Vandenberg, Jr., *Vandenberg*, p. 469; for a contrary view of Acheson's relations with Congress, see McLellan, *Acheson*, pp. 140–41, 407–10.

15. Walter LaFeber, *America, Russia, and the Cold War, 1945–1971* (New York: John Wiley and Sons, 1972), pp. 67–69; Joan Lee Bryniarsky, "Against the Tide: Senate Opposition to the Internationalist Foreign Policy of Presidents Franklin D. Roosevelt and Harry S Truman, 1943–1949"

(Ph.D. dissertation, University of Maryland, College Park, 1972), chapter 8; Robert E. Osgood, *NATO: The Entangling Alliance* (Chicago: University of Chicago Press, 1962); Timothy P. Ireland, *Creating the Entangling Alliance: The Origins of the North Atlantic Treaty Organization* (Westport, Conn.: Greenwood Press, 1981); Lawrence S. Kaplan, "Toward the Brussels Pact," *Prologue* 12 (Summer 1980): 72–86.

16. For the negotiations between the two senators and the Department, see memorandum of conversation, February 3, 1949, Decimal file, 1945–1949, 840.20/2-349, Records of the Department of State (RG 59), NA; Bohlen to Acheson, February 4, 1949, Decimal file, 1945–1949, 840.20/2-449, RG 59; memorandum of conversation, February 5, 1949, Decimal file, 1945–1949, 840.20/2-549, RG 59; Bohlen to Acheson, February 14, 1949, Decimal file, 1945–1949, 840.20/2-1449, RG 59; memorandum of conversation, February 14, 1949, Decimal file, 1945–1949, 840.20/2-1449, RG 59; Bohlen to Acheson and Webb, February 16, 1949, Decimal file, 1945–1949, 840.20/2-1649, RG 59; Acheson memorandum of conversation with Truman, February 17, 1949, DGA.

17. U.S. Congress, Senate, Committee on Foreign Relations, *Hearings Held in Executive Session on the North Atlantic Treaty*, 81st Cong., 1st sess., February 18, 1949, in U.S. Congress, Senate, Committee on Foreign Relations, *The Vandenberg Resolution and the North Atlantic Treaty* (Washington, D.C.: Government Printing Office, 1973), pp. 111, 114; Bohlen to Acheson, February 21, 1949, Decimal file 1945–1949, 840.20/2-2149, RG 59; Gross to Acheson, February 24, 1949, Decimal file, 1945–1949, 840.20/2-2449, RG 59; in *The Vandenberg Resolution and the North Atlantic Treaty*, March 8, 1949, pp. 131–44, specifically p. 134 for the quotation; Acheson to Truman, March 8, 1949, Decimal file, 1945–1949, 840.20/3-849, RG 59.

18. For Vandenberg, see *NYT*, March 20, 1949, p. 1; for Connally, see Connally press statement, March 18, 1949, Connally Papers; *The Vandenberg Resolution and the North Atlantic Treaty*, April 5, 12, 1949, pp. 169–200, specifically pp. 174, 184, and 187 for the quotations; for Gross's account, see Gross to Acheson, April 12, 1949, Decimal file, 1945–1949, 840.20/4-1249, RG 59.

19. *The Vandenberg Resolution and the North Atlantic Treaty*, April 21, 1949, pp. 213–14.

20. *The Vandenberg Resolution and the North Atlantic Treaty*, June 2, 6, 1949, pp. 251–324, specifically p. 319 for the quotation; U.S. Congress, Senate, Committee on Foreign Relations, *Report of the Committee on Foreign Relations on the North Atlantic Treaty*, 81st Cong., 1st sess., June 6, 1949, pp. 357–87, specifically p. 373 for the quotation.

21. *The Vandenberg Resolution and the North Atlantic Treaty*, June 6, 1949, pp. 369–70.

22. *The Vandenberg Resolution and the North Atlantic Treaty*, June 6, 1949, pp. 313, 318–19; Connally press statement, June 6, 1949, Connally Papers.

23. For a fine analysis of the opponents, see Bryniarsky, "Against the Tide," pp. 266–93.

24. Bryniarsky, "Against the Tide," pp. 268–79; July 21, 1949, *CR* 95: 9880, 9885–86, 9915.

25. Bryniarsky, "Against the Tide," pp. 279–88; July 21, 1949, *CR* 95: 9898–9900, 9915, 9901–04, 9916.

26. George Gallup, *The Gallup Poll: Public Opinion, 1935–1971* (New York: Random House, 1972), pp. 792–93, 800, 815, 820–21, and 829–30; for the Watkins quotation, see memo of conversation between Watkins and Darrell St. Claire, March 17, 1949, Decimal File, 1945–1949, 840.20/3-1749, RG 59.

27. *NYT*, July 26, 1949, p. 2; memorandum of conversation between Lodge and St. Claire, July 28, 1949, Decimal file, 1945–1949, 811.032/7-2849, RG 59; Vandenberg to his wife, July 25, 1949, in Vandenberg, Jr., *Vandenberg*, pp. 503–4, (emphasis in original).

28. U.S. Congress, Senate, Committee on Foreign Relations, *Military Assistance Program: 1949* (Washington, D.C.: Government Printing Office, 1974) July 29, August 2, 1949, 5–8, 20–24; Vandenberg to his wife, August 2, 1949, in Vandenberg, Jr., *Vandenberg*, p. 508.

29. Vandenberg to his wife, c. July 1949 and July 31, 1949, in Vandenberg, Jr., *Vandenberg*, pp. 500–501, 505–6 (emphasis in original); Acheson, *Present at the Creation*, pp. 309–10.

30. For a much different evaluation of Acheson and Vandenberg, see McLellan, *Acheson*, pp. 164–67, 409–10; for the Acheson quotation, see Acheson, *Present at the Creation*, p. 311.

31. Vandenberg to Lippmann, August 9, 1949, in Vandenberg, Jr., *Vandenberg*, pp. 508–9.

32. For Acheson's presentation, see *MAP*, August 5, 1949, pp. 48–49; for a copy of the new bill, see *MAP*, pp. 648–63; for Vandenberg's response, see particularly *MAP*, August 5, 1949, p. 52; Vandenberg to his wife, August 5, 1949, in Vandenberg, Jr., *Vandenberg*, p. 508; *MAP*, August 10, 1949, pp. 75–76, 82; Vandenberg to his wife, mid-August 1949, in Vandenberg, Jr., *Vandenberg*, p. 513 (emphasis in original); Gross to Acheson, and memorandum of conversation between Acheson and Connally, August 22, 1949, Decimal file, 1945–1949, 840.20/8-2249, RG 59.

33. *MAP*, August 25, 29, 1949, pp. 332, 343–50, 390–91.

34. *MAP*, September 12, 1949, p. 629; September 19, 20, 21, 22, 1949, *CR* 95: 13016-35, 13043-65, 13079-13113, 13130-68; Vandenberg, Jr., *Vandenberg*, pp. 516–17.

35. Norman Graebner, "Walter George," in John A. Garraty, ed., *Dictionary of American Biography, Supplement 6, 1956–1960* (New York: Charles Scribner's Sons, 1980), pp. 234–36; September 21–22, 1949, *CR* 95: 13179–83, 13090-97, 13142-45, 13148-50, 13160-61.

36. For the votes on the amendments and the final vote, see September 22, 1949, *CR* 95: 13165-66, 13168.

CHAPTER 3

1. General works on the subject include: Ross Y. Koen, *The China Lobby in American Politics* (New York: Octagon Books, 1974); Akira Iriye, *The Cold War in Asia: An Historical Introduction* (Englewood Cliffs, N.J.: Prentice-Hall, 1974); Lisle A. Rose, *Roots of Tragedy: The United States and the Struggle for Asia, 1945–1953* (Westport, Conn.: Greenwood Press, 1976); H. Bradford Westerfield, *Foreign Policy and Party Politics: Pearl Harbor to Korea* (New Haven, Conn.: Yale University Press, 1955); Anthony Kubek, *How the Far East Was Lost: American Policy and the Creation of Communist China, 1941–1949* (Chicago: Henry Regency, 1963); Ernest May, *The Truman Administration and China, 1945–1949* (Philadelphia: Lippincott, 1975); Dorothy Borg and Waldo Heinricks, eds., *Uncertain Years: Chinese-American Relations, 1947–1950* (New York: Columbia University Press, 1980); and William W. Stueck, Jr., *The Road to Confrontation: American Policy Toward China and Korea, 1947–1950* (Chapel Hill, N.C.: University of North Carolina Press, 1981); Nancy Bernkopf Tucker, *Patterns in the Dust: Chinese-American Relations and the Recognition Controversy, 1949–1950* (New York: Columbia University Press, 1983); Robert Blum, *Drawing the Line: The Origin of the American Containment Policy in East Asia* (New York: W. W. Norton, 1982); Michael Schaller, *The United States Crusade in China, 1938–1945* (New York: Columbia University Press, 1979); George Charles Roche III, "Public Opinion and the China Policy of the United States, 1941–1951" (unpublished Ph.D. dissertation, University of Colorado, Boulder, 1965); James Alan Fetzer, "Congress and China, 1941–1950" (unpublished Ph.D. dissertation, Michigan State University, East Lansing, 1969); James Fetzer, "Senator Vandenberg and the American Commitment to China, 1945–1950," *The Historian* 36 (Feb. 1974): 283–303.

2. "Patrick McCarran," "William F. Knowland," and "Styles Bridges," *Current Biography*, 1947, pp. 406–8, 359–61; idem, 1948, pp. 3–5; William A. Leary, "Smith of New Jersey: A Biography of H. Alexander Smith,

United States Senator from New Jersey, 1944–1959" (Ph.D. dissertation, Princeton University, Princeton, N.J., 1966); on Smith's earlier attitude, see U.S. Congress, Senate, Committee on Foreign Relations, *Hearings in Executive Session on Assistance to China*, 80th Cong., 2nd sess., March 22, 1948, in U.S. Congress, Senate Committee on Foreign Relations, *Foreign Relief Assistance Act of 1948* (Washington, D.C.: Government Printing Office, 1973), pp. 465–87; George Mazuzan, "Styles Bridges," in John A. Garraty, ed., *Dictionary of American Biography, Supplement 7: 1961–64* (New York: Charles Scribner's Sons, 1981), pp. 73–74.

3. Koen, *The China Lobby*, chapter 2.

4. Rose, *The Roots of Tragedy*, chapters 5 and 6; Gary May, *China Scapegoat: The Diplomatic Ordeal of John Carter Vincent* (Washington, D.C.: New Republic Books, 1979).

5. *Nashua Herald*, October 30, 1948, *New Hampshire Monitor*, November 12 and 16, 1948, Scrapbook 104, Styles Bridges Papers, New England College Library, Henniker, N.H.; *NYT*, November 27, 1948, pp. 1, 27; November 13, 1948, p. 9; report by Bullitt to the Joint Committee on Foreign Economic Cooperation, December 24, 1948, 80th Cong., Committee Print; report by Clark to the Joint Committee on Foreign Economic Cooperation, c. January 1949, 81st Cong., Committee Papers, Committee on Foreign Relations, Records of the U.S. Senate (Record Group 46), NA.

6. McNaughton report, November 12, 1948, Frank McNaughton Papers, Harry S Truman Presidential Library, Independence, Mo.; *NYT*, November 17, 1948, p. 3; Vandenberg to Charles Kersten, November 16, 1948, AHV; Vandenberg to Knowland, December 11, 1948, and Vandenberg to Lewis, December 14, 1948, in Arthur H. Vandenberg, Jr., ed., *The Private Papers of Senator Arthur H. Vandenberg* (Boston: Houghton Mifflin, 1952), pp. 527–29; *NYT*, December 2, 1948, p. 1; December 10, 1948, p. 1, December 11, 1948, p. 1; December 31, 1948, p. 4; *FRUS, 1948* 8: 296–306; the administration had considered barring Madame Chiang from the country, see notes of Cabinet meeting, November 26, 1948, Matt Connelly Papers, Truman Library; for Kennan's recommendation and subsequent action, see Kennan to Marshall and Marshall to Lovett, November 26, 1948, *FRUS, 1948* 8: 214–20; Walter Millis, ed., *The Forrestal Diaries* (New York: Viking Press, 1951), November 26, 1948 entry, p. 534.

7. Warren Cohen, "Acheson, His Advisors, and China, 1949–1950," in Borg and Heinrich, eds., *Uncertain Years*, pp. 13–52; Tucker, *Patterns in the Dust*, chapter 10; for Acheson's contempt for the Nationalists, see notes of conversation between Koo, Acheson, and Butterworth, February 15, 1949, Wellington Koo Papers, Columbia University, New York.

8. Democratic Senator Tom Connally of Texas, Vice President Alben

Barkley, Senator Vandenberg, Democratic Congressman Sol Bloom of New York, and Republican Congressman Charles Eaton of New Jersey were present. Vandenberg, Jr., *Vandenberg*, February 5, 1949, diary entry, pp. 530–31 (emphasis in original); Dean Acheson, *Present at the Creation: My Years at the State Department* (New York: W. W. Norton, 1969), p. 306; Sidney Souers to Truman, February 3 and 17, 1949, President's Secretary's File, HST; notes of cabinet meeting, February 4, 1949, Connelly Papers; Acheson's memorandum of conversation, February 4, 1949, DGA; Marshal Carter to Souers, February 7, 1949, and Acheson's memorandum of conversation, February 7, 1949, in *FRUS, 1949* 9: 485–86.

9. Acheson's memorandum of conversation with the president, February 14, 1949, DGA; for information on Acheson's meeting with the House Foreign Affairs Committee, see Acheson's notes, February 24, 1949, DGA; see also two memoranda, Chen Chih-mai to Koo, February 25 and 26, 1949, Koo Papers; for the letter from the representatives, see fifty-one representatives to Truman, February 7, 1949, Decimal File, 1945–1949, 893.00/2-749, Records of the U.S. Department of State (Record Group 59), NA; while it is unclear as to the exact beginning date of the *White Paper* project, it was "under way" by late April 1949, see *FRUS, 1949* 9: 1363 n.1.

10. Acheson, *Present at the Creation*, p. 306; Acheson conversation, July 22, 1953, Princeton seminars, DGA.

11. U.S. Congress, Senate, S. 1063, 81st Cong., in U.S. Congress, Senate, Committee on Foreign Relations, *Economic Assistance to China and Korea: 1949–1950* (Washington, D.C.: Government Printing Office, 1974), pp. 232–39; McCarran to Karl Mundt, February 26, 1949, papers accompanying S. 1063, Committee on Foreign Relations, 81st Cong., RG 46; see also McCarran to H. Alexander Smith, February 26, 1949, HAS.

12. Fifty senators to Connally, March 9, 1949, papers accompanying S. 1063, Committee on Foreign Relations, 81st Cong., RG 46; *Economic Assistance to China and Korea*, March 11 and 15, 1949, pp. 2, 9, 15; March 24, 1949, *CR* 95: 3088; Koo's memorandum of conversation with McCarran, c. March 1949, Koo Papers.

13. Acheson to Connally, March 15, 1949, committee papers, Committee on Foreign Relations, RG 46; *Economic Assistance to China and Korea*, March 15, 18, 22, and 24, 1949, pp. 5-112.

14. *Economic Assistance to China and Korea*, March 11 and 24, 1949, pp. 3–4, 110–11; March 24, 1949, *CR* 95: 3089; see also Acheson to Stuart, March 24, 1949, as cited in *FRUS, 1949* 9:304.

15. McNaughton report, April 16, 1949, McNaughton Papers; for Bridges's reluctance to support the McCarran bill, see Richard Weigle's memorandum of conversation with Bert Teague, April 26, 1949, Decimal File,

1945–49, 893.00/4-2649, RG 59; for Knowland, see April 21, 1949, *CR* 95: 4862-63; for the Vandenberg-Bridges quarrel, see *New Hampshire Leader*, April 2, 1949, Scrapbook, 25, Bridges Papers; *Washington Evening Star*, April 15, 1949, *New Hampshire Leader*, April 25, 1949, Scrapbook 105, Bridges Papers.

16. State Department records indicate that it was Truman's idea, but Truman's appointment books indicate Connally first suggested the meeting. Weigle's memorandum of conversation with Teague, April 26, 1949, Decimal File, 1945–1949, 893.00/4-2649, RG 59; Daily sheet, April 28, 1949, HST; for Wherry and Bridges's remarks, see McNaughton report, May 6, 1949, McNaughton Papers; *Washington Post*, April 29, 1949, p. 1; Acheson conversation, July 22, 1953, Princeton seminars, DGA.

17. U.S. Congress, Senate, Committee on Foreign Relations, *Hearings Held in Executive Session on the Nomination of Butterworth*, 81st Cong., 1st sess., June 14, 1949, p. 7, RG 46; for Butterworth's credentials, see June 21, 1949, pp. 28–29, for the controversy the issue caused in committee, see June 14, 1949, p. 8; June 21, 1949, pp. 34–35, 43, June 24, 1949, *CR* 95: 8292-97; *NYT*, June 25, 1949, pp. 1, 5; for the final vote, see September 26 and 27, 1949, *CR* 95: 13264-67, 13284-94.

18. Acheson to Truman, July 29, 1949, as cited in *FRUS, 1949* 9: 1389; for more on the *White Paper*, see Robert P. Newman, "The Self Inflicted Wound: The China White Paper of 1949," *Prologue* 14 (Fall 1982): 141–56; Acheson conversation, July 22, 1953, Princeton seminars, DGA; Butterworth to Acheson, July 15, 1949, as cited in *FRUS, 1949* 9: 1373–74; Gross memorandum of conversation between Acheson, Connally, and Francis Wilcox, July 19, 1949, as cited in *FRUS, 1949* 9: 1375-76; Acheson memorandum of conversation with Truman, July 18, 1949, DGA; see also David McClellan, *Dean Acheson: The State Department Years* (New York: Dodd, Mead, 1976), pp. 194–98.

19. Acheson appointment book, July 22, 1949, DGA. For more on Acheson's difficulties with the MAP, see chapter 2.

20. Acheson conversation, July 22, 1953, Princeton seminars, DGA; U.S. Department of State, *United States Relations with China with Special Reference to the Period 1945–1949* (Washington, D.C.: Government Printing Office, 1949).

21. For the "storm of attack" comment, see Acheson to Truman, July 29, 1949, as cited in *FRUS, 1949* 9: 1389; *NYT*, August 7, 1949, p. 2; for the memorandum, see August 22, 1949, *CR* 95: A5451-53; poll, August 14–19, 1949, in George H. Gallup, *The Gallup Poll: Public Opinion, 1935–1971*, vol. 2: *1949–1971* (New York: Random House, 1972), p. 852.

22. "William F. Knowland, *Current Biography*, 8: 29–30.

23. August 8, 1949, *CR* 95: 10976; U.S. Congress, Senate, Joint Armed

Services and Foreign Relations Committees, *Joint Hearings Held in Executive Session on S. 2388*, 81st Cong., 1st sess., August 12, 1949, as cited in U.S. Congress, Senate, Committee on Foreign Relations, *Military Assistance Program: 1949* (Washington, D.C.: Government Printing Office, 1974), pp. 177–78, 185–86; for Knowland see *MAP*, September 9, 1949, pp. 583–88; August 26, 1949, pp. 370–73; August 29, 1949, pp. 365–77; for the department, see *MAP*, August 30, 1949, pp. 473–74.

24. *MAP*, September 9, 1949, pp. 593–97; September 12, 1949, p. 629.

25. Blum, *Drawing the Line*, chapter 8; William M. Leary and William Stueck, "The Chennault Plan to Save China: U.S. Containment in Asia and the Origins of the CIA's Aerial Empire, 1949–1950," *Diplomatic History* (Fall 1984): 356–57.

26. See, for instance, Acheson to Stuart, May 13, 1949, in *FRUS, 1949* 9: 21–23; memorandum of Charlton Osborn, November 2, 1949, in *FRUS, 1949* 9: 160–61; see also Cohen, "Acheson," in *Uncertain Tradition*, pp. 32–42.

27. U.S. Congress, Senate, Committee on Foreign Relations, *Hearings Held in Executive Session on the Peace Treaty with Austria and Conditions in China*, 81st Cong., 1st sess., October 12, 1949, as cited in U.S. Congress, Senate, Committee on Foreign Relations, *Reviews of the World Situation: 1949–50* (Washington, D.C.: Government Printing Office, 1974), pp. 94, 95, 100.

28. *Reviews*, pp. 84–103, especially, pp. 100–101; for Hickenlooper's later behavior, see U.S. Congress, Senate, Subcommittee of Committee on Foreign Relations, *State Department Loyalty Investigation*, 81st Cong., 2nd sess., March 20, 1950, p. 258; April 6, 1950, p. 442; and May 3, 1950, pp. 899–910.

CHAPTER 4

1. On whether the State Department was ready to recognize, see, for instance, David S. McLellan, *Dean Acheson: The State Department Years* (New York: Dodd, Mead, 1976), pp. 198–201; Nancy Bernkopf Tucker, *Patterns in the Dust: Chinese-American Relations and the Recognition Controversy, 1949–1950* (New York: Columbia University Press, 1983), chapter 10; Warren Cohen, "Acheson, His Advisors, and China, 1949–1950," in Dorothy Borg and Waldo Heinricks, eds., *Uncertain Tradition: Chinese American Relations, 1947–1950* (New York: Columbia University Press, 1980), pp. 13–52.

2. For more information on Smith, see William H. Leary, "Smith of New Jersey: A Biography of H. Alexander Smith, United States Senator

from New Jersey, 1944–1959" (Ph.D. dissertation, Princeton University, Princeton, N.J., 1966), chapter 1.

3. Ibid., chapters 1, 6.

4. Smith to Twitchell, April 27, 1949, Smith memorandum, Re Far Eastern Situation, August 1, 1949, HAS; see also Smith to Twitchell, July 15, 1949, HAS.

5. For more details of Smith's trip, see Leary, "Smith," pp. 138–45; Smith to Connally, November 29, 1949, Records of the Committee on Foreign Relations, 81st Cong., Records of the U.S. Senate (RG 46), NA.

6. *NYT*, October 11, 1949, pp. 1, 36; October 20, 1949, pp. 1, 6; Truman speech, November 3, 1949, in *Public Papers, Harry S Truman, 1949*, pp. 549–53.

7. *Chicago Tribune*, November 8, 1949, p. 2; November 14, 1949, pp. 1, 2; November 16, 1949, p. 1; *New York Herald Tribune*, November 10, 1949, pp. 1, 2; December 16, 1949, p. 21; *Nebraska State Journal*, November 13, 1949, p. 1.

8. Arthur H. Vandenberg, Jr., ed., *The Private Papers of Senator Arthur H. Vandenberg* (Boston: Houghton Mifflin, 1952), pp. 546–47; Vandenberg to Lovett, October 26, 1949, AHV.

9. Vandenberg to Lawrence, November 15, 1949, Lawrence to Vandenberg, November 15, 1949, AHV.

10. Vandenberg to Lawrence, November 17, 1949, AVH (emphasis in original). Parts of the letter are in Vandenberg, Jr., *Vandenberg*, p. 550.

11. Truman press conference, November 10, 1949, *Public Papers, Truman, 1949*, p. 559.

12. Vandenberg to Dulles, November 19, 1949, AHV (emphasis in original). Most of the letter is cited in Vandenberg, Jr., *Vandenberg*, p. 551; Vandenberg to Lodge, November 19, 1949, AHV.

13. *NYT*, January 26, 1949, pp. 1, 4, August 5, 1949, pp. 1, 7; August 7, 1949, p. 34; *Nebraska State Journal*, December 14, 1949, p. 1.

14. *Nebraska State Journal*, November 30, 1949, p. 3, December 15, 1949, p. 4; *NYT*, December 14, 1949, pp. 1, 25.

15. Vandenberg press statement, December 21, 1949, Records of the Committee on Foreign Relations, 81st Cong., RG 46.

16. Vandenberg to Watkins, December 28, 1949, AHV (emphasis in original). See chapter 2 for Vandenberg's fight against the administration's version of MAP.

17. *NYT*, December 28, 1949, pp. 1, 2.

18. *NYT*, December 27, 1949, p. 10; December 30, 1949, p. 6, January 1, 1950, pp. 1, 15; January 4, 1950, p. 1.

19. January 5, 1950, *CR* 96: 83; Hoover to Knowland, December 31, 1949, HCH.

20. *NYT*, January 2, 1950, p. 1.

21. January 5, 1950, *CR* 96: 82; January 9, 1950, *CR* 96: 150.

22. January 13, 1950, *CR* 96: 388–92.

23. January 5, 1950, *CR* 96: 90–91.

24. Ibid.

25. *NYT*, January 6, 1950, p. 3; Vandenberg to Bernard Yunck, January 17, 1950, as cited in Vandenberg, Jr., *Vandenberg*, p. 539.

26. Chen Chih-mai to Wellington Koo, January 4, 1950, Wellington Koo Papers, Columbia University, New York.

27. Truman press conferences, January 5, 7, 1950, in *Public Papers, Truman, 1950*, pp. 11–12, 33; see also Battle's memorandum of conversation between Acheson and Truman, January 5, 1950, DGA. Acheson press conference, January 5, 1950, in U.S. Department of State, *Department of State Bulletin*, January 16, 1950, 22: 79–81. See also Dean Acheson, *Present at the Creation: My Years at the State Department* (New York: W. W. Norton, 1969), p. 351, and U.S. Congress, Senate, Committee on Foreign Relations, *Hearings Held in Executive Session in Review of the World Situation*, 81st Cong., 2d sess., January 10, 13, 1950, as cited in U.S. Congress, Senate, Committee on Foreign Relations, *Reviews of the World Situation: 1949–50* (Washington, D.C.: Government Printing Office, 1974), pp. 133–39, 146–47, 169, 184.

28. *NYT*, January 11, 1950, p. 1; *Reviews of the World Situation*, January 10, 1950, p. 163; January 11, 1950, *CR* 96: 300; *NYT*, January 14, 1950, p. 1. For a discussion of the advisability of calling on the JCS to discuss top secret matters before a Senate committee, see Vandenberg to Walter Lippmann, January 17, 1950, Lippmann to Vandenberg, January 18, 1950, and Vandenberg to Lippmann, January 19, 1950, AHV. The JCS reports were prepared in November 1948 and February, March, August, and December 1949. See also *Reviews of the World Situation*, January 26, 1950, pp. 239–40, 242, and Connally press conference, January 26, 1950, Tom Connally Papers, Library of Congress, Washington, D.C.

29. January 9, 1950, *CR* 96: 170.

30. Taft speech, January 11, 1950, RAT.

31. Ibid.

32. Smith to Howard Twitchell, August 15, 1949, HAS.

33. For the subsequent attacks on the Press Club speech, see chapters 6 and 8; for Acheson's thoughts on the speech before delivering it, see Acheson, July 23, 1953, Princeton Seminars, DGA; for the speech itself, see Acheson speech, January 12, 1950, as cited in *State Department Bulletin*, January 23, 1950, p. 22: 111–18; for a more detailed analysis of the speech, see David S. McLellan, *Dean Acheson: The State Department Years* (New York: Dodd, Mead, 1976), pp. 209–15.

34. *NYT*, December 14, 1949, pp. 1, 25, December 16, 1949, p. 24, December 26, 1949, p. 1; Minutes, January 3, 1950, Records of the Senate Republican Policy Committee.

35. Minutes, January 3, 1950, Records of the Senate Republican Policy Committee; statement by Mundt, c. January 30, 1950, RAT. See also statement of Republican Senator Hugh Butler of Nebraska, c. January 1950, and Dulles to Taft, January 19, 1950, RAT.

36. Vandenberg diary, c. February 1950, in Vandenberg, Jr., *Vandenberg*, pp. 553–56; Vandenberg to Heffelfinger, December 29, 1949, AHV; Acheson memorandum of conversation with Vandenberg, January 21, 1950, DGA.

37. Vandenberg to Taft, January 19, 1950, AHV.

38. Taft to Vandenberg, January 24, 1950, Vandenberg diary, c. February 1950, in Vandenberg, Jr., *Vandenberg*, pp. 553–56. See also Vandenberg to Heffelfinger, December 29, 1949, AHV; Acheson memorandum of conversation with Vandenberg, January 21, 1950, DGA.

CHAPTER 5

1. The literature on McCarthy and McCarthyism is voluminous and of high quality. The following works provide valuable insights: Richard Rovere, *Senator Joe McCarthy* (New York: Harcourt Brace, 1959); Robert Griffith, *The Politics of Fear: Joseph R. McCarthy and the Senate* (Lexington: University of Kentucky Press, 1970); Earl Latham, *The Communist Controversy in Washington from the New Deal to McCarthy* (Cambridge, Mass.: Harvard University Press, 1966); Michael P. Rogin, *The Intellectuals and McCarthy: The Radical Specter* (Cambridge, Mass.: Massachusetts Institute of Technology Press, 1967); Robert Griffith and Athan Theoharis, eds., *The Specter: Original Essays on the Cold War and the Origins of McCarthyism* (New York: New Viewpoints, 1974); Richard M. Fried, *Men Against McCarthy* (New York: Columbia University Press, 1976); David M. Oshinsky, *A Conspiracy So Immense: The World of Joe McCarthy* (New York: The Free Press, 1983); Thomas C. Reeves, *The Life and Times of Joe McCarthy: A Biography* (New York: Stein and Day, 1982); Alan Harper, *The Politics of Loyalty: The White House and the Communist Issue* (Westport, Conn.: Greenwood Press, 1969).

2. Fried, *Men Against McCarthy*, pp. 43–47; and Griffith, *Politics of Fear*, pp. 48–49.

3. U.S. Congress, Senate, *A Resolution to Investigate Whether There Are Employees in the State Department Disloyal to the United States*, 81st Cong., 2d sess., S. Res. 231. Other members of the subcommittee were Democrats Brien McMahon of Connecticut and Theodore Green of Rhode

Island, joined by Republicans Bourke Hickenlooper of Iowa and Henry Cabot Lodge, Jr., of Massachusetts. Connally was unsuccessful in persuading Republican H. Alexander Smith of New Jersy to join the subcommittee instead of Hickenlooper. Smith diary, February 25 and 26, 1950, HAS.

4. "Bourke Hickenlooper," *Current Biography, 1949*, pp. 302–4; for Lodge's background, see Henry Cabot Lodge, Jr., *The Storm Has Many Eyes: A Personal Narrative* (New York: W. W. Norton, 1973), pp. 70–71; for information about Lodge's move against Taft, see chapter 2; see also Fried, *Men Against McCarthy*, pp. 60–61.

5. U.S. Congress, Senate, Subcommittee of Committee on Foreign Relations, *State Department Employment Loyalty Investigation*, 81st Cong., 2d sess., March 20, 1950, p. 258; April 6, 1950, p. 442, and May 3, 1950, pp. 879–910 (hereafter referred to as *Tydings Committee Hearings*); for examples, see *Tydings Committee Hearings*, May 3, 1950, pp. 913–19 and April 25, 1950, pp. 571–78; for Lodge's resolution, see *NYT*, April 4, 1950, p. 24.

6. Fried, *Men Against McCarthy*, pp. 60–61, 91–94.

7. *NYT*, March 19, 1950, p. 11, *NYT*, March 21, 1950, p. 1; Webb notes of meeting with Truman, March 26, 1950, HST.

8. *Tydings Committee Hearings*, March 21, 1950, pp. 277–84.

9. Minutes, March 22, 1950, Records of the Senate Republican Policy Committee, U.S. Senate, Washington, D.C.; *NYT*, March 23, 1950, p. 1; Smith diary, March 21, 1950, HAS; *NYT*, March 25, 1950, p. 2; for Taft, see James T. Patterson, *Mr. Republican: A Biography of Robert A. Taft* (Boston: Houghton Mifflin, 1972), pp. 444–49.

10. Fried, *Men Against McCarthy*, p. 72; for examples of how McCarthy could frustrate the Democrats, see McCarthy to Tydings, April 5, 1950, Tydings to McCarthy, April 4, 1950, McCarthy to Tydings, April 5, 1950, Millard Tydings Papers, University of Maryland, College Park.

11. *NYT*, March 26, 1950, pp. 1, 3, 4, 23; March 27, 1950, pp. 1, 2.

12. Truman to Vandenberg, March 27, 1950, official file, HST; Vandenberg to Truman, March 29, 1950, AHV; *NYT*, April 1, 1950, pp. 1–2.

13. For an exhaustive study of the Hiss case, see Allan Weinstein, *Perjury: The Hiss-Chambers Case* (New York: Alfred A. Knopf, 1978).

14. *NYT*, March 27, 1950, p. 2.

15. U.S. Congress, Senate, Committee on Foreign Relations, *Hearings on the Nominations of Dean Acheson*. 81st Cong., 1st sess., January 13, 1949, p. 6; David S. McLellan, *Dean Acheson: The State Department Years* (New York: Dodd, Mead, 1976), pp. 138–40; *NYT*, January 26, 1950, p. 1; *NYT*, March 26, 1950, p. 1.

16. Truman to Bridges, March 26, 1950, AHV; *NYT*, March 27, 1950, p. 22, March 28, 1950, p. 1.

17. *NYT*, March 28, 1950, p. 4.

18. Truman press conference, March 30, 1950, in *Public Papers, Harry S Truman, 1950*, pp. 235–36; Truman to Acheson, March 31, 1950, HST; he repeated the same sentiments in a letter to a friend, Nellie Noland, March 31, 1950, in Robert H. Ferrell, ed., *Off the Record: The Private Papers of Harry S Truman* (New York: Harper and Row, 1980), pp. 176–77.

19. For McCarthy and Wherry's retorts, see *NYT*, March 31, 1950, p. 3; for Styles Bridges's comments, see Bridges's statement, March 31, 1950, Styles Bridges Papers, New England College Library, Henniker, N.H.; for Taft's charges, see Taft statement, March 31, 1950, RAT.

20. *NYT*, March 28, 1950, p. 4; Rusk, March 14, 1954, Princeton Seminars, DGA; Warren I. Cohen, *Dean Rusk*, vol. XIX of *The American Secretaries of State and Their Diplomacy* (Totowa, N.J.: Cooper Square, 1980), pp. 44–46.

21. U.S. Congress, Senate, Committee on Foreign Relations, *Review of the Situation in the Far East*, 81st Cong., 2d sess., March 29, 1950, in U.S. Congress, Senate, Committee on Foreign Relations, *Reviews of the World Situation: 1949–50* (Washington, D.C.: Government Printing Office, 1974), pp. 251–54, 265, 271–76.

22. *NYT*, March 29, 1950, p. 1; Dulles memorandum of conversation, March 30, 1950; Vandenberg to Acheson, March 31, 1950, JFD; Webb notes of meeting with Truman, March 26, 1950, HST.

23. Townshend Hoopes, *The Devil and John Foster Dulles* (Boston: Little, Brown, 1973), pp. 79–82; Webb notes of meeting with Truman, March 26, 1950, HST.

24. Hoopes, *The Devil and John Foster Dulles*, chapters 1–4.

25. John Foster Dulles, *War or Peace* (New York: Macmillan Co., 1950), pp. 95–99, 122–27; for his comments on China, see chapters 12 and 18.

26. Dulles memorandum of conversation with Vandenberg, March 30, 1950; Dulles to Acheson, March 29, 1950, Dulles memorandum of conversations with Rusk and Acheson, March 30, 1950, JFD; Dulles to Truman, March 31, 1950, and Truman to Dulles, April 4, 1950, HST; Acheson, March 14, 1954, Princeton Seminar, DGA; Acheson, memorandum of conversation with Truman, April 4, 1950, DGA; Acheson to Truman, April 5, 1950, HST.

27. Acheson's memorandum of conversation with Truman, April 6, 1950, DGA; Truman to Acheson, April 7, 1950, HST; Dulles statement, April 6, 1950, JFD.

28. *NYT*, April 7, 1950, p. 5; Smith diary, April 6 and 8, 1950, HAS; Vandenberg to Dulles, April 10, 1950, AHV.

29. *NYT*, April 7, 1950, p. 5; Taft statement, March 31, 1950, RAT.

30. Acheson memorandum to Truman, April 26, 1950, HST; Acheson memorandum of conversation with Truman and Connally, April 27, 1950, DGA; Acheson memorandum of conversation with Wiley and McFall, April 28, 1950, DGA.

31. Vandenberg to Acheson, March 29, 1950, AHV; *NYT*, April 20, 1950, p. 6, April 16, 1950, pp. 1, 52; see also U.S. Congress, Senate, Committee on Foreign Relations, *Executive Hearings on Committee Organization*, 81st Cong., 2d sess., April 18, 1950, Committee on Foreign Relations, Records of the U.S. Senate (RG 46), NA. During early 1950, Assistant Secretary of State for Congressional Relations Jack McFall had suggested the subcommittee approach to Connally without success. By April, however, the political situation made the idea a lot more attractive, especially when McFall diplomatically allowed Connally to claim credit for it. The plan called for establishing eight subcommittees for consultative purposes that corresponded with the new organization of the State Department. Oral history interview with Jack McFall, Harry S Truman Presidential Library, Independence, Mo.

32. For Truman's earlier comment on Bridges, see Truman's press conference, March 30, 1950, *Public Papers, Truman, 1950*, pp. 235–36; for Truman's characterization of his discussion with Bridges, see Truman's statement, April 18, 1950, ibid., pp. 258–59; for Acheson's subsequent action, see Acheson's memoranda of conversations, April 18 and 20, 1950, DGA.

33. Minutes, April 19, 1950, Records of the Senate Republican Policy Committee; *New York Tribune*, April 19, 1950, in Scrapbook 111, Bridges Papers; *NYT*, April 20, 1950, p. 6.

34. U.S. Congress, Senate, Committee on Foreign Relations, *Hearings in Executive Session on S. Res. 231*, 81st Cong., 2d sess., July 18, 1950, as cited in U.S. Congress, Senate, Committee on Foreign Relations, *Executive Sessions of the Foreign Relations Committee* (Washington, D.C.: Government Printing Office, 1976), pp. 551–97.

35. July 20, 1950, *CR* 96: 10686-89, 10691-707.

CHAPTER 6

1. The following works were helpful in composing this chapter: Lisle A. Rose, *Roots of Tragedy: The United States and the Struggle for Asia, 1945–53* (Westport, Conn.: Greenwood Press, 1976), chapters 4 and 7;

Glenn D. Paige, *The Korean Decision, June 24–30, 1950* (New York: Free Press, 1968); David McLellan, *Dean Acheson: The State Department Years* (New York: Dodd, Mead, 1976), chapters 14 and 15; Ronald J. Caridi, *The Korean War and American Politics: The Republican Party as a Case Study* (Philadelphia: University of Pennsylvania Press, 1968); William Whitney Stueck, Jr., *The Road to Confrontation: American Policy toward China and Korea, 1947–1950* (Chapel Hill: University of North Carolina Press, 1981); Russell Buhite, *Soviet-American Relations in Asia, 1945–1954* (Norman: University of Oklahoma Press, 1981); Charles Dobbs, *The Unwanted Symbol: America's Foreign Policy, the Cold War, and Korea, 1945–1950* (Kent, Ohio: Kent State University Press, 1981); for a different view, see I. F. Stone, *The Hidden History of the Korean War* (New York: Monthly Review Press, 1952); Bruce Cummings, ed., *Child of Conflict: The Korean American Relationship, 1943–1953* (Seattle: University of Washington Press, 1983); James Richard Riggs, "Congress and the Conduct of the Korean War," (Ph.D. dissertation, Purdue University, Lafayette, Ind., 1972).

2. Jessup memorandum of conversation, June 25, 1950, *FRUS, 1950* 7: 157–61; Jessup memorandum of conversation, June 26, 1950, *FRUS, 1950* 7: 178–83; editor's note, *FRUS, 1950* 7: 170–71; Elsey to Murphy, c. July 1, 1950, Elsey Papers; Lucius Battle, memoranda of telephone conversations between Acheson and Kee, and Acheson and Wiley, June 26, 1950, DGA; see also Harry S Truman, *Memoirs*, vol. 2: *Years of Trial and Hope* (New York: Doubleday, 1956), pp. 377–86.

3. June 26, 1950, *CR* 96: 9154-59.

4. *NYT*, June 27, 1950, p. 12, June 26, 1950, p. 4.

5. The congressmen present were Senators Lucas, Tydings, Connally, Wiley, H. Alexander Smith, Bridges, and Elbert Thomas of Utah, and Congressmen John McCormack of Massachusetts, John Kee of West Virginia, Charles Eaton of New Jersy, Carl Vinson of Georgia, and Dewey Short of Mississippi. The vice president and Democratic Senator Walter George of Georgia were invited too but were out of town. Elsey memorandum, June 27, 1950, Elsey Papers.

6. Ibid.; Dean Acheson, *Present at the Creation: My Years at the State Department* (New York: W. W. Norton, 1969), pp. 408–10; Jessup memorandum of conversation, June 27, 1950, *FRUS, 1950* 7: 200–02; for Truman's statement, see Truman's message to Congress, June 27, 1950, *Public Papers, Harry S Truman, 1950*, p. 492.

7. *NYT*, June 28, 1950, p. 1; for Smith and Lodge, see June 27, 1950, *CR* 96: 9230; for Bridges, see Bridges's statement, June 27, 1950, Styles Bridges Papers, New England College Library, Henniker, N.H.; for Hoover, see Hoover release, June 28, 1950, HCH: for Dewey, see Dewey to

Truman, June 27, 1950, *Public Papers, Truman, 1950*, p. 496; for Vandenberg, see Vandenberg to Truman, July 3, 1950, AHV; see also Caridi, *The Korean War and American Politics*, pp. 33–38.

8. For Kem, see *NYT*, June 28, 1950, p. 5, and June 27, 1950, *CR* 96: 9230; for Watkins, see June 27, 1950, *CR* 96: 9229; for Malone, see June 27, 1950, *CR* 96: 9238-39.

9. Eric Goldman, *The Crucial Decade—and After: America, 1945–60* (New York: Vintage, 1960), pp. 164–65; June 28, 1950, *CR* 96: 9319-24.

10. June 28, 1950, *CR* 96: 9320.

11. Taft to Harold Henderson, July 25, 1950, RAT, in James Patterson, *Mr. Republican: A Biography of Robert A. Taft* (Boston: Houghton Mifflin, 1972), p. 455; see Patterson, *Taft*, pp. 451–55, for an explanation of Taft's behavior.

12. Elsey memorandum, June 30, 1950, Elsey Papers; unsigned memorandum of NSC meeting, June 30, 1950, HST; Tom Connally, *My Name Is Tom Connally* (New York: Thomas Crowell, 1954), pp. 346–48.

13. Jessup memorandum of conversation, July 3, 1950, *FRUS, 1950*, 7: 286–91; Elsey memorandum, c. July 1950, Elsey Papers; Acheson, February 13, 1954, Princeton Seminars, DGA; Acheson memorandum of conversation with Louis Johnson, July 3, 1950, DGA.

14. Elsey to Beverly Smith, July 16, 1951, Elsey Papers; Department of State memorandum, July 3, 1950, in U.S. Department of State, *Bulletin*, 23 (July 31, 1950): 173–80.

15. David S. McLellan, *Dean Acheson*, pp. 270–72; Acheson, *Present at the Creation*, pp. 373–81; John Lewis Gaddis, *Strategies of Containment: A Critical Appraisal of Postwar American National Security Policy* (New York: Oxford University Press, 1982), chapter 4; NSC 68, April 7, 1950, HST; Acheson, February 14, 1954, Princeton Seminars, DGA. For a different view, see Joyce and Gabriel Kolko, *The Limits of Power: The World and United States Foreign Policy, 1945–1954* (New York: Harper and Row, 1972), chapter 24.

16. Acheson's notes of cabinet meeting, July 14, 1950, DGA; Truman's message to Congress, July 19, 1950, *Public Papers, Truman, 1950*, pp. 527–37.

17. Connally statement, July 19, 1950, Tom Connally Papers, Library of Congress, Washington, D.C.; *NYT*, July 20, 1950, p. 12; Dulles to Truman, July 20, 1950, HST; U.S. Congress, Senate, Committee on Foreign Relations, *Hearings Held in Executive Session in Review of the World Situation*, 81st Cong., 2d sess., July 24, 1950, as cited in U.S. Congress, Senate, Committee on Foreign Relations, *Reviews of the World Situation* (Washington, D.C.: Government Printing Office, 1974), pp. 318–28.

18. *NYT*, July 12, 1950, p. 4; Smith diary, July 12, 14, 1950, HAS.

19. Smith diary, July 2, 1950, Smith memorandum, July 24, 1950; Smith to Dulles, July 24, 1950, HAS.

20. Smith memorandum, July 26, 1950, HAS.

21. Vandenberg to Lodge, July 29, 1950, AHV.

22. Statement of Taft and Martin, July 18, 1950, RAT; for Gabrielson, see *NYT*, August 1, 1950, p. 17; for Wherry, see *NYT*, August 7, 1950, p. 2.

23. Smith memorandum, August 8, 1950, HAS.

24. Smith to Vandenberg, August 9, 1950, HAS; Vandenberg's note penciled in on Smith to Vandenberg, July 29, 1950, AHV.

25. *NYT*, August 14, 1950, p. 10.

26. Ibid.; Smith diary, August 15, 1950, HAS.

27. Tannenwald memorandum, August 15, 1950, Frank Tannenwald Papers, Truman Library; Ayers diary, August 14 and 17, 1950, Eben Ayers Papers, Truman Library; for Connally's comments, see *NYT*, August 15, 1950, p. 22; for McMahon's speech, see August 14, 1950, *CR* 96: 12417.

28. August 14, 1950, *CR* 96: 12417-19.

29. For the Democrats, see Ken Hechler to Spingarn and Neustadt, July 18, 1950, Stephen Spingarn Papers, Truman Library; *NYT*, July 28, 1950, p. 8; Richard M. Fried, *Men Against McCarthy* (New York: Columbia University Press, 1976), p. 108; for the Republicans, see Republican National Committee, "Bipartisan Foreign Policy," c. late August 1950, Bridges Papers; *NYT*, August 29, 1950, p. 14; Caridi, *The Korean War and American Politics*, pp. 77–78.

30. Henry Cabot Lodge, Jr., "Lodge Defines the Minority Role," *NYT*, September 17, 1950, VI, pp. 22, 58.

31. For Harriman's statement, *NYT*, September 20, 1950, p. 34; for Lloyd, see Lloyd to Murphy, September 28, 1950, David Lloyd Papers, Truman Liberary; see also Lloyd to Murphy, September 21, 1950, Charles Murphy Papers, Truman Library; Hechler to Tannenwald, September 6, 1950, Tannenwald Papers; for Truman, see Truman news conference, September 21, and Truman speech, November 4, 1950, *Public Papers, Truman, 1950*, pp. 643, 698–99.

32. For Wherry, see Wherry to James Austin, August 18, 1950, Kenneth S. Wherry Papers, Nebraska State Historical Society, Lincoln, Nebraska, and *NYT*, August 7, 1950, p. 2; for Bridges, see *NYT*, September 15, 1950, p. 51; for Taft, see Taft speech, October 24, 1950, RAT; also see Taft's speeches, October 26 and November 4, 1950, RAT; for Smith, Flanders, and Ives, see *NYT*, November 7, 1950, p. 9; Caridi, *The Korean War and American Politics*, pp. 93–100.

33. Brewster to Vandenberg, November 1, 1950; Vandenberg to Brewster, c. November 1, 1950, AHV.

34. Fried, *Men Against McCarthy*, pp. 109–21.

CHAPTER 7

1. David S. McLellan, *Dean Acheson: The State Department Years* (New York: Dodd, Mead, 1976), chapter 17; Arthur M. Schlesinger, Jr., *The Imperial Presidency* (Boston: Houghton Mifflin, 1973), chapter 6; Jacob Javits and Don Kelleman, *Man Who Makes War: The President versus Congress* (New York: William Morrow, 1973), chapter 16; Justus Doenecke, *Not to the Swift: The Old Isolationists in the Cold War Era* (Lewisburg, Pa.: Bucknell University Press, 1979); Gabriel and Joyce Kolko, *The Limits of Power: The World and United States Foreign Policy, 1945–1954* (New York: Harper and Row, 1972); H. Bradford Westerfield, *Foreign Policy and Party Politics: Pearl Harbor to Korea* (New Haven, Conn.: Yale University Press, 1955); Richard Grimmett, "The Politics of Containment: The President, the Senate, and American Foreign Policy, 1947–1956" (Ph.D. dissertation, Kent State University, Kent, Ohio, 1973); John Lewis Gaddis, *Strategies of Containment: A Critical Appraisal of Postwar American National Security Policy* (New York: Oxford University Press, 1982).

2. Taft press conference, November 13, 1950, RAT; *NYT*, November 18, 1950, pp. 1, 7; November 19, 1950, pp. 1, 36; November 21, 1950, p. 25; November 25, 1950, p. 6.

3. *NYT*, December 8, 1950, p. 1; Minutes, December 7 and 12, 1950, Records of the Senate Republican Policy Committee, U.S. Senate, Washington, D.C.; Smith diary, December 2, 1950, HAS; Richard M. Fried, *Men Against McCarthy* (New York: Columbia University Press, 1976), p. 157; William H. Leary, "Smith of New Jersey: A Biography of H. Alexander Smith, United States Senator from New Jersey, 1944–1959" (Ph.D. dissertation, Princeton University, Princeton, N.J.: 1966), p. 165; *Concord Monitor*, December 8, 1950, Scrapbook 116, Styles Bridges Papers, New England College Library, Henniker, N.H.; Truman news conference, December 19, 1950, in *Public Papers, Harry S Truman, 1950*, pp. 351–53.

4. U.S. Congress, Senate, Committee on Foreign Relations, *Hearings in Executive Session on the Situation in Korea*, 81st Cong., 2d sess., November 28, 1950, in U.S. Congress, Senate, Committee on Foreign Relations, *Reviews of the World Situation: 1949–50* (Washington, D.C.: Government Printing Office, 1974), pp. 372–78; Truman press conference, November 30, 1950, in *Public Papers, Truman, 1950*, p. 725; Tru-

man message to Congress, December 1, 1950, in ibid., pp. 728–31; Timothy Ireland, *Creating the Entangling Alliance: The Origins of the North Atlantic Treaty* (Westport, Conn.: Greenwood Press, 1981), chapter 6.

5. Elsey memorandum, December 13, 1950, George Elsey Papers, Harry S Truman Presidential Library, Independence, Mo.; Truman speech, December 15, 1950, in *Public Papers, Truman, 1950*, pp. 741–46; Truman message, December 19, 1950, in ibid., p. 750.

6. Hoover speech, December 20, 1950, in *Vital Speeches of the Day* 17 (January 1, 1951): 165–67; see also *NYT*, December 24, 1950, IV, p. 3; for Kennedy's speech, see *Vital Speeches of the Day* 17 (January 1, 1951): 170–73.

7. *NYT*, December 23, 1950, p. 3; Truman press conference, December 28, 1950, in *Public Papers, Truman, 1950*, p. 761.

8. *NYT*, December 28, 1950, pp. 1, 6; December 30, 1950, p. 4; Dulles to Taft, December 29, 1950; Dulles to Hoover, December 28, 1950, RAT.

9. James T. Patterson, *Mr. Republican: A Biography of Robert A. Taft* (Boston: Houghton Mifflin, 1972), pp. 474–76; Taft speech, January 9, 1951; Taft to Ethan Shepley, January 8, 1951, RAT.

10. January 5, 1951, *CR* 97: 54–61; Taft on "Meet the Press," January 7, 1951; Taft speech, January 9, 1951, RAT.

11. Taft speech, January 9, 1951, RAT; for Acheson's assurances, see U.S. Congress, Senate, Committee on Foreign Relations, *Hearings on the North Atlantic Treaty*, 81st Cong., 1st sess., April 27, 1949, p. 42; January 8, 1951, *CR* 97: 94; for Wherry's reasons for introducing the resolution, see January 16, 1951, *CR* 97: 318–32.

12. Truman speech, January 8, 1951, in *Public Papers, Truman, 1951*, pp. 9–10; Truman press conference, January 11, 1951, in ibid., pp. 18–22.

13. Vandenberg to Gilmore, February 12, 1951; Vandenberg to Aiken, January 18, 1951; Vandenberg to Lovett, January 11, 1951, AHV.

14. January 11, 1951, *CR* 97: 147–49, 154–55; Arthur H. Vandenberg, Jr., ed., *The Private Papers of Senator Vandenberg* (Boston: Houghton Mifflin, 1952), p. 467.

15. *NYT*, January 9, 1951, p. 14; January 14, 1951, p. 14; January 16, 1951, pp. 1, 9, January 17, 1951, p. 1, January 18, 1951, p. 17; George H. Gallup, *The Gallup Poll: Public Opinion, 1925–1971*, vol. 2: *1949–1971* (New York: Random House, 1972), p. 964; Truman press conference, January 19, 1951, in *Public Papers, Truman, 1951*, p. 112.

16. January 22, 1951, *CR* 97: 477; January 23, 1951, *CR* 97: 544–46; U.S. Congress, Senate, Committees on Foreign Relations and Armed Services, *Executive Session Hearings on S. Res. 8*, 82nd Cong., 1st sess., January 25, 1951, in U.S. Congress, Senate, Committee on Foreign Re-

lations, *Executive Sessions of the Senate Foreign Relations Committee*, vol.
3, pt. 1 (Washington, D.C.: Government Printing Office, 1976), pp. 1–
10.

17. Vandenberg to Duff, February 17, 1951, Vandenberg to Lodge,
February 26, 1951, AHV (emphasis in original); see also Vandenberg to
Wherry, February 2, 1951, AHV; Vandenberg to Wherry, January 30,
1951, Wherry to Vandenberg, January 31, 1951, Kenneth S. Wherry Papers, Nebraska State Historical Society, Lincoln, Neb.

18. U.S. Congress, Senate, Senate Joint Resolution 34, 82d Cong., 1st
sess., February 19, 1951; *Executive Sessions*, January 25, 1951, vol. 3, pt.
1, p. 3.

19. Draft of a resolution, February 27, 1951, Elsey Papers; Connally-
Russell resolution, Committee Papers, Committee on Foreign Relations,
82nd Cong., Records of the U.S. Senate (RG 46), NA.

20. Smith diary, January 8, 21, and February 16, 1951, HAS; Smith to
Wiley, February 19, 1951, Alexander Wiley Papers, State Historical Society of Wisconsin, Madison, Wisconsin; Smith to Walter George, March
3, 1951, HAS; for the compromise resolution, see *Executive Sessions*, March
6, 1951, vol. 3, pt. 1, pp. 131–33.

21. For Knowland, see *Executive Sessions*, March 6, 1951, vol. 3, pt.
1, pp. 150–51; for Byrd, see ibid., pp. 145, 148–50; for George, see ibid.,
March 7, 1951, pp. 172–75.

22. *Executive Sessions*, March 7, 8, 1951, vol. 3, pt. 1, pp. 167–258,
for the Russell quotation specifically see p. 244.

23. Actually the committees reported two resolutions, S. Res. 99 and
S. Con. Res. 18, which were identical except that the former expressed
the sense of the Senate and the latter the sense of the Congress. This
chapter will refer to them in the singular, since amendments to one automatically extended to the other.

24. U.S. Congress, Senate, Senate Resolution 99 and Senate Concurrent Resolution 18, 82nd Cong., 1st sess., emphasis added.

25. For McCarthy's amendment, see April 3, 1951, *CR* 97: 3161–73.

26. April 2, 1951, *CR* 97: 3089-95, for the Lodge quotation, specifically
see p. 3094. The twelve cosponsors of the amendment were Republicans
Lodge, Ives, Aiken, James Duff of Pennsylvania, and Smith of Maine, and
Democrats Paul Douglas of Illinois, Herbert Lehman of New York, Russell Long of Georgia, Clinton Anderson of New Mexico, Brien McMahon
of Connecticut, John Sparkman of Alabama, and Robert Hendrickson of
New Jersey.

27. April 2, 1951, *CR* 97: 3095.

28. Ibid., pp. 3075, 3080.

29. Ibid., pp. 3082, 3096.

30. April 3, 1951, *CR* 97: 3173.

31. For Smith, see ibid., p. 3181; for Saltonstall, see ibid., p. 3180; for Lodge, see ibid., p. 3175; for McClellan, see ibid., p. 3181; for the votes, see ibid., pp. 3075–91.

32. The votes referred to were the Kem amendment, April 3, 1951, *CR* 97: 3160; the Mundt amendment, ibid., 3194; and the final vote on S. Res. 99, April 4, 1951, *CR* 97: 3288.

33. For the vote on the McClellan amendment, see April 2, 1951, *CR* 97: 3082–83, 3095–96.

34. For the vote on the Ives amendment, see April 2, 1951, *CR* 97: 3095.

35. For the final vote on Sen. Con. Res. 18, see April 4, 1951, *CR* 97: 3293–94.

CHAPTER 8

1. Lisle Rose, *Roots of Tragedy: The United States and the Struggle for Asia, 1945–1953* (Westport, Conn.: Greenwood Press, 1976), pp. 233–37; Dean Acheson, *Present at the Creation: My Years in the State Department* (New York: W. W. Norton, 1969), pp. 469–73.

2. Douglas MacArthur, *Reminiscences* (New York: McGraw-Hill, 1964), p. 379.

3. Ronald J. Caridi, *The Korean War and the American Politics: The Republican Party as a Case Study* (Philadelphia: University of Pennsylvania Press, 1968), chapters 5 and 6. This writer sees three major factions of the Republican party on East Asian policy, while Caridi sees two.

4. December 4, 1950, *CR* 96: 16047-50.

5. Caridi, *Korean War*, pp. 79–93; James T. Patterson, *Mr. Republican: A Biography of Robert A. Taft* (Boston: Houghton Mifflin, 1972), pp. 451–55. This writer prefers Patterson's interpretation of Taft with its emphasis on the conflicting forces that worked on Taft, as opposed to Caridi's, which postulates that his contradictory behavior was strictly a function of politics.

6. Hoover speech, December 20, 1950, *Vital Speeches of the Day* 17 (January 1, 1951): 165–67; January 5, 1951, *CR* 97: 54–61; Taft "Meet the Press" interview, January 7, 1951; Taft speech in the Senate, January 5, 1951, RAT; *NYT*, January 8, 1951, p. 1.

7. *NYT*, January 5, 1951, p. 3.

8. January 11, 1951, *CR* 97: 160–62.

9. Ives, for instance, attacked Acheson. *NYT*, December 8, 1951, p. 1.

10. For background on MacArthur, see D. Clayton James, *The Years of MacArthur, Vol. 1: 1880–1941* (Boston: Houghton Mifflin, 1970); for

examples of MacArthur's vanity, see MacArthur, *Reminiscences*, p. 413; for the general's explanation of the Japanese attack, see ibid., pp. 125–33; for Hoover's comment, see Smith memorandum of conference with Hoover, April 14, 1951, HAS.

11. For Republican reaction to MacArthur in the fall of 1950, see Caridi, *Korean War*, pp. 85–88; *NYT*, November 29, 1950, p. 4; December 2, 1950, p. 4; MacArthur, *Reminiscences*, p. 379.

12. For a good summary of MacArthur's actions in the spring, see Caridi, *Korean War*, pp. 142–45; MacArthur to Martin, March 20, 1951, in April 11, 1951, *CR* 97: 3380.

13. Harry S Truman, *Memoirs*, vol. 2: *Years of Trial and Hope* (Garden City, N.Y.: Doubleday, 1956), p. 412; Truman address, April 11, 1951, in *Public Papers, Truman, 1951*, pp. 222–27; Truman to Eisenhower, April 12, 1951, DDE; Truman diary, April 6, 8, 9, 1951, in Robert H. Ferrell, *Off the Record: The Private Papers of Harry S Truman* (New York: Harper and Row, 1980), pp. 210–11; Truman memorandum, April 28, 1951, HST.

14. Letters supporting MacArthur: 5986, against: 32; telegrams supporting MacArthur: 42,024, against: 334; telephone calls supporting the general: 1775, against: 13; *NYT*, April 13, 1951, p. 7; special release, American Institute of Public Opinion, May 3, 16, 1951; *Appendix to CR* 97: A2017-18, A1989, A2014, A2015, A2037, A2049, A2050.

15. Joseph Martin, *My First Fifty Years in Politics* (New York: McGraw-Hill, 1960), pp. 207–11; *NYT*, April 12, 1951, p. 3; Minutes, April 11, 1951, Records of the Republican Policy Committee, U.S. Senate, Washington, D.C.; Smith diary, April 12, 1951, HAS; Dulles memorandum, April 12, 1951, JFD; April 11, 1951, *CR* 97: 3608; Taft speech, April 12, 1951, RAT.

16. Martin, *First Fifty Years*, p. 208; Fellers to Herbert Hoover, April 14, 15, 1951, HCH.

17. *NYT*, April 22, 1951, p. 1; April 28, 1951, p. 3; April 13, 1951, pp. 1, 4; April 14, 1951, p. 1; April 15, 1951, p. 11; April 16, 1951, p. 1; April 18, 1951, p. 9; April 20, 1951, p. 4; Taft to Elmer Bruss, April 19, 1951, RAT.

18. *NYT*, April 12, 1951, p. 31; April 16, 1951, p. 6; April 18, 1951, p. 5.

19. *NYT*, April 17, 1951, p. 1, 8; April 18, 1951, p. 9; Minutes, April 17, 1951, Records of the Republican Policy Committee; see also Taft to Foster Arnett, April 24, 1951, RAT; *NYT*, May 3, 1951, pp. 1, 5; May 5, 1951, pp. 1, 3.

20. Douglas MacArthur, *Revitalizing a Nation: A Statement of Beliefs, Opinions, and Policies Embodied in the Public Pronouncements of General*

of the Army Douglas MacArthur (Chicago: The Heritage Foundation, 1952), p. 83; MacArthur, *Reminiscences*, pp. 337, 390; U.S. Congress, Senate, Committees on Armed Services and Foreign Relations, *Hearings on the Military Situation in the Far East*, 82nd Cong., 1st sess., May 4, 1951, p. 83; May 3, 1951, pp. 29, 40, 68, hereafter referred to as *MacArthur Hearings*.

21. For the Bradley quotation, see *MacArthur Hearings*, May 15, 1951, p. 732; for Marshall, see May 7–14, 1951, pp. 322–724; for Bradley, see May 15–24, 1951, pp. 729–1151; for Acheson, see June 1–9, 1951, pp. 1667–2291.

22. *MacArthur Hearings*, May 11, 1951, pp. 549–59; June 2, 1951, pp. 1778–79; for evidence of the department's considering recognition, see memorandum by Charlton Osborn, Jr., November 2, 1949, *FRUS, 1949* 9: 160–61; for material on the American stance toward the British, see memorandum by Acheson, September 17, 1949, *FRUS, 1949* 9: 88–91, and memorandum by Troy Perkins, November 5, 1949, *FRUS, 1949* 9: 168–72.

23. For Knowland, see *MacArthur Hearings*, May 4, 1951, pp. 121–29; for Bridges, see May 3, 1951, pp. 26–28; for Smith, see May 3, 1951, pp. 36–39.

24. Smith memorandum, April 14, 1951, HAS; Smith to William Castle, May 1, 1951, in William Leary, "Smith of New Jersey: A Biography of H. Alexander Smith, United States Senator from New Jersey, 1944–1959," (Ph.D. dissertation, Princeton University, Princeton, N.J., 1966), p. 181; Smith memorandum, May 15, 1951, HAS; for Smith's views on the MacArthur controversy, see Leary, "Smith," pp. 179–87.

25. Taft press release, April 12, 1951, RAT; *NYT*, April 24, 1951, p. 4; April 19, 1951, p. 9; May 1, 1951, pp. 1, 16; May 10, 1951, *CR 97*: 5172–73; see also Patterson, *Taft*, pp. 492–96.

26. MacArthur, *Reminiscences*, pp. 331, 341; *MacArthur Hearings*, pp. 213–14.

27. For Taft, see Taft to J. Thomas Baldwin, July 31, 1951, RAT, as cited in Patterson, *Taft*, p. 491. For Hickenlooper's questioning of MacArthur, for instance, see *MacArthur Hearings*, May 3, 1951, pp. 51–60; for Hickenlooper's questioning of Marshall, see *MacArthur Hearings*, May 10, 1951, p. 490–96.

28. U.S. Congress, Senate, Joint Committees on Armed Services and Foreign Relations, *Individual Views of Certain Members of the U.S. Senate, Relating to Hearings Held on the Dismissal of General MacArthur and the Military Situation in the Far East*, September 5, 1951, S. Doc. 69, 82nd Cong., 1st sess., pp. 48, 49, 51; see Ross Y. Koen, *The China Lobby in American Politics* (New York: Octagon, 1974), pp. 104–6.

29. For Saltonstall, see *MacArthur Hearings*, May 3, 1951, pp. 39–42 and August 17, 1951, pp. 3559–60; for Lodge, see *MacArthur Hearings*, May 4, 1951, pp. 115–21, and August 24, 1951, pp. 3659–62.

30. *MacArthur Hearings*, May 3, 1951, pp. 65–67 and May 5, 1951, pp. 226–32, 234–86, 3662–65.

CHAPTER 9

1. Townshend Hoopes, *The Devil and John Foster Dulles* (Boston: Little, Brown, 1973), chapter 7; David McClellan, *Dean Acheson: The State Department Years* (New York: Dodd, Mead, 1976), pp. 323–26; Dean Acheson, *Present at the Creation: My Years at the State Department* (New York: W. W. Norton, 1969), pp. 539–50, 603–5.

2. Dulles memorandum, April 12, 1951, JFD; *NYT*, September 2, 1951, p. 3; Smith diary, April 12, 1951; Smith memorandum of conversation with Dulles, May 6, 1951, HAS; Dulles to Alexander Wiley, September 11, 1951, Alexander Wiley Papers, State Historical Society of Wisconsin, Madison, Wis.

3. September 11, 1951, *CR* 97: 11121, 11127–28.

4. September 11, 1951, *CR* 97: 11126, 11128–29.

5. Smith diary, January 13, 1952, HAS.

6. Fifty-six senators to Truman, September 12, 1951, HCH; March 18, 1952, *CR* 98: 2451; Yoshida to Dulles, December 24, 1951, in Acheson, *Present at the Creation*, p. 759.

7. For texts of the treaties, see U.S. Department of State, *United States Treaties and Other International Agreements*, vol. 3: 1952, pp. 3171–91, 3331–32, 3422–25, and 4644–45; U.S. Congress, Senate, Committee on Foreign Relations, *Hearings in Executive Session on the Japanese Peace Treaty*, 82nd Cong., 2d sess., February 5, 1952, p. 41, Committee on Foreign Relations, Records of the U.S. Senate (RG 46), NA.

8. March 20, 1952, *CR* 98: 2578. Herbert Hoover was particularly concerned that the treaty not ratify Yalta. Hoover to Hickenlooper, January 28, 1952, HCH.

9. March 14, 1952, *CR* 98: 2327–43; March 17, 1952, *CR* 98: 2357–59.

10. January 20, 1952, *CR* 98: 1175–83; March 17, 1952, *CR* 98: 2365–66.

11. March 19, 1952, *CR* 98: 2507; March 18, 1952, *CR* 98: 2449–50; and March 18, 1952, *CR* 98: 2442, 2454–55, 2473.

12. March 18, 1952, *CR* 98: 2473; March 19, 1952, *CR* 98: 2501–3.

13. March 20, 1952, *CR* 98: 2561–62, 2567, 2571, 2574, 2578, 2593–94, 2604–5; Connally news release, March 24, 1952, Connally Papers.

14. Useful literature on the election includes Herbert S. Parmet, *Eisenhower and the American Crusades* (New York: Macmillan, 1972), part 1; Robert A. Divine, *Foreign Policy and U.S. Presidential Elections, 1952–1960* (New York: New Viewpoints, 1974), chapters 1–2; James T. Patterson, *Mr. Republican: A Biography of Robert A. Taft* (Boston: Houghton Mifflin, 1972), part 6; Jerome Nashorn, "Choosing the Candidates, 1952" (Ph.D. dissertation, Harvard University, Cambridge, Mass., 1974).

15. Patterson, *Taft*, pp. 499–506; Nashorn, "Choosing the Candidates, 1952," chapter 2; Robert A. Taft, *A Foreign Policy for Americans* (Garden City, N.Y.: Doubleday, 1951), pp. 6–8, 12, 14, 17–18, 48–63.

16. Taft, *Foreign Policy*, pp. 60–63, 66–67, 74, 78, 79, 88, 91, 99, 100, 108–9, 117–20.

17. For a good discussion of Eisenhower's background, see Parmet, *Eisenhower*, chapters 2, 6, and 7.

18. Lodge memorandum of conversation, June 9, 1950, Henry Cabot Lodge, Jr. Papers (on microfilm), Dwight D. Eisenhower Presidential Library, Abilene, Kans.; Nashorn, "Choosing the Candidates, 1952," pp. 40–42. In his book, Lodge does not quote his earlier memorandum accurately. Henry Cabot Lodge, Jr., *The Storm Has Many Eyes: A Personal Narrative* (New York: W. W. Norton, 1973), p. 77.

19. Eisenhower to Hazlett, November 1, 1950, DDE; see chapter 6 for background on the Great Debate; *NYT*, February 2, 1951, p. 4; see also Eisenhower to J. Lawton Collins, February 28, 1951; Eisenhower to Truman, February 24, 1951, (emphasis in original), DDE. Eisenhower's statement was: "Having been called back to military duty, I want to announce that my name may not be used by anyone as a candidate for President—and if any do I will repudiate such efforts." Dwight D. Eisenhower, *At Ease: Stories I Tell To Friends* (Garden City, N.Y.: Doubleday, 1967), pp. 371–72; Eisenhower oral history interview, Eisenhower Library.

20. Taft to White, October 29, 1951, RAT; C. L. Sulzberger, *A Long Row of Candles: Memoirs and Diaries, 1934–54* (New York: Macmillan, 1969), pp. 693–94, 702; *NYT*, March 7, 1952, p. 15; March 8, 1952, p. 8.

21. *NYT*, March 18, 1952, p. 16, March 28, 1952, p. 15; March 30, 1952, p. 49; March 22, 1952, p. 7, April 29, 1952, p. 17; Eisenhower to Clay, March 19, 1952; Eisenhower to Robinson, March 21, 1952; Eisenhower to Truman, April 2, 1952, DDE.

22. Townshend Hoopes, *The Devil and John Foster Dulles* (Boston: Little, Brown, 1973), pp. 124–28; John Foster Dulles, "A Policy of Boldness," *Life*, May 19, 1952, pp. 146, 148, 151–52, 154, 157–58, 160.

23. Dulles, "A Policy of Boldness," p. 146.

24. Ibid., pp. 151, 154, 158 (emphasis in original).

25. Ibid., p. 158.

26. Eisenhower to Clay, April 10, 1952; Eisenhower to Dulles, April 15, 1952; Dulles to Eisenhower, May 20, 1952, DDE.

27. Dulles to Eisenhower, May 20, 1952, DDE; John B. Hollister oral history interview, Seeley G. Mudd Library, Princeton University, Princeton, N.J.

28. *NYT*, June 2, 1952, p. 14; June 22, 1952, p. 37.

29. *NYT*, June 5, 1952, p. 16; June 6, 1952, p. 10; June 24, 1952, p. 20; June 25, 1952, p. 20; Dulles memorandum, June 18, 1952; Dulles to Millikin, June 20, 1952, JFD.

30. Dulles Draft #7, c. June 1952, JFD.

31. Eisenhower to Dulles, June 20, 1952, JFD; Schulzberger, *A Long Row of Candles*, pp. 767–70; Kirk H. Porter and Donald B. Johnson, ed., *National Party Platforms, 1840–1956* (Urbana: University of Illinois Press, 1956), pp. 496–500.

32. Divine, *Foreign Policy and U.S. Presidential Elections: 1952*, p. 37; Nashorn, "Choosing the Candidates, 1952," pp. 396–405.

33. Truman speech, March 29, 1952, in *Public Papers, Harry S Truman, 1952–1953*, pp. 220–25; Divine, *Foreign Policy and U.S. Presidential Elections, 1952–1960*, pp. 37–41.

34. *NYT*, August 27, 1952, pp. 1, 15; August 26, 1952, p. 12; Truman speech, September 2, 1952, in *Public Papers, Truman, 1952–53*, pp. 550–51; *NYT*, August 27, 1952, p. 15; Divine, *Foreign Policy and U.S. Presidential Elections, 1952–1960*, p. 52; Parmet, *Eisenhower*, pp. 124–25.

35. Patterson, *Taft*, pp. 569–72; *Newsweek*, September 1, 1952, pp. 19–20; Hoover to Taft, July 11, 1952, HCH; Taft to Herman Welkey, August 18, 1952, RAT; *NYT*, August 5, 1952, p. 13; Patterson, *Taft*, pp. 572–73.

36. Taft, "Memorandum on Eisenhower," c. early August, 1952; Taft to Dirksen, August 6, 1952; see also Taft to Hugh Butler, August 13, 1952, RAT; Patterson, *Taft*, pp. 576–77; Parmet, *Eisenhower*, pp. 129–30; Taft statement, September 12, 1952, DDE; Taft notes on Morningside Heights meeting, c. September 1952, RAT; *NYT*, September 13, 1952, pp. 1, 6.

37. *NYT*, September 14, 1952, p. 12.

38. Sherman Adams, *Firsthand Report: The Story of the Eisenhower Administration* (New York: Harper and Brothers, 1961), p. 33; *NYT*, September 10, 1952, p. 19; Parmet, *Eisenhower*, pp. 127–28.

39. Kohler to Adams, August 28, 1952; Adams to Kohler, September 9, 1952; Vandenberg, Jr., to Adams, October 4, 1952, DDE; Adams, *Report*, pp. 31–32; Parmet, *Eisenhower*, pp. 130–32.

40. Parmet, *Eisenhower*, pp. 145–49; Divine, *Foreign Policy in U.S. Presidential Elections, 1952–1960*, pp. 84–85.

Note on Sources

Sources on the study of the effect of foreign policy on Congress are numerous and varied, but in some cases they are scattered. Scholars interested in studying Congress are fortunate in that more than any other agency of government, much of the activities of Congress are published and have been disseminated in libraries around the country. Speeches that are delivered on the floor of Congress, for instance, are reproduced in the *Congressional Record*. While I found that the *Record* was a valuable source for congressional opinion, scholars should be aware that its text can be altered by members after the fact and that some of the speeches were not actually delivered, only presented to a clerk for later inclusion. Nonetheless, the *Record* does document the public position of senators and contains some extremely valuable colloquies between senators which proved quite useful in delineating their positions. Because all roll-call votes are also reproduced in the *Record*, it is also an excellent source for gathering that type of information.

While floor debates are useful, the substantive work of the modern Congress is performed in its committees. Committee hearings and reports, the records of the Foreign Relations and Armed Services Committees at the National Archives, and the private papers of the senators who served on the committees were the most important sources I consulted to piece together this committee activity. Public hearings held by the committees were published at the time and are available throughout the country. Scholars are deeply indebted to the foresight of Senator J. William Fulbright, who during the 1970s initiated a program to declassify and publish the Foreign Relations Committee's executive-session hearings. For the late 1940s and early 1950s, these are widely available in the committee's "Historical Series."

The greatest strength of congressional hearings as historic documents is that they often capture unguarded exchanges among committee members and between committee members and witnesses. Their greatest weakness grows out of senatorial courtesy: each senator is permitted to question witnesses, which means that the same ground is frequently covered several times by different senators. Unfortunately, the index to the hearings usually only indicates the page numbers on which witness testimony is recorded, but not the subjects covered. Committee reports are another valuable source documenting committee activity. When a bill is presented on the floor by the committee chairman, it is almost always accompanied by a formal committee report, which is in effect an argument for the bill. These reports are published in the Congressional Serial Set and are widely available around the country.

The unpublished, archival record of the workings of the Senate is widely scattered and of uneven quality. The official records of the committees at the National Archives are useful but often disappointing. The scholarly utility of the private papers of individual senators depends on the file-keeping practices of the senator's office, the work habits of the senator, and the extent to which the collection has been weeded. The most useful senatorial collections to this study were the papers of Arthur H. Vandenberg, Robert A. Taft, Tom Connally, H. Alexander Smith, and John Foster Dulles. Collections that were less fruitful included the papers of Kenneth S. Wherry, Alexander Wiley, Homer E. Capehart, Styles Bridges, Henry Cabot Lodge, Jr., John W. Bricker, James E. Kem, Millard Tydings, and Hugh Butler.

It will come as no surprise to scholars of this period that the presidential library system contributed much of value to this study. Collections at the Herbert C. Hoover, Dwight D. Eisenhower, and, particularly, the Harry S Truman Presidential Libraries, were important. At the Truman Library the Papers of Truman, Dean G. Acheson, and George Elsey were indispensable, especially when used in conjunction with the records of the Department of State at the National Archives and the *Foreign Relations of the United States*. Other collections at the Truman Library that provided occasional insights were the papers of Frank McNaughton, Stephen Spingarn, Eban Ayers, James Webb, Clark Clifford, Matt Connelly, David Lloyd, and Frank Tannenwald. At the Eisenhower Library, the papers of Eisenhower, Sherman Adams, Harry A. Bullis, and Edward J. Bermingham were useful. The papers of Herbert Hoover are also a rich source for this period.

Other archival sources that provided some occasional insights include the papers of Philip C. Jessup and Claire Chennault (Library of Congress), Wellington Koo (Columbia University), Douglas MacArthur (MacArthur

Memorial), and the records of the Senate Republican Policy Committee (United States Senate).

Because senators have always been figures of great public interest, the newspaper and periodical literature frequently provides much useful information. I used the *New York Times* extensively for the entire period of this study, because it is so well indexed and so comprehensive in its treatment of national news. I also consulted a number of local newspapers to learn more about certain senators during particularly critical periods.

Many public figures from this era have contributed memoirs or have had significant portions of their papers published. The most helpful to the preparation of this book were those written by or about Truman, Eisenhower, Vandenberg, Connally, Ralph Flanders, Acheson, Lodge, and MacArthur.

I only hope that the numerous citations to the works of others in the notes will bear testament to their importance to this study.

Index

About the Author

DAVID R. KEPLEY is an Archivist for the National Archives and an instructor at Northern Virginia Community College. His publications include works on archives administration and the history of Congress.